WISCONSIN IN 1865
Map prepared by the Author
(Revised 1971)

ECONOMIC HISTORY OF WISCONSIN
DURING THE CIVIL WAR DECADE

PUBLICATIONS OF THE STATE HISTORICAL SOCIETY
OF WISCONSIN

ECONOMIC HISTORY OF WISCONSIN DURING THE CIVIL WAR DECADE

BY

FREDERICK MERK

PUBLISHED BY THE SOCIETY
MADISON, 1916

Published by The State Historical Society of Wisconsin

Manufactured in the United States of America
Standard Book Number 87020-117-4

CONTENTS

Preface to the Second Edition

For the states of the Union the opening of the Civil War in 1861 was a traumatic experience. Half a century later a proper observance of it was under consideration in Wisconsin well before the semicentennial year. In 1905 a commission was authorized by the legislature to draw plans for the observance by stimulating commemorative historical works describing the part played by Wisconsin soldiers in the war, of which every citizen of the state was believed to be "justly proud." The Commission was to consist of the Governor of the state, the head professor of American history at the University of Wisconsin, the Secretary of the State Historical Society, the Secretary of the Wisconsin Free Library Commission, and a survivor of the war who was to be selected at the next annual encampment of the Grand Army of the Republic.

A scholars' plan was prepared by this Commission which was embodied in a new law in 1907. Its basic recommendation was a widening of the scope of the initial act so as to embrace the civilian as well as the military contributions of Wisconsin to the successful outcome of the war. It emphasized attracting the youth in the state to working in the field, producing monographs and papers from materials already gathered and to be gathered in the State Historical Society. An annual appropriation was voted of $2,000 for two years, and this was renewed in 1909 and in 1911 for further two years in each case, to finance the work.

In 1911 the writer of this preface was invited to participate in the enterprise. He met the specifications of the legislation in one respect—he was among the younger generation of students of American history. He was raw from his undergraduate degree at the University of Wisconsin. He was informed of his duties at a conference with Dr. Reuben Gold Thwaites, Secretary of the State Historical Society. One duty was immediate—to get educated in the arts of copy editing, proofreading, and indexing. This could be accomplished by work on manuscripts under preparation in the Society for the press. One, among a number jointly sponsored by the Commission and the Society, was "Civil War Messages and Proclamations of Wisconsin War Governors," which was published in 1912. The salary was a beginner's, $1000 a year, and this was increased by increments of $100 as proficiency increased. A greater inducement to proficiency was the prospect of writing an economic history of Wisconsin during the Civil War which would implement one of the legislature's purposes and incidentally end the apprenticeship.

This assignment was of high interest, for it was an opportunity. It meant research, adventures in historical discovery, and the pleasures of describing them. It was an incentive to hours of work beyond the call of duty. Much of the *Economic History of Wisconsin During the Civil War Decade* was written after hours, between five o'clock and the next morning, under a special key arrangement with his good friend, Dr. Milo M. Quaife, the successor to Dr. Thwaites. The completion of the manuscript came after the demise of the Commission, and the State Historical Society published it as the first of a series of *Studies*. The total of the publications of the Civil War History Commission was eight volumes of *Original Papers*, chiefly reminiscences of participants in the war, and two volumes of *Reprints*, one, a reminiscence, the other, the *Civil War Messages and Proclamations of Wisconsin War Governors*.

The central theme of the *Economic History of Wisconsin During the Civil War Decade* was the impact of a great war on the life of a state and of the geographic province of which it was a part. This theme has a perennial interest, as wars still shape the lives of states and nations. It contains lessons for the present in parallels that are at least suggestive.

One parallel in the Civil War years was inflation. Inflation became a major problem for the State. The war produced a doubling and even a trebling of the costs of essential services. In transportation the rise was especially severe for wheat farmers. The rate on wheat by river and rail from the Mississippi River to points on Lake Michigan rose from 12 cents a bushel in 1861 to 35 cents in 1865. A like skyrocketing of other costs occurred. This brought outcries from the farm areas of the State and generated an antimonopoly revolt which eventuated in early attempts at state regulation of public carriers.

Shortages of labor on farms were a product of the recruitment of armies. They were met by increasing mechanization of agriculture and increasing reliance on the labor of women and children. The interruption of the importation of Southern staples produced Northern shortages and in Wisconsin led to the production of substitutes — sorghum to replace sugar, wool to replace cotton, and tobacco to replace the Southern product.

Not all Wisconsin citizens took pride in the State's contribution to the winning of the war. Draft riots occurred in some lakeshore counties where part of the population was of German origin, and there was also dissent by Democrats who had Southern leanings, and wished compromise with the Confederates. These interesting subjects lie outside the realm of economic history. They are dealt with by Frank L. Klement in *Wisconsin and the Civil War,* published by the Society Press in 1963 for the State's Civil War Centennial Commission.

The close of the war and the return of the soldiers from the front brought dislocations. These were, however, less marked than in the older parts of the Union. Wisconsin was still a frontier state, with unexploited resources of virgin lands, forests, and iron mines, especially in the north and the northwest, which cushioned the return to peace.

If war — with its harsh impacts on life — is no longer expected to arouse "just pride" on the part of youth, an understanding of war's perennial dislocation of society will seem important to all. A reissue of this volume, in essentially the form in which it originally appeared, needs no apology, for new readers will bring to it the insight which the present bestows upon the past — a more vivid understanding of the problems confronting Wisconsin and the nation in the years of the Civil War.

Frederick Merk

Cambridge, Massachusetts
September, 1971

AUTHOR'S PREFACE

As an industrial community Wisconsin during the Civil War was typical of the Northwest. In all its important aspects her economic life reflected that of the states adjoining her borders. Agriculturally her development found its counterpart in Minnesota and Iowa; her lumber industry repeated that of Michigan and Minnesota; her lead mining was a duplication of what obtained in the region about Galena and Dubuque. Milwaukee paralleled Chicago. In trade, commerce, and railroad expansion the metropolis of Wisconsin followed in the footsteps of its great southern rival. Upon the Mississippi, La Crosse occupied a commercial position similar to those of St. Paul and Dunleith. Nearly all the industrial interests of the region west of Lake Michigan were represented in some degree in the Badger State. The account which follows, therefore, typifies the history of the larger economic unit—the area later known as the Granger Northwest—of which Wisconsin was but a part.

Industrial changes work themselves out only with the lapse of decades. To attempt to chronicle economic progress during the brief span of four or five years must always prove unsatisfactory. History is a stream of events. To cut across it arbitrarily is to record developments but barely begun, or only partially completed, or just come to a close. However profoundly the Civil War affected the economic life of the State and nation, the historian who reviews it should not, it seems to me, limit his discussion to the four years in which the armies of the North and the South were clashing on the battlefield. If he does, his picture will be but a static, panoramic view, and not, as it should be, a moving film of events. My design in this volume has been to limit myself as closely as possible to the period of the Civil War. Yet when it has seemed desirable I have not hesitated to range over the entire period between the two years of financial crisis, 1857 and 1873. Developments brought to a close during the war I have attempted to trace to their origin; changes begun during the war I have briefly carried either to their conclusion or to the point at which it has seemed profitable to leave them. Thus the industrial history of Wisconsin during the war has been placed in what has seemed to me to be its proper setting.

The historical sources for this volume have been scattering, often fragmentary. The generation of the Civil War was less interested in preserving records of its industrial than of its military achievements. Newspaper files necessarily constituted the chief source of information. Fortunately, the great newspaper collection of the State Historical Society of Wisconsin was at my constant disposal. Reports of boards of trade and publications of similar industrial associations were useful as repositories of statistical information. Legislative journals, local laws, and court proceedings likewise yielded much valuable data. To manuscript materials, on the other hand, I had only limited access. From local histories and personal interviews some help was obtained, but was accepted only when it could be corroborated by other testimony.

Much of the ground covered in this volume is broken for the first time. The field has been surveyed nationally several times, but never, so far as I know, intensively for a single state. Whatever errors of fact or of judgment the future discloses in this work will find in this fact at least partial extenuation.

I am under heavy obligations to Dr. M. M. Quaife, superintendent of the State Historical Society of Wisconsin, who with great care has read and corrected my manuscript. My thanks are due also to Dr. Carl Russell Fish of the University of Wisconsin, who has read a number of the chapters, and has given valuable suggestions for improving them. Finally, I am deeply indebted for the national background of this book to J. F. Rhodes' *History of the United States*, and E. D. Fite's *Social and Industrial Conditions in the North During the Civil War.*

Frederick Merk

Madison, Wisconsin

CHAPTER 1

AGRICULTURE

The 80,000 boys in blue, sent by Wisconsin to southern battle-fields during the Civil War, constituted but one of the armies that the State consecrated to the preservation of the Union. At home another army toiled in field and workshop, rendering less thrilling but not less important service to the imperiled cause of the national government. The men and women who made up this army of peace, stimulated by much the same spirit that moved the soldiers at the front, wrought with ever increasing productiveness to supply the food and clothing that maintained the Federal forces. The material development of the State continued throughout the war almost as if no gigantic military struggle were going on.

Wisconsin was young among the great agricultural commonwealths of the Union. She was one of the group of northwestern states which but a decade prior to the war had wrested from the older sections of the East their supremacy in the production of wheat. During the war she produced for exportation larger crops of wheat than ever before in her history. Her surplus fed the armies battling at the front and the mill operatives toiling in New England, and entered conspicuously into the commerce of drought-stricken England and France.[1] During the dark days of 1862, when these countries seemed about to intervene on behalf of the Confederacy, this food supply exerted an undoubted influence in holding them to neutrality.[2]

The State gloried in the new importance of its agricultural products. Its sentiments were expressed by the Milwaukee *Sentinel* in a triumphant editorial published early in the war under the caption "A Greater than King Cotton." "The flocculent monarch no longer commands the world. Just now Breadstuffs have the throne. Shut up by an iron blockade, the textile scepter no longer sways. But there is going forward to foreign markets from the loyal states the greatest quantity and greatest value of crop export this, or any other country has ever seen. Wheat is king, and Wisconsin is the center of the Empire."[3]

Wheat was truly king in Wisconsin. The decade opened with the greatest crop in the history of the State. The stored-up fertility of three previous short years, 1856, 1858, and 1859, seemed to have crowded itself under unusually favorable conditions into this one extraordinary harvest. Between 27,000,000 and 29,000,000 bushels were garnered, almost twice the

[1] In 1864 J. C. Kennedy, superintendent of the eighth census declared: "There can be no doubt that the West, directly or indirectly, is the source of all the wheat that is exported from the United States, and this in addition to supplying New England with breadstuffs." U. S. *Census*, 1860, Introduction to agricultural statistics, p. xliii.

[2] See Emerson D. Fite, *Social and Industrial Conditions in the North During the Civil War* (N. Y., 1910), 17–21.

[3] Milwaukee *Sentinel*, Nov. 8, 1861. The same sentiment was expressed in a memorial sent by citizens of Milwaukee to Congress late in 1861: "Whatever may be said of the power of Cotton as influencing the conduct of Foreign Nations towards us, the power of food (which, in times of famine, can be furnished by the Northwest alone,) is still greater."

amount of any previous yield. In addition to the immensity of the crop, prices during the early months of autumn ruled high, higher indeed than at any corresponding time since the panic of 1857. Everywhere the industrial depression which had been hanging over the State lightened, and indications pointed to an era of unprecedented prosperity.

Under such circumstances the presidential election of 1860 approached. Some weeks before the canvass closed it became evident that Lincoln would be elected. The disaffected in the South openly threatened that such a choice would be followed by secession, and war clouds gathered ominously over the nation. The bonds and stocks of southern and border states, which as will be seen in a succeeding chapter formed the basis for most of the currency of Wisconsin, declined sharply in value, carrying with them into discredit a large part of the money necessary to move the crop. No farmer with hard wheat in his bins would exchange it, if he could possibly hold off, for bank notes that might over night become worthless. The price of wheat, too, came tumbling down as the prospect of the closing of southern markets against northern grain became more certain. From 94 cents per bushel at the beginning of August it sank by the close of navigation in December to 65 cents.[1]

The situation steadily became worse during the spring of 1861 as the nation helplessly drifted into civil war. With the price of wheat ruling 20 to 30 cents lower per bushel than during the previous year[2]

[1] Milwaukee Chamber of Commerce, *Report*, 1860, 22.
[2] *Id.*, 1861, 11–12.

and payment in currency that was daily depreciating in value, the discouraged farmers found their anticipated profits from the fine crop of 1860 rapidly vanishing. On April 12 the Confederate batteries opened fire on Fort Sumter. A sharp financial panic at once swept over the State. The banking system, undermined by previous months of strain, collapsed with a crash. The wildcat currency which was held largely by the agricultural classes sank to 50 cents on the dollar,[1] and business everywhere came to an abrupt standstill. The brief period of prosperity was over.

The crop of 1861 yielded excellent returns,[2] but prices remained low, and depression continued unabated throughout the ensuing winter and spring.[3] The summer of 1862, however, marked a turning point in the industrial situation as it did likewise in the affairs of the national government. Though the yield of wheat was somewhat unsatisfactory, prices rose, as the result of greenback inflation and of crop shortages in Europe, at just the time when the grain was ready for market. In 1863 nature once more responded generously to the efforts of the agriculturist,[4] while prices continued to rise as heavy issues of greenbacks followed one another and the

[1] See *post*, chap. vii.

[2] Wisconsin State Agricultural Society, *Transactions*, 1861–68, 33, 83.

[3] During the week before Christmas, 1861, when it seemed that the United States would become involved in war with England over the Trent affair, the price of wheat sank abruptly on the Milwaukee Exchange from 75 cents per bushel to 68 cents. "We are informed," observed the Milwaukee *Daily Wisconsin* on Dec. 23, 1861, "that our farmers, under the apprehension of a war with England, have been rushing in their grain [to Milwaukee] and selling at the ruling very low prices."

[4] Wis. Agric. Soc., *Trans.*, 1861–68, 33.

demands of the Federal government for its armies continued to increase.

Drought and chinch bugs almost ruined the crop of 1864. Prices, too, as a result of Federal reverses in the South, fluctuated during the year with a violence never before known. In July, 1864 the value of wheat in depreciated greenbacks was $2.26 per bushel in the Milwaukee market,[1] almost three times the amount which it had brought during the same month three years before. Upon the return of peace in the spring of 1865 the price slumped for a short time; it recovered, however, in 1866, and by May, 1867 it reached the highest point ever attained in the history of the State, $2.96 per bushel.[2]

During the five crucial years from 1860 to 1865 Wisconsin produced approximately 100,000,000 bushels of wheat,[3] of which probably two-thirds was exported. In 1860 she ranked second among the great wheat-producing states of the Union, being surpassed in that year only by her southern neighbor, Illinois. Until the close of the decade, with but few intervals, she maintained this high position in the ranks of the wheat-producing states of the nation.

Wheat completely dominated Wisconsin agriculture; other grains were raised only in sufficient quantity to supply local needs. During the five years from 1860 to 1865 the State produced not more than 45,000,000 bushels of corn, 75,000,000 bushels of oats, 4,500,000 bushels of rye, and 4,000,000 bushels of barley.[4]

[1] Milwaukee Chamber of Commerce, *Report*, 1864, 14.

[2] *Id.*, 1867, 18.

[3] U. S. Commissioner of Agriculture, *Reports*, 1862–65; Wis. Agric. Soc., *Trans.*, 1860–68; Milwaukee Chamber of Commerce, *Reports*, 1860–65.

[4] *Ibid.*; U. S. Comr. of Agric., *Reports*, 1862–65; Wis. Agric. Soc., *Trans.*, 1860–68.

Sheep husbandry was a branch of agriculture which enjoyed unusual prosperity during the Civil War. Wool was at a premium. Not only was it needed to replace southern cotton in northern homes but to supply the enormous demands of the Federal government for army cloth. The coarser fleeces were in especial demand, for they entered conspicuously into the manufacture of soldiers' uniforms. The Wisconsin grades, which were of this character, rose in value from 25 cents per pound at the beginning of the war to the unprecedented height of $1.05 in the fall of 1864.[1]

In the southern and eastern counties of the State, where wheat, owing to soil exhaustion, no longer adequately repaid the labor of the farmer, this stimulus to wool raising came as a blessing. It was here that the industry assumed its first and greatest importance. The Wisconsin Wool Growers' Association, organized at Janesville in September, 1864[2] for the discussion of trade matters and protective tariff legislation, was one of the numerous manifestations of this development. County associations of the same nature flourished in all the surrounding region. The wool product of the State rose from approximately 1,000,000 pounds in 1860[3] to 4,000,000 pounds in 1865,[4] a more than fourfold increase in five

[1] Milwaukee Chamber of Commerce, *Report*, 1861, 16–17; *id.*, 1864, 29–30. Common wool was in especial demand since army cloth was manufactured almost exclusively from it. Its price during the war was but little less than that paid for fine grades.

[2] Milwaukee *Sentinel*, Oct. 6, 1864; Wis. Agric. Soc., *Trans.*, 1861–68, 501–2.

[3] U. S. *Census*, 1860, *Agriculture*, 167; Milwaukee *Sentinel*, Jan. 1, 1861.

[4] The Chicago *Tribune* of May 1, 1866, in a carefully prepared article on the wool industry of the Northwest, estimated the wool product of

years. The number of sheep in the State increased in the same proportion from 332,954 in 1860[1] to 1,260,900 at the end of 1865.[2] Optimistic growers, encouraged by this rapid progress, predicted that at no distant date Wisconsin would rival Ohio in the wool industry.

Unhappily, with the return of peace this hope vanished. During the entire season of 1865 the price of wool ranged at scarcely half the level of the previous year. Nor was the slump merely temporary as in the case of wheat. On the contrary, as southern cotton fields once more became productive, the market value of wool continued to decline. Between 1864 and 1867 the price of Wisconsin grades fell from $1.05 to 29 cents per pound.[3] Despite this discouragement Wisconsin farmers continued to maintain their flocks. The impulse given to the industry during the war and the capacity it disclosed of thriving on worn-out wheat fields were sufficient to sustain it. The wool product of the State in 1868 was about 4,500,000 pounds;[4] in 1872, approximately the same.[5] The industry held its own, but little more.

Wisconsin for 1865 at 5,000,000 pounds. This estimate appears, however, to have been somewhat high.

[1] U. S. *Census*, 1860, *Agric.*, 166.

[2] U. S. Comr. of Agric., *Report*, 1865, 68. The shipment of wool from Milwaukee, nearly all of which was produced in Wisconsin, increased from 669,375 pounds in 1860 to 1,000,225 pounds in the first year of the war and 2,277,850 pounds in 1865. Altogether Milwaukee exported, during the years from 1860 to 1865, 8,610,411 pounds of common wool.

[3] Milwaukee Chamber of Commerce, *Report*, 1867, 39. In response to a memorial of the Wisconsin Wool Growers' Association the State legislature in 1869 adopted a joint resolution requesting Congress to raise the tariff on raw wool to 10 cents per pound plus 10 per cent ad valorem.

[4] *Id.*, 1868, 51. It was estimated that in 1868 Wisconsin and Minnesota together produced 5,000,000 pounds of wool, of which Minnesota produced approximately 500,000.

[5] *Id.*, 1872, 79.

Another interest, however, was now attracting the attention of many farmers in southern and eastern Wisconsin. This was dairying, and in particular the manufacture of cheese. Until near the close of the war this industry had been carried on, by those who engaged in it at all, merely as a diversion from the serious business of wheat raising. Each farmer maintained his own primitive kitchen dairying establishment in which the wife and children churned the butter and manufactured the cheese for the family table or the irregular local trade. Cheese was still largely imported from New York; butter was exported only in limited quantities.[1]

However, the unprofitableness of wheat raising in the exhausted fields of eastern and southern Wisconsin and the high prices paid for cheese during the closing years of the Civil War were factors influential enough to bring about a desired change. Enterprising farmers throughout this region now heeded the oft-repeated advice of their agricultural journals to "substitute the cow for the plow." At the same time there was introduced into the State the highly important American factory system of associated dairying. To the dairy industry of Wisconsin this meant what the cotton gin had meant to the plantations of the South and the reaper to the wheat fields of the West. Inaugurated in New York in 1851, by 1860 it had revolutionized the processes of dairying in that greatest of dairy states. In 1864 it invaded Wisconsin, when Chester Hazen, an

[1] Milwaukee exported butter for the first time in 1858. In 1861 shipments from that city amounted to 637,706 pounds, in 1865 to 1,263,740 pounds.

enterprising immigrant from the Empire State, established at Ladoga, in Fond du Lac County, the first cheese factory built in Wisconsin.[1] So far superior were the factory methods, whereby the milkings of an entire neighborhood were thrown together and the whole manufactured into cheese or butter by an expert, to the old private dairying methods that by the end of the Civil War thirty cheese factories were already in successful operation in Wisconsin, chiefly in Kenosha and other southeastern counties.[2] By the end of the decade more than a hundred were in business in the State.[3] The amount of cheese which

[1] It should be noted in this connection that the definition of a cheese factory is more or less arbitrary. It is not easy to say with precision what a factory is, or just when a private dairying establishment may be said to have ceased to be such and developed into a cheese factory. During the fifties many Wisconsin farmers manufactured butter and cheese in coöperation; instead of conducting their dairying individually, four or five neighbors would bring their milk to some one of the group who would carry on the manufacture of butter and cheese for the entire group. Such coöperation as this approximates the factory system of production, but does not in itself constitute it. The manufacturing families are producing butter and cheese as a side line to their main occupation, which is the regular pursuit of agriculture. In other words, the procedure under discussion constitutes only the household stage of the dairy industry. The factory system may be said to have been reached only when some individual agrees to take the milkings of so large a number of cows (usually regarded as about 100) as to necessitate giving all, or at least the major portion, of his time and attention to cheese manufacture. The first example of such an enterprise in Wisconsin was afforded by Chester Hazen in 1864.

[2] The earlier factories were usually coöperative in form, the farmers who owned them and produced milk for them merely hiring expert cheese-makers at a salary to operate them. Later factories came to be privately owned, the farmer paying the cheese-maker a stipulated price per pound for manufacturing and marketing the products of his milk. The modern practice, whereby the factory owner buys the milk which he uses and assumes the risks of marketing his cheese, was also coming into vogue in the early seventies.

[3] Estimate of W. D. Hoard, Northwestern Dairymen's Association, *Report*, 1873, 66.

they and the private dairies in Wisconsin produced increased from 1,104,300 pounds in 1860[1] to approximately 6,000,000 pounds in 1871,[2] and to almost 10,000,000 pounds in 1873.[3]

The production of butter by the factory or creamery plan secured a less rapid hold in Wisconsin. In Illinois, where in 1870 the first creamery in the Northwest was established at Elgin,[4] this branch of the dairy industry attained large proportions. Wisconsin dairymen from the beginning, however, specialized in cheese, leaving butter chiefly to the province of the private dairy. The output of dairy butter in the State increased from 13,611,328 pounds in 1860 to 22,473,036 pounds in 1870.

Wisconsin was well adapted to the dairy industry by reason of her favorable climate, her excellent grasses, and pure water. She was favored also by a social factor, the character of the immigrants who early settled within her borders. From New York came the descendants of pioneer English dairymen, who introduced into the Lake counties, the Fox River Valley, and the southern counties, the art of making the English cheddar cheese. From the mountain cantons of Switzerland came the hardy Swiss, traditional experts in cheese manufacture, who introduced into the northern hills of Green and the surrounding counties, the making of Swiss and Limburg "kase."[5] When to the natural aptitude of

[1] U. S. *Census*, 1860, *Agric.*, 168.

[2] Wis. Agric. Soc., *Trans.*, 1870, 55–58; Milwaukee *Sentinel*, Jan. 7, 1871.

[3] Estimate of W. D. Hoard, Wisconsin Dairymen's Association, *Report*, 1874, 13.

[4] Northwestern Dairymen's Assn., *Report*, 1880, 29.

[5] Green County led the State in cheese manufacture in 1870, its product being chiefly of the Swiss and the Limburg variety. Its 358,830 pounds

these immigrant dairymen were added the efficient methods of factory production, success was already half won.

Several obstacles, however, stood in the way of progress. Chief among these was the evil repute of western dairy products in the eastern markets. Wisconsin dairymen were obliged in the beginning to submit to the humiliation of concealing the identity of their cheeses, while their butter was contemptuously quoted on eastern exchanges as "Western grease." In order to win a market it was necessary to lift the quality of the Wisconsin product conspicuously above that of surrounding states,[1] a difficult task of education and coöperation. Fortunately for the State, a number of earnest and public-spirited leaders were ready to devote their energies to it. W. D. Hoard, the great dairy editor[2] and the future governor of the State, Stephen Faville, an early president of the Northwestern Dairymen's Association, Chester Hazen, the first president of the Wisconsin Dairymen's Association and one of the greatest cheese-

were, however, produced chiefly in private dairies, the factory system having spread slowly among the Swiss dairymen. By tradition, habit, and pride the foreign cheese-makers were individualistic, and not until 1870 was the first factory established in Green County. Much interesting data concerning the rise of the Swiss-cheese industry in Wisconsin may be found in *Wisconsin Historical Collections*, VIII, 411–45; *id.*, XII, 335–82; Wisconsin Historical Society, *Proceedings*, 1899, 226–30; Wis. Dairymen's Assn., *Report*, 1881, 50–54; *id.*, 1908, 167–75; Wisconsin Cheese Makers' Association, *Report*, 1902, 63–70; *id.*, 1908, 182–88; *id.*, 1911, 52–54.

[1] In 1866 was enacted the first dairy law passed in Wisconsin, "An act to prevent fraud in the manufacture of cheese." Wisconsin *General Laws*, 1866, chap. 6.

[2] In 1870, W. D. Hoard established at Lake Mills the *Jefferson County Union*, a weekly devoted to the improvement of Wisconsin dairying. It is the best existing source of information for the early history of the subject. *Hoard's Dairyman* was founded fifteen years later as the dairy edition of the *Union*.

makers in the Northwest, Hiram Smith, A. D. De-Land, Charles R. Beach, Robert Houston, and others scarcely less noteworthy led the way in the effort of Wisconsin to win recognition.

Concerted action, which was essential to the improvement of the cheese and butter product of Wisconsin, could be secured only by the organization of dairymen's associations. The initial step toward this end was taken on Mar. 6, 1867, when a convention of Illinois and Wisconsin dairymen was called together at Rockford, Illinois, where the Illinois and Wisconsin Dairymen's Association was formed, the first such organization to be established west of Lake Michigan.[1] In 1869 it developed into the present Northwestern Dairymen's Association, in whose deliberations Wisconsin cheese-makers took prominent part. Within the State the first dairymen's association to be organized was that of Fond du Lac County, established at Brandon on Jan. 15, 1870.[2] Two years later, on Feb. 15, 1872, the present Wisconsin Dairymen's Association was organized at Watertown, an event full of significance in the dairy history of the State.[3]

[1] Chicago *Times*, Mar. 8, 1867.

[2] Brandon *Times*, Jan. 19, 1870. The association was organized under the leadership of Chester Hazen, who was its first president. The Jefferson County Dairymen's Association followed soon after.

[3] Watertown *Democrat*, Feb. 22, 1872; *Jefferson Co. Union*, January to March, 1872. One of the purposes of the organization was declared by Stephen Faville to be the securing of "some united action with regard to the marketing of dairy products. As the matter now stands, the producers of butter and cheese were at the mercy of a disorganized market, or at least what organization existed was against rather than for them." For additional data concerning the early history of the Association see Wis. Dairymen's Assn., *Reports*, 1879, 121–29; 1900, 10–16; 1903, 15–22; 1905, 60–65; 1906, 168–76; 1911, 140–44. See also Wis. Cheese Makers' Assn., *Report*, 1901, 16–19; *id.*, 1908, 178–81.

These and similar associations subsequently organized were able, by discussion, investigation, and coöperation, to bring about a rapid improvement in the quality of the dairy products of the State. Careless and ignorant methods gave way to the scientific procedure and expert skill of the factory. Before the end of the seventies Wisconsin was carrying away at eastern dairy exhibitions coveted prizes, which had hitherto uniformly gone to New York and Ohio. Wisconsin dairymen no longer found it necessary to parade their cheese as "New Hamburg" or "New York Factory"; they now rested securely upon the reputation of their own brands.

The concerted efforts of dairymen's associations likewise made possible a close study of marketing methods and conditions. This was a matter of especial importance to Wisconsin dairymen in the early seventies. Until 1872 Wisconsin cheese exports had been manufactured almost exclusively for the consumption of the West and the Southwest. So rapid had been the development of the dairy industry in the Northwest, however, that these markets no longer sufficed. Each summer in the markets of Chicago and St. Louis the supply was greater than the demand, and as a consequence prices declined to a point that precluded profit. "We must make our cheese, like our flour, for the markets of the world," was the lesson which this condition enforced upon Wisconsin dairymen.[1]

The cheese that was suitable for the western trade, however, was unsuited to the requirements of the

[1] The best source of information concerning the marketing problems of Wisconsin cheese-makers at this time is the *Jefferson Co. Union*.

East and Europe. The West demanded a large, soft, and slightly colored variety; the eastern and English markets wished a brand of smaller size, of finer and firmer texture, and more color. The soft cheese was open to other objections besides its limited market. Dairymen had not yet learned the secret of manufacturing a product that would keep without deterioration during the hot summer months, and the soft variety in particular was likely to become strong and spoil. It was the practice of Wisconsin and other dairymen to rush to market without delay all the cheese made during June, July, and part of August, with the obvious result that prices were regularly depressed during the summer season.

During the summer of 1871 conditions were particularly bad,[1] and it was chiefly as a means of escape from them that the Wisconsin Dairymen's Association was organized early in 1872. The advantages of coöperative effort were quickly demonstrated. From addresses and exchanges of opinion at the regular conventions the dairymen of the State acquired information about such important trade matters as the variety of shapes, sizes, texture, coloring, and packing of cheese demanded by the home and foreign markets. It was no mere coincidence that Wisconsin cheese-makers first successfully invaded the East within a few years after the Association was organized.

One of the first steps of the Association was to organize at Watertown in February, 1872 a dairy board of trade patterned after that of Little Falls,

[1] Good Wisconsin cheese sold during the summer of 1871 for as low as 8 cents a pound.

New York.[1] Its purpose was to maintain regular dairy market days, at which cheese producers and wholesale dealers could meet for the purpose of buying and selling. Its success was immediate, and it was speedily followed by others at Kenosha and Sheboygan Falls. Wisconsin dairymen were enabled thus to establish direct relations with eastern and English markets, and gradually to shake off the Chicago middlemen who had hitherto dominated the industry.

Successful shipment for long distances of a perishable commodity like cheese depended upon swift transportation and a minimum of handling. Fortunately for the dairymen of Wisconsin these were secured during the later sixties by the organization of through-freight lines, which carried consignments from western producers to eastern consumers in guaranteed time and without change of cars.[2] Quite as important were the perfection and successful employment of refrigerator cars for the first time in 1871 or 1872, just when the Badger dairy farmers were in a position to make extensive use of them.[3] A few months after the Wisconsin Dairymen's Association was organized, its representative was able to procure from a prominent transportation company the new and highly important refrigerator service, as well as rates of freight so favorable that Wisconsin cheese could be shipped to London or Liverpool for but little more than the New York product.[4] Wisconsin dairymen, who enjoyed an

[1] *Jefferson Co. Union*, for the year 1872.

[2] See *post*, 383–87.

[3] Chicago *Prairie Farmer*, June 22, 1872; *Jefferson Co. Union*, July 19, 1872.

[4] For an interesting account of how these concessions were secured by

important advantage over their New York rivals by reason of the relative cheapness of their lands, were now in a position to compete with them on at least equal terms. Today, after the lapse of scarcely half a century, Wisconsin ranks as the greatest dairy state of the Union.

A number of interesting experiments were tried in Wisconsin as a result of the war, some of which were destined to affect significantly the future agricultural development of the State. Sugar cane and flax, which before the war had received but slight attention at the hands of the farmers, were taken up with new interest when war suddenly cut off the southern supply. Sugar cane of two varieties, Chinese imphee and African sorghum, had been introduced into the State by the State Agricultural Society as early as 1857.[1] Its culture had not been entirely satisfactory, however, and at the beginning of the Civil War only a few hundred farmers were raising the new plant. Even these, moreover, commonly produced only sufficient cane to supply their own family table with molasses.

In January, 1861, Alexander Randall, the far-sighted governor of Wisconsin, urged the legislature, "in view of the probable difficulties which may

W. D. Hoard as the representative of the Wisconsin Dairymen's Association and the Watertown Dairy Board of Trade see Wis. Dairymen's Assn., *Report*, 1900, 12–13; *id.*, 1903, 17–19; *Jefferson Co. Union*, July 5, 1872; Northwestern Dairymen's Assn., *Report*, 1873, 66–70; Wis. Agric. Soc., *Trans.*, 1872, 35–36, 90; Milwaukee Chamber of Commerce, *Report*, 1872, 34. For freight rates prior to 1872 see *Jefferson Co. Union*, Jan. 27, 1871 and Feb. 23, 1872.

[1] Wisconsin was one of the first states in the Union to experiment with sorghum.

embroil the States of the Union," to establish special premiums for the further encouragement of the growth of sugar cane.[1] His recommendations were disregarded in the excitement of the year, but the unusual price to which sugar rose following the opening of hostilities, soon furnished sufficient stimulus to stir the farmers of southern and eastern Wisconsin to action. Sorghum culture became the subject of interested discussion and experimentation throughout the region. In 1863 and for a number of years thereafter State sorghum conventions annually assembled at Madison, the center of sorghum culture in Wisconsin, and a monthly paper devoted to the new crop, the *Northwestern Sorgho Journal*, was established there in 1865. At every State and county agricultural fair enthusiastic sorghum growers exhibited their toothsome products, while manufacturers of rival cane crushers and syrup evaporators gave practical demonstrations before interested crowds of the art of preparing the syrup from the cane.[2]

Each year during the war the number of acres planted to sorghum revealed an increase over the acreage of the preceding year, and the hope was entertained by many well-informed citizens that Wisconsin would some day be independent of foreign sources for its supply of sugar and syrup.[3] In the census year of 1860 but 19,854 gallons of sorghum

[1] Wisconsin *Governor's Message and Accompanying Documents* (Madison, 1861), 13–14.

[2] See Wis. Agric. Soc., *Trans.*, 1861–68, 238–39, for a description of the sorghum exhibition at the State Fair in 1865.

[3] *Ibid.*, 101. Some attempts were made in Wisconsin to manufacture sorghum flour from the seed of the cane.

syrup were produced within the State.[1] In 1863 this amount had risen to 600,000 gallons, if we may trust an estimate made by Secretary O. S. Willey at the convention of 1864,[2] and in 1866, the year when the sorghum fever reached its height, nearly 1,000,000 gallons were reported as the product of the State.[3] "It is safe to assume," wrote the secretary of the State Agricultural Society in his report for 1868, "that in 1866 the value of the product considerably exceeded half a million of dollars. * * * At that time hundreds of fields in every section of the State greeted the eye of the traveler with the pleasing spectacle of this luxuriant crop, lifting its millions of plume-like panicles rejoicingly in the autumn sun. On every hand groaned and creaked the crowded mill, and upward curled the cloud of vapor and smoke as incense to Ceres for this, her latest and most wonderful gift."[4]

Despite such apparent success, however, it was impossible to escape the fact that the Wisconsin summer was too short fully to ripen the cane. In favorable seasons it matured sufficiently to permit of the manufacture of excellent molasses, but never sufficiently to produce sugar. Both during and after the conclusion of the war the State Agricultural Society persistently offered a handsome premium for ten pounds of dry sorghum sugar made within the State, but the prize was never awarded.[5] When sugar prices again fell to normal, the conviction—strongly

[1] U. S. *Census*, 1860, *Agric.*, 169.

[2] E. W. Skinner, *Sorgho Hand Book* (Madison, 1864), 13.

[3] *Wisconsin Farmer*, 1866, 119.

[4] Wis. Agric. Soc., *Trans.*, 1861–68, 35.

[5] *Ibid.*, 36.

rebutted during the war—that Wisconsin lay too far north for successful sugar-cane production gained ground. In the lower latitudes of Ohio, Indiana, Illinois, and Missouri sorghum continued to flourish, but in Wisconsin it practically disappeared when the war-time emergency passed.

A new sugar plant, however, the sugar beet, seemed to hold out better prospects. It had long been successfully cultivated in Central Europe, but until the close of the Civil War had almost entirely escaped the notice of American agriculturists. In Wisconsin a vague project for an experimental beet-sugar farm and refinery was under consideration in Oconto County as early as 1863.[1] Not until 1868, however, were any real experiments made. In the spring of that year two enterprising German immigrants, one of whom had been employed in the Fatherland for many years as foreman in a beet-sugar refinery, rented a tract of land near the city of Fond du Lac and planted it to sugar beets. Such time as they could spare during the summer was devoted to the erection of a primitive though complete sugar refinery. By 1869 they were manufacturing sugar at the rate of 1,000 pounds per day,[2] a feat which enabled the Milwaukee *Sentinel* to boast early in 1870 that Wisconsin was producing more beet sugar than all the other states of the Union combined.[3] It was one of the earliest attempts at beet-sugar manufacture in the United States and

[1] La Crosse *Democratic Journal*, Aug. 12, 1863.

[2] This account is constructed from random items gathered from the Fond du Lac *Saturday Reporter*, 1868–71; Wis. Agric. Soc., *Trans.*, 1861–71; U. S. Comr. of Agric., *Report*, 1869, 349–50. Late in 1869 the proprietors became discouraged and removed their works to California.

[3] Milwaukee *Sentinel*, Jan. 11, 1870.

as such received wide notice throughout the Northwest. Other companies were induced to follow the example thus set, and between the years 1869 and 1871 approximately a dozen beet-sugar companies were organized in the southern and eastern counties of the State.[1] The most successful of these, the First Sauk County Farmers' Association for the Fabrication of Beet Sugar, an interesting company of some fifty German farmers, which had secured the services of a German expert, manufactured in 1871 as much as 134,400 pounds of beet sugar and 72,350 pounds of molasses.[2]

In spite of every effort, however, it was impossible to compete successfully with the cheaper and better southern product, and after one or two years of discouragement all these pioneer companies disappeared. Yet they served a useful purpose, for they demonstrated that the soil and climate of Wisconsin were well adapted to the growth of the root. A quarter of a century later Wisconsin made a second attempt, this time to persevere, until today she ranks well up among the great beet-sugar states of the Union.

We have already seen how the disappearance of southern cotton from northern markets during the war stimulated the wool industry in Wisconsin. It likewise stimulated flax, a crop which prior to the war had been steadily declining in importance not only in Wisconsin but throughout the country. The

[1] In 1870 the State legislature in order to encourage the manufacture of beet sugar in the State passed an act which exempted from taxation for a period of ten years all property and capital stock engaged in beet-sugar refining. Wis. *Gen. Laws*, 1870, chap. 62.

[2] For additional data concerning this and other early beet-sugar projects in Wisconsin see Wis. Agric. Soc., *Trans.*, 1861–68, 388; 1869, 27, 223; 1870, 25; 1871, 350.

decline had been due in part to the immense development of cotton during the decade of the fifties; in a measure, also, to the expense of converting the raw flax into linen. During the war the North turned eagerly to the task of cheapening the processes of linen manufacture. Large premiums were offered in several eastern states for the discovery of methods whereby flax fiber could easily be spun on cotton machinery, and in 1863 Congress appropriated $20,000 to this end.[1]

Governor Randall of Wisconsin, who confidently believed that these efforts to "cottonize flax," as the process was called, would soon be successful, urged the State legislature in 1861 to encourage the cultivation of the crop by offering special premiums.[2] His recommendation bore no fruit, but in 1863 the farmers of the State spontaneously took up the work. In 1864 a number of prominent corporations, notably the New York and De Pere Flax Company, and the Northwestern Flax Company of Chicago, sent agents throughout the southern and eastern counties distributing free seed and contracting for the crop which the farmers agreed to raise. Enough flax was soon produced to justify the erection of several linen factories and linseed-oil mills, and the new industry seemed to flourish. However, no substantial progress was made in the art of cottonizing flax, the expense of manufacturing linen remained prohibitive, and when southern cotton again appeared on the market flax culture suffered a decline.

Strangely enough the war gave almost no impetus to the cultivation of tobacco in Wisconsin. The

[1] *Id.*, 1870, 28–33.

[2] Wis. *Mess. and Docs.*, 1861, 13–14.

tobacco plant had originally been introduced into the State during the early territorial days. To its present favorite abode in the rich limestone fields of Dane and Rock counties it came somewhat later. It was brought thither by immigrants from the tobacco districts of Ohio in 1853.[1] Nowhere, however, had it been able to secure a substantial footing. Wheat was the all-absorbing interest, and tobacco was raised, where raised at all, only in quantities sufficient to supply home requirements. Some few farmers, it is true, particularly immigrants from the tobacco regions of Connecticut and Ohio, were encouraged during the war to take up the new crop, and the product of the State increased from 87,595 pounds in 1860[2] to 162,891 pounds in 1865.[3]

Toward the close of the sixties the farmers of southeastern Wisconsin were forced by the bitter experience of continuous short crops to abandon the old ruinous policy of unrotated wheat. The price of tobacco at the same time increased, after a heavy decline in 1865, to approximately 18 cents per pound by 1868,[4] and now for the first time Wisconsin farmers turned their attention seriously to it. In 1870, 960,813 pounds were produced, almost all of it in Rock and Dane counties.[5]

[1] Ralph and Orrin Pomeroy and J. R. Hiestand are usually credited with introducing tobacco into Wisconsin. While they were by no means the first white men to raise tobacco in the State, they were probably the first to raise it in the present tobacco region and the first to make it a major farm interest. University of Wisconsin, *Bulletin*, No. 101 (Madison, 1904), 155–75; Wis. Agric. Soc., *Trans.*, 1870, 364.

[2] U. S. *Census*, 1860, *Agric.*, 167.

[3] U. S. Comr. of Agric., *Report*, 1865, 55.

[4] University of Wisconsin, *Bulletin*, No. 101, 175.

[5] U. S. *Census*, 1870, III, 282.

The Norwegians, who predominated in the tobacco region, soon acquired from their American neighbors the art of tobacco culture. They proved to be well adapted to the industry, for not only were they industrious and painstaking, but they were able to employ in the light work involved in tobacco raising the large families with which immigrants were always blessed. To this day Scandinavians are the chief tobacco growers of the State.

Wisconsin tobacco was almost exclusively of the variety used for the manufacture of cigars and known to the trade as seed leaf. At first considered inferior, it soon came to be ranked with Connecticut tobacco for cigar-wrapping purposes. Edgerton, in Rock County, early assumed importance as a tobacco center and continued to grow until it is now one of the greatest primary cigar-wrapper markets in the country.

Perhaps the most interesting episode in the agricultural history of the period is the hop craze which swept over the State during the years between 1864 and 1870. The hop vine seems originally to have been brought to Wisconsin by pioneers from the great hop districts of the Empire State. Like tobacco, however, its early efforts to secure a footing in competition with wheat were attended with little success. In 1860 the product of the State was but 135,587 pounds.[1] During the war a slight improvement took place. A discriminatory tax on whisky and the development of a new taste for lager beer in the United States stimulated the numerous breweries of Wisconsin to increase largely their output. As a

[1] *Id.*, 1860, *Agric.*, 168.

result the hop growers of the State found a profitable market for their crop at their very doors. The development of the industry under such influences was gradual and healthy.

Toward the close of the war, however, a new factor entered. In New York and other eastern hop centers the louse, a traditional enemy of the vine, swept over the fields, and for a succession of years the eastern crops were almost ruined. Prices as a result went soaring. In the fall of 1861 the best Wisconsin grades ranged in the New York market at from 15 to 25 cents per pound;[1] by 1865 they were 50 to 65 cents per pound,[2] and in 1867, 55 to 70 cents per pound.[3]

The profits held out to hop growers by such prices were extraordinary. In 1865 numbers of growers in Sauk County were said to have realized from their crop $800 to $1,200 per acre, and one farmer was reported to have sold the product of fifteen-sixteenths of an acre for $1,600.[4] In 1867 the *Wisconsin State Journal* contained an account of a farmer who was reported to have raised on a single acre 3,100 pounds of hops worth 58½ cents per pound.[5] "Cases are numerous," declared the secretary of the State Agricultural Society in 1868, "in which the first crop has paid for the land and all the improvements; leaving subsequent crops a clear profit, minus the cost of cultivation and harvesting."[6] The Milwaukee

[1] New York *Herald*, 1861, market quotations.

[2] *Id.*, 1865, market quotations.

[3] *Id.*, 1867, market quotations.

[4] *Dodge County Citizen*, Nov. 16, 1865.

[5] *Wisconsin State Journal*, Dec. 6, 1867.

[6] Wis. Agric. Soc., *Trans.*, 1861–68, 37.

Sentinel in 1867 estimated that of $2,000,000 paid to the hop growers of Sauk County during the year, $1,500,000 was clear profit.[1]

Whether or not such accounts were true, and they were no doubt highly exaggerated, their effect was the same upon the popular mind. Hop growing developed into a veritable craze. "Gathering renewed force with every new acre planted in the county of Sauk, where it may be said to have originated, and where the crop of 1865 was over half a million of pounds, it spread from neighborhood to neighborhood, and from county to county, until by 1867 it had hopped the whole State over; so completely revolutionizing the agriculture of some sections that one in passing through them found some difficulty in convincing himself that he was not really in old Kent, of England."[2] In 1867 the product of the State was between 6,000,000 and 7,000,000 pounds, valued at $4,200,000;[3] by the next year it had leaped almost to 11,000,000 pounds.[4] Sauk County alone produced in 1867 upon 2,548 acres of land approximately 4,000,000 pounds, or one-fifth of all the hops raised in the entire country,[5] and the next year, upon a more than doubled acreage, her product was even larger. In 1867 Kilbourn (Wisconsin Dells), the chief shipping

[1] Milwaukee *Sentinel*, Nov. 13, 1867.

[2] Wis. Agric. Soc., *Trans.*, 1861–68, 37.

[3] Baraboo *Republic*, Dec. 11, 1867. This weekly paper, published in the heart of the hop district, is the best source of information concerning the hop episode. In the interests of the hop-growers it probably understated rather than overstated the annual crop. See also Milwaukee Chamber of Commerce, *Report*, 1867, 47.

[4] Baraboo *Republic*, July 22, 1868; *Emmet Well's Weekly Hop Circular*, Aug. 1, 1868, printed in Baraboo *Republic*, Aug. 5, 1868; Milwaukee Chamber of Commerce, *Report*, 1868, 57–58.

[5] Milwaukee *Sentinel*, Nov. 13, 1867.

center of the Wisconsin hop district, ranked, according to the *Wisconsin Mirror*, as "the greatest primary hop depot in the United States—perhaps in the world."[1]

Harvest time in the hop district was a season of unusual and picturesque animation. Far and near from the surrounding country girls and women of every class and condition, in response to the call for pickers, streamed into the hop gardens. "The railroad companies are utterly unable to furnish cars for the accommodation of the countless throngs who daily find their way to the depots * * * to take the cars for the hop fields. Every passenger car is pressed into service, and freight and platform cars are fixed up as well as possible for the transportation of the pickers. Every train has the appearance of an excursion train, on some great gala day, loaded down as they are with the myriads of bright-faced, young girls * * *."[2]

In 1868 the *Wisconsin Mirror* estimated that 30,000 girls were at work picking hops in the region tributary to Kilbourn, of whom 20,000 had been brought in from outside.[3] "Truly Hops are King, and in this region 30,000 Queens are waiting on the old fellow."[4]

The girls, in addition to receiving their board, were ordinarily paid at the rate of 50 cents per ten-pound box, a rate which permitted industrious workers to earn readily from $1.75 to $2.25 a day. Nor were wages the only attraction. The picking season was

[1] *Wisconsin Mirror*, June 17, 1868.
[2] *Wisconsin State Register*, Aug. 29, 1868.
[3] *Wis. Mirror*, Aug. 12 and Sept. 2, 1868.
[4] *Ibid.*, Sept. 2, 1868.

a time of feasting and merrymaking. Each night when darkness put an end to labor, the well-used fiddle was fetched from its case, and to its merry strains, under the mellow autumn moon the unwearied tripped the jovial steps of the hop dance.

It was not long before the inventive Yankee mind was at work upon the problem of substituting machinery for the costly labor of the pickers. In 1868 the Baraboo *Republic* listed nine such machines invented during the year by men residing in the Wisconsin hop region.[1] None of these mechanical hop pickers, however, was ever successful, though great things were predicted for them.

The magnificent profits realized by hop growers were usually as royally spent. If one may credit the tales still told in Sauk and adjoining counties, farmers' daughters rustled in silks and satins, purchased pianos, and visited foreign courts, while sons exchanged overalls for broadcloth and sported blooded horses and fancy phaetons. Hop growers, who at first proceeded cautiously, soon threw discretion to the winds and sank not only their profits, but as much more as they could raise on credit, into the purchase of more acres and the poling of more yards. No words of warning or advice could at such a time gain a hearing. Even the farsighted, who realized that a crash must inevitably come, took a gambler's chance of winning before luck changed.

The change came sooner and more disastrously than even the worst fears anticipated. In 1868, owing to an unfavorable growing season and the inroads of the recently arrived louse, the average

[1] Baraboo *Republic*, July 22 and 29, 1868.

yield of Wisconsin yards sank from 1,400 to 800 or 900 pounds per acre,[1] while the quality of much of the crop was inferior. Yet even this was but the beginning of the misfortune. No sooner did the new hops begin to move than it became evident that the bottom had dropped out of the market. The eastern growers, having successfully banished the louse, had again produced a normal crop. The necessity for the Wisconsin product had disappeared at just the time when the output had increased, in spite of the small yield per acre, to almost 11,000,000 pounds. The blackest predictions were fulfilled; the New York market was hopelessly glutted.

Prices swiftly declined. The growers who first sent their crop to market were fortunate to receive from 25 to 35 cents per pound for it, though they bitterly protested at the time that they were being robbed. As the season advanced, prices sank lower and lower, until at length hops became practically unsalable. It is probable that the average price realized by the growers did not exceed 10 cents per pound, or a trifle over half the cost of production.[2] A large part of the crop was held over until the next year in the hope that the situation might improve, but ultimately it had to be sold at from 3 to 5 cents per pound.[3]

Some growers courageously attempted in 1869 to retrieve their lost fortunes, and a fair yield was secured, but prices continued to range between 10 and 20 cents, and the net result of the effort was only

[1] *Ibid.*, July 22, 1868.

[2] Milwaukee Chamber of Commerce, *Report*, 1868, 41. It was usually estimated that the cost of raising, picking, and curing hops in the West amounted to 18 or 20 cents a pound.

[3] *Id.*, 1869, 57–58.

to increase the general distress. Hundreds of farmers were ruined, other hundreds lost the savings of a lifetime. Depression succeeded feverish enthusiasm. The hop bubble had burst.[1]

It has no doubt been observed in these pages that the southern and eastern counties of Wisconsin were the scene of most of the innovations in the agriculture of the State during the war. Here the wool and dairy industries first took root, here the substitutes for southern crops received their testing, and here the hop episode reached its climax. The influence of the war in stimulating these experiments has already been noticed. A more fundamental influence, however, was the increasing soil deterioration of the region, caused by decades of unrotated wheat growing. Meager harvests of inferior wheat were forcing even the most unintelligent farmers to look about them for new crops and a better system of agriculture. The innovations which the Civil War encouraged mark the first sustained effort of Wisconsin to advance to a rational system of mixed agriculture. They represent the transition from an old to a new kind of farming.

The agricultural system from which these early Wisconsin farmers were trying to escape was characteristic of the frontier. It was a one-crop system in which every interest was sacrificed to wheat. Wheat was the obvious crop to grow. It required little care and less equipment, two extremely important considerations in a new community where

[1] The depression in the hop market continued unrelieved until 1871, when owing to the failure of the eastern crop, prices again became normal. A large proportion of Wisconsin growers had in the meantime plowed up their yards. After 1871 the industry became comparatively steady.

both labor and capital were scarce and expensive. It could be marketed to advantage for its value was high compared with its bulk. It undoubtedly exhausted the soil, but to the pioneer this was a minor matter. The original cost of the farm was "an insignificant fraction of its intrinsic value, which is more than repaid by the net proceeds of a single crop. He cares little for a small diminution of productive capacity, while he can fence and stock his farm, and place money in bank, from the sale of successive crops of wheat, and then sell the naked land for ten-fold its original cost."[1] Onward toward the setting sun uncounted millions of fresh acres held out their invitation to the enterprising. There wheat would once more spring up at the very touch of the plow.

The pioneer farmer should not be harshly condemned for thus exploiting the richness of the soil. He himself was a victim of circumstances.[2] Usually he was poor and saddled with debt. He was obliged to capitalize the fertility of his soil as quickly as possible in order to free himself from embarrassing encumbrances, and to secure necessary improvements. Impractical eastern theorists might easily preach the beauty and dignity of crop rotation and scientific agriculture; he knew that such a system was unsuited to conditions on the frontier. If he neglected or destroyed the small quantities of manure that accumulated on his meagerly stocked farm, if he burned his strawstacks in midnight celebration, that, too, was part of an unescapable system.[3] "Bet-

[1] U. S. Comr. of Agric., *Report*, 1868, 18.

[2] U. S. *Census*, 1860, *Agric.*, pp. viii–x.

[3] In 1868 when conditions were improving, the secretary of the Wisconsin State Agricultural Society wrote: "Fewer of the old barns lie inaccessible

ter tillage, accompanied by the use of manures and other fertilizers, would not, upon the virgin soils, have added sufficiently to the yield to pay the cost of applying them. Hence, to the first farmers of the State poor farming was the only profitable farming, and consequently the only good farming, an agriculturo-economical paradox from which there was no escape."[1]

No doubt this system of agriculture persisted for many years after it had ceased to be even economically advantageous in southern and eastern Wisconsin. As early even as the decade of the fifties soil exhaustion was making itself evident in short crops of inferior grain. But settled habits of single cropping, ignorance of better methods of farming, and the high price to which wheat rose on occasions when a change seemed imminent maintained the preëminence of the great staple. Toward the end of the fifties, after a succession of unfruitful years, a change seemed to be at hand, when there came the tremendous crop of 1860, rousing new hopes that the soil was still undiminished in its richness. The war followed soon after, during which, unhappily, the movement for reform suffered another setback. Southern battlefields called from the farms of the State the labor which was necessary for a thorough system of agriculture; the rapid introduction of agricultural machinery, particularly harvesting machinery, and the

and useless in the steaming, stenchy craters of surrounding manure heaps; and a less number of those newly built are found standing on the brow of a hill or on the brink of some stream, with a view to an easy riddance of such 'miserable offal' as, somehow, will accumulate in and about every stable and cow-yard!" *Trans.*, 1861–68, 32.

[1] W. W. Daniells, "Agriculture," in *History of Dodge County, Wisconsin* (Chicago, 1880), 151.

passage of the Homestead Act in 1862 encouraged as never before the cultivation of broad acres. More important than all else, the unusual prices to which wheat rose during and after the conflict tempted agriculturists to continue raising it even though the yield per acre was declining and the quality of the grain was inferior.[1] Those who at the beginning of the war were contemplating careful and thorough methods of agriculture now reverted to old practices, and wheat was once more planted in fields too impoverished adequately to sustain it. The southern and eastern counties of the State continued throughout the decade to specialize in the staple and easily maintained their leadership in its production. To the observing, however, it was evident that a change was at hand.

Fortunately a good share of the farmers of the State were immigrants of European origin. The Yankee farmer has been characterized as a depleter of soils and destroyer of forests, and certain it is that his restless spirit and eager enterprise fitted him rather to be an exploiter than a conserver of natural resources. The European immigrant who followed in his footsteps knew the value of land, was accustomed to careful farming, and was by nature pains-

[1] During the closing years of the decade Wisconsin was producing only slightly more wheat than at the beginning, though the number of acres devoted to it had increased over 50 per cent. The decline in the quality of the Wisconsin grain was even more striking. In 1865, 77 per cent of the wheat shipped to Milwaukee was graded "No. 1"; in 1870 only 30 per cent attained this standard. Much of the grain received in Milwaukee, it should further be observed, was raised in Minnesota and Iowa, a larger proportion in 1870 than in 1865. Were it possible to exclude from the Milwaukee receipts this high-grade wheat, it would be seen that the decline in the quality of the Wisconsin product was even more rapid than has been indicated.

taking and industrious. Many of the early arrivals were, it is true, driven by poverty and the force of surroundings to adopt the land-skimming methods of the Americans. But those who came when the first era of exploitation was over exerted a powerful influence for a change to a more rational system of agriculture.

The expansion of the agricultural borders of Wisconsin proceeded with some interruption during the war. In 1860 only the southern half of the State was settled and under cultivation. The northern half was still for the most part an unbroken forest, disturbed only by the hunter, the trapper, and the lumberman.[1] During the war two projections of settlement were thrust northward into this region, one in the northwestern portion, the other, of smaller dimensions, in the northeastern portion. Between the two, and in the far northern counties, there remained a practically unexplored and somewhat uninviting wilderness, the subjugation of which was left to a later generation.

The extension of the agricultural frontier of the State was reflected in a rapid increase in farm acreage. Between 1860 and 1870 the amount of land in farms increased from 7,893,587 acres to 11,715,321 acres, more than 48 per cent, while the number of acres of improved land increased from 3,746,167 to 5,899,343, more than 57 per cent.[2] Most pronounced was the expansion in the northwestern counties, where farm acreage increased 225 per cent and im-

[1] Among the minor products of the northern forests and marshes were maple sugar, furs, cranberries, and ginseng.

[2] U. S. *Census*, 1860, *Agric.*, 166; *id.*, 1870, III, 280.

proved lands 275 per cent. In the northeastern counties the increases were 115 and 135 per cent, respectively.[1] It was the addition of these new acres that maintained Wisconsin high in the ranks of the wheat-producing states of the nation at a time when the yield per acre of her southern farms was swiftly declining.

In the settled portions of the State the new farm acreage represented lands which in the first rush of development had for one reason or another been passed by. In the northwest and the northeast, however, it represented the conquest of the public domain. The Federal government, the State, the land-grant railroads, and the various canal and plank-road companies were all at this time competing with one another in the sale of their lands in this frontier region. The Federal government, moreover, inaugurated on Jan. 1, 1863 its new policy of giving away 160-acre homesteads to actual settlers, and by the end of the war had thus disposed of 351,833 acres in Wisconsin, chiefly in the northwestern counties.[2]

Although Wisconsin was thus rapidly expanding, her rate of growth was far less than that of her neighbors, Minnesota and Iowa. Indeed it was but a fourth as rapid as her own growth during the decade of the fifties. The war was perhaps responsible in a small measure for this check, but the chief cause lay elsewhere. In 1860 practically all the choice

[1] The counties grouped as northwestern are St. Croix, Pierce, Pepin, Dunn, Chippewa, Buffalo, Eau Claire, Trempealeau, Jackson, La Crosse, Monroe, and Polk. The counties grouped as northeastern are Door, Kewaunee, Brown, Outagamie, Waupaca, Shawano, Marathon, Portage, Waushara, Manitowoc, Winnebago, and Calumet.

[2] U. S. Commissioner of General Land Office, *Reports*, 1860–70.

public lands in Wisconsin, with the exception of those in the northwestern and the northeastern counties, were gone. The only stretches of unoccupied land in the State lay in the north-central and the far northern sections, and these were burdened for the most part with timber and stumps. They were, moreover, distant from any means of transportation and, still more important, were generally believed to be unfit for cultivation. The wash of glacial streams in this region has formed along its valleys great sand streams and flats, constituting what we know as the "plains" or "barrens." Unfortunately, these occurred mainly along the earlier lines of travel, giving to the section an appearance of barrenness that was quite untrue of it as a whole.[1] Even as late as 1868 this erroneous idea found confirmation in a report of the United States Commissioner of Agriculture. "The principal part of the unsold government lands in Wisconsin," it is declared, "are situated in the northern portion of the State and are more especially important on account of their timber. * * * A large portion of the soil in the region of the unsold lands is not generally adapted to purposes of agriculture, being wet and marshy, or a dry drift sand."[2] It is not strange that the great bulk of immigrants who came to Wisconsin passed on to the fertile prairies of Minnesota. Only the

[1] T. C. Chamberlin, *Geology of Wisconsin, 1873–1879* (Madison, 1883), I, 681. This impression of the barrenness of north and north-central Wisconsin was confirmed by some of Wisconsin's early geologists who characterized the region as an alternation of sand ridges and impenetrable swamps.

[2] U. S. Comr. of Agric., *Report*, 1868, 456. With the completion of the Wisconsin Central Railroad through this region its true character became better known, and thereafter settlement was rapid.

easily accessible and therefore well-known northwestern and northeastern counties were able to compete with the western neighbor of Wisconsin in the race for development.[1]

Agricultural education suffered an unfortunate check in the State during the adverse years between 1861 and 1863, when popular interest was diverted to southern battle-fields and financial support was cut off by the more pressing demands of the war. In 1861 the Wisconsin State Agricultural Society, perhaps the most effective single agent for agricultural education, lost its annual legislative appropriation and was for a time practically suspended. The Wisconsin Fruit Growers' Association, a flourishing organization founded in 1853, was even harder hit, being obliged to disband formally in the first year of the war. Of the thirty-seven county agricultural societies active at the beginning of the war, only eighteen survived the year, and not until the end of the decade did the number again reach its former proportions. Upon the outbreak of hostilities the Wisconsin State Agricultural Society patriotically turned over its fairground to Governor Randall for use as a military camp,[2] and partly for this reason, partly because of popular indifference, omitted its annual State Fair in the years 1861, 1862, and 1863.

[1] That the war did not materially check Wisconsin's agricultural expansion may be seen from the fact that the average number of homesteads annually entered between 1863 and 1865 was only slightly less than during the following years of the decade. The quantity of land sold during the period offers no evidence of agricultural expansion. A large part of the public domain was disposed of to lumber speculators who had an eye solely to the timber contained on it.

[2] From Camp Randall, as the fair ground came to be called, approximately two-thirds of Wisconsin's soldiers went forth to battle.

The various county societies that survived the year 1861 continued to hold their annual fairs as before, chiefly, it seems, to earn the bonus allowed by the State, for the exhibitions usually ended in partial or complete failure.

The prosperous closing years of the war, however, brought a revival of interest. In 1864 the State Agricultural Society once more held its annual State Fair, and scored a success that was surpassed only in the following year when the national war hero, Gen. William T. Sherman, delivered the principal address. In rapid succession the sorghum growers, wool growers, and fruit growers organized new State societies or reorganized lifeless ones, while in most of the older counties discussion clubs and district associations of one kind or another sprang into vigorous life.[1] In 1866, in accordance with the Federal College Land Grant Act of 1862,[2] the State University was reorganized so as to include a department of agriculture and mechanical arts, an event little appreciated at the time, but highly significant for the future of agricultural education in the State.

Wisconsin sent into the Federal armies, east and west, approximately 80,000 of her sturdiest sons. To the newly opened prairies of Minnesota and Iowa she sent, during the war, a good many thousand more. Other thousands were lured away to the mining camps of Idaho, Colorado, Nevada, and California. This depletion of labor in a State in which

[1] The Granger movement in Wisconsin originated in the revival of interest in agricultural education which followed the Civil War. In 1872 there were approximately one hundred granges of the Patrons of Husbandry in the State. Wis. Agric. Soc., *Trans.*, 1872–73, 91.

[2] Wis. *Gen. Laws*, 1866, chap. 114.

five-sixths of the population were farmers was a particularly severe blow to agriculture. How did Wisconsin in spite of the loss manage, as we have seen, to expand her agricultural borders and harvest her extraordinary crops? The answer is to be found in the substitution of agricultural machinery for hand labor, the employment of women and children to a greater extent than formerly, and the acquisition of thousands of hardy German and Scandinavian immigrants from Europe.

Agricultural machinery had been employed in the State to a limited extent long before the war. Indeed, the reaper and the mower, which were revolutionizing American agriculture, had been brought into Wisconsin as early as 1844.[1] The Northwest was particularly adapted to the use of such machinery because of its broad and level prairies, its chronic scarcity of labor, and its peculiar mode of single cropping. The spread of the new appliances was more rapid, therefore, in this portion of the country than in the older communities of the East. It was estimated in 1861 that not less than 3,000 reapers of different patterns, but all using patented portions of the McCormick reaper, had been sold in Wisconsin during the previous year.[2] However, even in Wisconsin a large proportion of farmers was still, at the beginning of the war, sowing and reaping by the old laborious methods of their forefathers.

The war gave a tremendous stimulus to the spread

[1] R. G. Thwaites, "Cyrus Hall McCormick and the Reaper," in Wis. Hist. Soc., *Proc.*, 1908, 234–59.

[2] Memorial adopted by the executive committee of the Wisconsin State Agricultural Society on Feb. 6, 1861 against the extension of patent rights to Cyrus W. McCormick. *Wis. Farmer*, 1861, 94.

of agricultural machinery. Even the most conservative farmers, who had been wont to sniff at the newfangled devices while labor was comparatively plentiful, now eagerly adopted them as a means of saving their crops. At the very outbreak of hostilities the *Wisconsin State Journal* in an earnest editorial thus warned its agricultural readers:

> But this season the prospect is almost certain, that many thousands of our most active and efficient harvest hands, the very bone and sinew of the harvest fields, will be called away to other fields of toil and danger. * * * The only way to make up for short manual help, is to substitute as far as possible, the horses and machinery. In fact, that is all that has saved the State for years past. Every good reaper counts daily equal to from five to ten men. Hence the thousands of reapers in the State, represent from five to ten times as many thousand men. Then fix up your reapers, farmers, all of you that have them, put them in the best possible condition at the earliest opportunity, for even now harvest is close upon you. The tiny green blades that are just now piercing the soil, will in sixty days expand into the ripening yellow fields, calling for the reaper and harvest hands. Then look up your reapers we repeat and those of you who have not already got them and intend to buy this season, look around you in time to get what you want.[1]

Labor-saving appliances became everywhere the subject of earnest discussion and experimentation. Swarms of rival agents proclaiming the superiority of their wares penetrated to the most remote parts of the State; public trials, at which rival machines were put to test before crowds of delighted farmers, became a common occurrence; at every State and county fair the department of machinery was a chief center of attraction.

The amount of machinery sold was enormous. A single railroad leading out of the city of Milwaukee moved, during the years from 1861 to 1865, 3,951,096 pounds of machinery and 22,214,094 pounds of

[1] *Wis. State Jour.*, May 6, 1861.

agricultural implements.[1] In 1868 the secretary of the Wisconsin State Agricultural Society observed:

> As to the mechanical branch of agriculture, we may safely assert that it has made more progress during the years embraced in this Report [1861–1868] than ever before within the same length of time. * * * The number of reapers and mowers annually sold in Wisconsin, during the period under review, is really marvellous; compelling the conviction that at present there must be very few farmers unsupplied. One single firm in the city of Madison is this year selling no less than six thousand machines of a particular patent. And judging from the equal activity and large income returns, of other agents, not only at this one point, but in various portions of the State, this number will be many times multiplied.[2]

The importance of agricultural machinery in the economy of the war can scarcely be overemphasized. Without the mechanical reaper for instance, each one of which released from the harvest fields of the State from four to six able-bodied men,[3] it is impossible to conceive how the enormous wheat crops of the war period could have been garnered. Besides the reaper there were dozens of other machines of less importance, mechanical threshers, seed drills, harrows, rollers, horserakes, hay loaders, and sulky cultivators, in new and modified forms, as well as scores of varieties of improved agricultural implements, all aiding to produce the food of the nation during the years of the crisis.[4]

[1] Milwaukee & Prairie du Chien Railway Company, *Reports*, 1861–66. See also U. S. Comr. of Agric., *Report*, 1866, 7.

[2] Wis. Agric. Soc., *Trans.*, 1861–68, 38–39.

[3] U. S. Comr. of Agric., *Report*, 1867, p. vi.

[4] "No matter how great the industry and patriotism of the people, it is universally conceded that the success of our Government in bringing the late war to a favorable issue in so short a time and without serious financial distress or disturbance of social order, is very largely due to the numberless labor-saving inventions with which American industry has been so preeminently blessed." Wis. Agric. Soc., *Trans.*, 1861–68, 39. The Wisconsin legislature in 1864 expressed similar sentiments when it memorialized

Until the beginning of 1863 the absence of 35,000 boys in blue was thus partly compensated for by agricultural machinery. Women and children, particularly those of the foreign immigrants, performed much labor on the farms, but not in noticeably greater numbers than before the war. Agricultural wages did not increase materially from the standard of 1860, and agricultural papers contained no unusual complaints of scarcity of labor. During the closing years of the war, however, when calls for troops followed one another with startling rapidity and wages of farm hands rose in harvest season to $2 and $2.50 per day, women and children were required to do more and more of the labor of the farm.

They rose to their responsibility with noble zeal. In 1864 the editor of the Green Bay *Advocate* wrote: "But we have a great element of strength up here which goes far toward repairing the loss in farm hands by the war. The sturdy, muscular German and Belgian women plough and sow and reap with all the skill and activity of men, and we believe are fully their equals in strength. If need be they will even go into the pineries and do the logging."[1] The Milwaukee *Daily News* in the spring of 1864 contained this statement from "a reliable and intelligent gentleman who has just returned from a recent visit to some of the northern counties." "A grown man at work in the field is a rare sight. The farm labor is mostly being done by women and children."[2] On the opposite side of the State the La Crosse *Democrat* observed

Congress to lower the tax on the sale of agricultural machinery. Wis. *Gen. Laws*, 1864, Memorial no. 18.

[1] Green Bay *Advocate*, June 9, 1864.

[2] Excerpt from Milwaukee *Daily News* in *Wis. State Jour.*, June 1, 1864.

in 1864: "It is not an uncommon thing to find half a dozen farms adjoining where there is not a man or boy to harvest the grain crop, and where the women are half unsexed in their efforts to keep body and soul together against the return of a husband or brother from the wars."[1]

The war closed in the summer of 1865, and before the end of the year 39,865 of the soldiers of Wisconsin, nearly all who were then in the service,[2] were back in the State seeking the places which for several years had been doing without them. At the same time the return of peace swelled to unusual proportions the stream of immigrants pouring into the State. It seemed for a brief space that Wisconsin would be swamped by the sudden deluge of labor power; that unemployment would follow, as in fact it did follow in the industrial centers of the East. Not so, however; to Wisconsin's rescue came again the superior elasticity of agricultural organization. Thirty-five thousand of the returning veterans came during the late summer and autumn,[3] when they were readily absorbed by the harvest fields. No doubt many farmers in the older portions of the State took advantage of the return of sons and brothers to make the beginnings of a more thorough

[1] La Crosse *Democrat*, July 19, 1864. In 1863 a group of farmers in the town of Trenton, Dodge County, imported from Cairo, Ill., a crew of about forty emancipated negroes to labor as farm hands. The experiment does not seem to have been repeated elsewhere. A strong feeling against permitting the settlement of free negroes in the State developed shortly after the Emancipation Proclamation went into effect, which found expression at the legislative session of 1863 in about sixty petitions requesting that negro immigration to Wisconsin be prohibited.

[2] Wisconsin Adjutant General, *Report*, 1865, 22–25, 28–30.

[3] *Ibid.*

and intensive system of agriculture. Such of the veterans as did not easily fit themselves into this old environment emigrated to the fertile prairies of Iowa, Minnesota, and northwestern Wisconsin, where they either entered homesteads upon the government domain or purchased land from private agencies.

Astonishing as it may seem, the return of the soldiers did not even completely supply the demand for agricultural laborers. From many of the newly settled portions of Wisconsin complaints still arose at the close of 1865 of the scarcity of help. Thus the Hudson *Star*, published in St. Croix County, observed in October: "Notwithstanding the return of so many soldiers, there is a great scarcity of labor in this section. Farmers are behind in their fall work, being unable to get hands, and all kinds of mechanics are in great demand. Many improvements intended to be made this fall will have to be deferred on account of the lack of labor."[1] On Jan. 11, 1866 Governor Fairchild, speaking for the country as a whole, though his observation was limited to the Northwest and was correct only for that section, declared: "A million of men have returned from the war, been disbanded in our midst and resumed their former occupations, and yet from all sides we hear the surest of all signs of national prosperity, complaints of the scarcity of labor."[2]

Thus the farmers of Wisconsin met and solved the problems arising out of the Civil War. During its last three years and the three years immediately

[1] Printed in *Wis. State Jour.*, Nov. 7, 1865. See also *Shawano County Journal*, Oct. 12 and 26, 1865; *Wis. Farmer*, 1865, 338.

[2] Wis. *Mess. and Docs.*, 1866, I, p. iii.

following its close, they enjoyed an era of prosperity such as they had never before known. The heavy burdens of the war they cheerfully bore, and only one grievance, the arbitrary exactions of grain-carrying railroads in the State,[1] marred the universal contentment. With the handsome profits which they realized from their crops they were improving their farms, purchasing new lands, and paying the debts accumulated during a previous decade of speculation. They were proudly conscious of the important services they were rendering the cause of the Union. Early in the war the Milwaukee *Daily Wisconsin* effectively stated a thought, frequently expressed in the press and on the platform during and after the conflict: "Not only has the want of this surplus grain [of the Northwest] put England and France under bonds to keep peace with us, but the specie proceeds have given the sinews that now maintain our patriotic defenders. The farmers of the Northwest, in producing this surplus grain, have fought a battle for the Union of greater significance than any possible achievement of the Grand Army of the Potomac."[2]

[1] See chap. xii.
[2] Milwaukee *Daily Wisconsin*, Nov. 1, 1861.

CHAPTER II

LUMBERING

The lumber industry in Wisconsin, though still in its infancy in 1860, ranked second only to agriculture in importance. The Wisconsin forest covered roughly all of the northern three-fifths of the State, forming part of that vast timber belt which originally stretched almost unbroken over northern Michigan, Wisconsin, and Minnesota. It consisted in part of mixed growths of pine and hardwood, in part of solid stands of pine. The mixed forests, which occurred usually on loamy and clay soils, were in this early period of Wisconsin lumbering considered valuable only in so far as they contained quantities of white pine. Hardwoods and hemlock had as yet little commercial value except in the lower Fox River Valley and along the shores of Lake Michigan. The pine forests, which occurred usually on sandy soils and in particular along the banks of the northern streams, contained the prize of every lumberman's heart. In Wisconsin were to be found some of the finest stands of pine timber in the entire world.[1]

This magnificent forest was drained by a dozen or more useful logging streams, which divided it into clearly defined lumbering districts. At the beginning

[1] For a detailed description of the original Wisconsin forest see Filibert Roth, *Forestry Conditions of Northern Wisconsin* (Madison, 1898), 10–12; and Mary Dopp, "Geographical Influences in the Development of Wisconsin," in American Geographical Society, *Bulletin*, 1913, 737–49.

of the Civil War six of these had already come into prominence, the Wolf River and Green Bay districts in northeastern Wisconsin, and the Wisconsin, Black, Chippewa, and St. Croix in northwestern Wisconsin.[1] Lumbering operations had been carried on in all of them since 1830, the first sawmill in the State having been erected at De Pere as early as 1809.[2] The total cut of pine prior to the war had, however, been comparatively small, and in 1860 the invading loggers were yet thundering only at the outer gates of the vast forest solitudes of Wisconsin.

The lumber produced in the State at this time was consumed almost entirely west of Lake Michigan. The Badger pineries were consequently dependent for their progress upon the industrial development of this region. In a period of boom immigrants pouring in upon newly opened lands required large amounts of lumber for their homes, barns, and fences; rapidly growing cities and villages sent out their calls for ever more building material; and railroads, hurrying their lines across the prairies, consumed quantities of ties and bridge timbers. In a period of depression, however, expansion and building ceased, and the pineries were the first to feel the lack of a market. Thus during the boom years from 1850 to

[1] At the beginning of the Civil War the Black, Chippewa, and St. Croix pineries which were the least developed were often grouped together as one.

[2] The Green Bay and the Wisconsin River pineries were perhaps the most extensively exploited at the beginning of the Civil War. For accounts of early lumbering in Wisconsin see W. B. Judson, "Lumber Manufacture," in *History of Dodge County, Wisconsin*, 185–91; R. G. Thwaites, *Wisconsin* (Boston, 1908), 281–82; Amer. Geog. Soc., *Bulletin*, 1913, 737–49; *Wis. Hist. Colls.*, III, 435–52; E. B. Usher, *Wisconsin* (Chicago, 1914), I, 153–219.

1856 the lumber industry of Wisconsin flourished and grew as never before, while prices just prior to the panic of 1857 were the highest that the Badger lumbermen had ever enjoyed. But the panic of 1857 put a disastrous end to expansion, and for three years the Wisconsin pineries knew only discouragement and failure.

In the autumn of 1860 prospects brightened. The slowly recovering energies of the Northwest were being quickened into new life by the wonderful grain crop of that year, and farmers once more prepared to purchase lumber for long-delayed improvements. The revival was but short-lived, however. The election of Lincoln, followed by the gathering of the war cloud in the South and the financial crisis in the North, destroyed the hope of a new period of expansion, and the Wisconsin pineries relapsed once more into depression. The price of mixed lumber in cargo lots sank in the Chicago market from a maximum of $12 per thousand feet in the middle of October, 1860 to a maximum of $6.75 per thousand in the beginning of May, 1861, and continued to range at ruinous figures until well into the next year.[1] It was not until the end of 1862 that fortune once more smiled upon the lumbermen of the State.

Prosperity, so long delayed, was of generous proportions when it finally returned. In the fall of 1863 prices rose with a bound. There followed a crusade into the pineries that was likened by a Wisconsin newspaper to the Pike's Peak gold rush of 1859–60.[2] The value of pine continued to soar.

[1] Chicago Board of Trade, *Reports*, 1860–75.

[2] Appleton *Crescent*, Oct. 24, 1863.

In the season of 1864 in the Chicago market it attained the unprecedented height of $23 per thousand feet for cargo lots.[1] Unhappily the pineries of northwestern Wisconsin were unable to take full advantage of this good fortune, for in 1863 and 1864 a large portion of their logs was tied up by an unusually low stage of water in the tributaries of the upper Mississippi. Lumbermen in northeastern Wisconsin, however, were prosperous as never before. Their products were distributed by the lumber-carrying railroads of Chicago not only to the southward and southwest but to those western regions which the pineries of the upper Mississippi customarily supplied. During the year 1864 Chicago received from northern Wisconsin and western Michigan more than half a billion feet of pine, to say nothing of vast quantities of shingles, lath, and pickets. In 1864 the receipts of the Illinois metropolis surpassed for the first time the previous record of 1857.

Temporary depression succeeded this period of unusual prosperity. In the spring of 1865 the Mississippi and its tributaries were visited by raging floods, and every stick of timber accumulated on the banks during the two preceding seasons was floated to market. The return of peace likewise depressed the sensitive lumber market. In June, 1865 pine in cargo lots could be purchased in Chicago for $10 per thousand. The rapid expansion of the Northwest, however, quickly dispelled the cloud. The railroads of Chicago and Milwaukee, in their efforts to capture the grain trade of Iowa and Minnesota, and the Union Pacific on its way to the western coast were speeding

[1] Chicago Board of Trade, *Report*, 1869, 65.

their construction as never before. The treeless prairies which they opened for settlement were peopled by soldiers returning from the war and by immigrants coming hither from abroad. The demand for lumber exceeded the supply. Prices rose during 1866 and the early part of 1867 to a higher average even than during the most prosperous years of the war.[1] Never had the ax and saw found such busy and profitable employment in the forests of Wisconsin.

Industrial depression, a delayed but inevitable consequence of the Civil War, sent prices sharply downward during the season of 1867. For three years the markets now ranged uniformly low, and in spite of a sharp curtailment of expenses the profits of Wisconsin lumbermen were very much reduced. There was a quick improvement in 1871 and 1872 in response to returning prosperity, stimulated in the autumn of 1871 by the great October fires, one of which destroyed a large part of the city of Chicago while the other swept over the rich forest areas of northeastern Wisconsin. With the panic of 1873, however, all industry was again prostrate.

It is extremely difficult to determine accurately the extent of Wisconsin lumbering operations during the period under review. This is owing in part to the nature of the industry, in part to the lack of dependable statistics. An approximation of the activities of the State has been secured, however, by carefully collating and checking scattering data found in the files of nearly a score of representative pinery newspapers with materials found in other

[1] *Ibid.*

sources.[1] From such information it appears that in the winter of 1860–61 the total product of the northern forests of Wisconsin in lumber sawed and logs rafted down the Mississippi was about 375,000,000 feet, a decrease from the season of 1856–57, when the industry was at its height, of some 100,000,000 feet. The various river and lake districts contributed toward this total in about the following proportions: the Wisconsin, 90,000,000; the Black, 40,000,000; the Chippewa, 60,000,000; the St. Croix, including only the Wisconsin side, 40,000,000; the Wolf, 75,000,000; the Green Bay, including only the Wisconsin side, 60,000,000; and the western shore of Lake Michigan with Manitowoc as a center, 10,000,000.[2]

During the winter which followed the outbreak of the war the lumber cut of the State was, as in 1860–61, far below normal. In 1863, however, began a period of rapid expansion. By the season of 1866–67 the pineries were yielding to the ax and the saw an annual tribute of 800,000,000 feet. By 1868–69 the product had reached the total of 1,200,000,000 feet, more than a threefold increase within eight years.

[1] A valuable source of information is the annual lumber circular issued by Bogy & Fry (later Berthold & Jennings) of St. Louis from 1870 to 1873, printed in St. Louis Union Merchants' Exchange, *Reports*, 1869–73; also Chicago Board of Trade, *Reports*, 1860–75; *Wisconsin Lumberman*, February, 1874, 339; *id.*, January, 1875, 204–6; *id.*, February, 1875, 395–424; J. S. Ritchie, *Wisconsin and Its Resources* (Philadelphia, 1857), 66–71; G. W. Hotchkiss, *History of the Lumber and Forest Industry of the Northwest* (Chicago, 1898), 501; Silas Farmer, *Map of Wisconsin for 1872* (Detroit, 1872).

[2] It should be remembered that these statistics refer to the annual cut, not to the amount of lumber brought to market. The latter varied greatly with conditions of stream flow. Half of the product of the Green Bay and St. Croix pineries is usually credited to Wisconsin.

Thereafter for a time the rate of development was somewhat checked, but by the winter of 1870–71 the camps were again as busy as ever. In the season of 1871–72 every logging crew redoubled its efforts to gather a rich harvest, and the cut attained the enormous total of 1,600,000,000 feet. It was a record that remained unequalled for the next nine years, for with the panic of 1873 expansion came to a close.

The several pinery districts of the State shared unequally in the growth of the years 1862 to 1872. The Wisconsin district shared least of all, and was rapidly surpassed by the others. The chief cause for its slow development was the nature of the stream upon which its products were sent to market. The Wisconsin River, because of its extreme length, its sweeping bends, and its frequent rapids and dangerous waterfalls, was the most expensive rafting stream in the State. It was likewise the most difficult of access for supplies. The latter had to be hauled into its pineries long distances by team at great expense. Its lumbermen were quite unable to compete, at least in the manufacture of common lumber, with their more favored rivals of the Chippewa, Black, and St. Croix rivers.

The Chippewa region was coming to the front with giant strides. It contained a magnificent stand of pine timber, the finest, its lumbermen maintained, in the entire country. One-sixth of all the white pine to be found within the United States was said to be standing within its confines. Prior to 1863 these immense riches were but little known even within the State. During the closing years of the war, however, speculators and operators from the whole

Northwest were rushing thither to invest. The product of the Chippewa leaped from 60,000,000 feet in the season of 1860–61 to 285,000,000 feet in 1868–69 and 436,000,000 feet in 1871–72, more than a sevenfold increase in a period of eleven years.[1] In the quantity of its annual yield the Chippewa district by 1870 held undisputed leadership over all others; in the quality of its lumber it was surpassed by none.

In the season of 1871–72 the Green Bay district, including only the Wisconsin portion, produced 300,000,000 feet, an amount somewhat in excess of its usual yield. This increase is accounted for by the necessity of immediately converting into lumber the deadened and fallen pine stumps upon the wide area that had been burned in the Peshtigo fire of the previous October. The Wolf River pineries produced in 1871–72, 180,000,000 feet, the Wisconsin, 200,000,000 feet, the Black, 300,000,000 feet, and the St. Croix, including only the Wisconsin side, 105,000,000 feet.[2]

A typical lumber camp in any of the Wisconsin pineries presented to the spectator a combination of animated sights and sounds. The rapid tap of the chopper's ax, the sudden crash as here and there a majestic pine thundered to earth, the intermittent rip of the saw as it rent the fallen giant into logs, the jingle of bells on the ox-drawn sled as it slowly moved off with its load to the river bank, or returned

[1] See newspaper exchanges from La Crosse *Republican* printed in *Wis. State Jour.*, Feb. 19, 1861; St. Louis Union Merchants' Exchange, *Report*, 1869, 72; *id.*, 1872, 95.

[2] The sources from which these statistics have been secured are *ibid.*, 91–92; *Wis. Lumberman*, February, 1875, 395–424.

on the run for a new burden of logs, the hearty shouts of the red-shirted lumberjacks as they hastened about their work in the keen and exhilarating winter air, all this was the foreground for which, in strange contrast, the background was the solemn grandeur of the forest.

With the coming of spring and the disappearance of the snow from the logging roads, labor in the forest came to an end. The lumbermen now turned their energies to the log drive. Presently rivers were freed of their imprisoning coat of ice and spring floods were at hand to carry the logs to the mills. Unhappy the logger, particularly when his operations took him far up stream, if the melting snow and the spring rains produced only a slight rise of water. Then his logs were tied up, and he must wait for a more favorable year to carry them to market. But when the river was high the red-shirts, handspike in hand, gaily set about the hazardous work of "breaking" the rollways and delivering to the swollen stream the accumulated harvest of the winter's work.

The drive was the most picturesque as it certainly was the most dangerous portion of the season's operations. Down the ice-cold torrent thousands upon thousands of logs went surging and hurtling, sometimes halting at an obstruction as if in hesitation and piling up in rude masses, then rushing onward again with greater momentum than before. It was the business of the drivers to keep this unstable mass constantly moving over obstructions, across waterfalls, and around bends of the stream. Occasionally, in spite of precautions, a jam was formed to which, unless it could be quickly broken, the charging mass behind soon added huge dimensions. On the wild Chippewa River, in particular, jams reached great proportions. In the spring of 1869 one gathered that was variously estimated to contain from 100,000,000 to 130,000,000 feet of logs. For two miles up the river to the depth of from twenty to fifty tiers, the pine was piled and wedged, completely obliterating for that distance all sight of water.[1] Upon such a confused and treacherous mass the hardy drivers ventured with their iron-shod spikes, seeking with practiced eye to discover, and if possible to dislodge, the logs that formed the key to the tangle.[2] Many a daring fellow lost his life in the wild rush of struggling pine that followed the successful breaking of a jam.

With the growth of the lumber industry in Wisconsin its pinery streams underwent many needed improvements. Rapids, bars, and waterfalls were rendered less dangerous for driving logs and running rafts; sloughs and bayous in which lumber was likely to be lost were closed; and booming works and log harbors of immense capacity were erected for the safe storing of pine during the annual freshets. This was the work partly of individual millmen and loggers, partly of organizations among them. It made excellent progress on all the important logging streams of the State, but particularly on the Chippewa, the unruly waters of which required especial measures of control. The system of log markings and log exchanges in vogue among millmen was

[1] Eau Claire *Free Press*, May 6, 1869. See also letter of George F. Train in Chippewa *Herald*, June 4, 1870.

[2] Several years after the close of the Civil War steam engines were introduced to aid in breaking log jams.

likewise extended and more scrupulously observed, a matter that became of increasing importance as the operations on each river assumed ever greater proportions.

On the Chippewa River a notable invention was made in 1862 by Levi W. Pond, a lumberman of Eau Claire. This consisted of the sheer or fin boom, an ingenious device for intercepting and turning logs from the drive into the pond or pocket of the sawmill for which they were destined. It consisted of a chain of logs, secured at one end to the river bank, upon which had been arranged a number of sturdy, collapsible rudders or fins. By merely opening or closing the fins with a rope held by the operator on shore, the boom could be thrown diagonally across the river and held in the current so as to steer the oncoming logs to their proper destination or, when necessary, could be withdrawn to permit the passage of boats and rafts. It was an application of the principle of the current ferryboat to the old windlass or anchored boom hitherto in general use. Patented by Pond in 1868,[1] it was soon in use on every logging stream in the country that was subject to much traffic, and it played a part by no means unimportant in the expansion of the logging industry of Wisconsin.

Sawmill methods were similarly undergoing a rapid development. In the late fifties and early sixties the circular or rotary saw was just coming into general use in Wisconsin as the main saw of the mill, replacing the slower "muley," the cutting

[1] U. S. Patent Office, *Report*, 1868, 305. See also *Wis. Lumberman*, March, 1874, 386–91; *id.*, June, 1874, 249–57; *id.*, February, 1875, 425–26; T. E. Randall, *History of Chippewa Valley* (Eau Claire, 1875), 90–94.

capacity of which it exceeded more than ten times. It had been brought to the State as early as 1854, but for some years remained an uncertain experiment. Few sawyers knew how to dress or operate it properly, and the woes of those who were hardy enough to give it a trial were such as to lead to the coinage of a popular expression, "Don't monkey with the buzz-saw." The early circular saws were exceedingly wasteful of lumber, sawing out at each cut a half-inch kerf. It was feared that a thinner saw would burst, or become heated, or fail to find proper clearance in its passage through the log.[1] It is to be noted as a characteristic of all sawmill innovations of this day that they were calculated solely to secure an increased output or a saving of labor. Little effort was made toward effecting a saving of lumber since timber was still cheap and abundant. To a later generation remained the task of eliminating waste in the operations of the sawmill.

The new circular saws, supplementing the improved gang saws of various patterns in use at the time, so greatly increased the sawing capacity of the mills that a prompt speeding up of all other operations became necessary. The changes that were introduced to meet these new requirements completely transformed the average lumber mill within a few years. The movements of the log carriage, which carried the log to the saw, were found to be too slow, and they were accelerated by the inventions, one after another, of the friction feed, the wire rope feed, and the steam

[1] The double rotary, consisting of two circulars, one running above the other, was an important improvement over the single rotary. It came into use in Wisconsin during the Civil War.

feed.[1] In 1863 or 1864 the double edger was introduced, which at a single cut trimmed both edges of the sawed board instead of but one as heretofore. The gang edger, which followed almost immediately, carried this invention still further toward perfection.

Near the close of the sixties steam took the place of manual labor in handling logs on their passage from the mill pond to the saw, the "steam nigger" and other similar devices rendering this possible. Somewhat earlier, "live rolls," driven by chains, for carrying sawed boards from one operation to another and finally depositing them in the mill yard, found their way into the larger mills. In the steam mills, where sawdust was burned for fuel, the labor of rows of shovelers was dispensed with by an invention perfected in a Chippewa River mill in 1869, which automatically carried the waste from the saws to the boiler.[2] These and dozens of other improvements of less importance were accompanied by an ever-increasing efficiency and power of the driving engines, not only in the steam mills but also in the water-power mills. The up-to-date sawmill of 1870 bore slight resemblance in its construction or equipment to the sawmill of 1860, and the process of development was still rapidly going on.[3]

These changes were reflected in the growing output

[1] One of the best steam feeds on the market was perfected and patented by D. C. Prescott of Marinette in 1873. The steam feed was often referred to as the "shot gun feed," for when the steam was turned on it literally shot the log carriage down the track to the saw. See U. S. Patent Office, *Report*, March, 1873, 173–74.

[2] Chippewa *Herald*, April 30, 1870; U. S. Patent Office, *Report*, 1869, 282; *Wis. Lumberman*, October, 1874, 152–54.

[3] For an excellent account of the evolution of sawmill machinery see Hotchkiss, *Lumber Industry*, 649–60.

of the mills. It was an unusual sawmill in 1860 that produced more than 50,000 feet of sawed lumber in a twelve-hour day. In 1870 the great mills of the Chippewa Valley were tearing out lumber at the rate of 100,000 to 200,000 feet per day. The millmen gloried in the increasing capacity of their establishments, and their trials of speed were the subject of frequent boasts in the journals of rival pinery cities. The immense mill of Pound, Halbert & Company at Chippewa Falls was able in 1867 to turn out in a twelve-hour run 207,400 feet.[1] By 1873 this mill could maintain during an entire month an average daily cut of 325,000 feet to say nothing of shingles, lath, and pickets.[2] In 1860 forty mills along the shores of Green Bay turned out in a year but 80,000,000 feet of lumber.[3] In 1873 a single great corporation in the Chippewa Valley turned out under one roof more than half that amount.[4]

This increasing efficiency and the growing costliness of sawmill machinery not only stimulated large-scale production in the manufacture of lumber but encouraged a new tendency towards integration in the industry. Prior to the fifties sawmill owners, with some notable exceptions, were persons of limited capital, whose means centered in their equipment and working stock. They usually purchased raw materials delivered to them at their mills; often they sawed logs merely upon commission or at a stipulated price per thousand feet. Land speculators commonly owned the standing pine. Men of capital

[1] Chippewa *Union and Times*, Aug. 24, 1867.
[2] *Wis. Lumberman*, January, 1874, 204–5.
[3] Wis. Agric. Soc., *Trans.*, 1858–59, 401–5.
[4] *Wis. Lumberman*, January, 1874, 204–54.

as well as foresight, they bought great stretches of the forest areas as soon as the State, the nation, or the numerous land-grant companies opened them for sale. Upon the heels of the surveyors they sent their "timber cruisers" or "explorers," wizards of wood lore, to select and enter for them the most desirable tracts. When with the lapse of time such holdings had acquired value they disposed of them in small tracts, sometimes selling land and all, more often parting only with their timber rights, "stumpage" as it was called, and retaining title to the land itself, which they subsequently sold to incoming settlers.[1] Logging contractors were the lumbermen of that day, who for a stipulated price per thousand feet hewed out the pine, drove it down the streams, and delivered it to the waiting millmen.[2] Other contractors, owners of lake vessels in the northeastern pineries, and master raft pilots in the Northwest carried the sawed lumber from the mills to market.[3] The sorting, seasoning, and distributing of the mill product were still other operations that were left to the wholesalers in the large lumber centers.

This entire procedure underwent a rapid change with the emergence during our period of mammoth corporations. The millmen now acquired vast tracts

[1] Ritchie, *Wisconsin and Its Resources*, 67–68. See also Cyrus Woodman Manuscripts for the years 1857 to 1867 in Wisconsin Historical Library. The rates paid for stumpage varied with the quality of the pine and its distance from an available stream. During the early years of the Civil War stumpage rates for good pine in northwestern Wisconsin were $1 or less per 1,000 feet. Pine owners sometimes contracted to sell stumpage to loggers or mill owners for a stipulated percentage of the lumber manufactured therefrom.

[2] Isaac Stephenson, *Recollections of a Long Life* (Chicago, 1915), 106–89.

[3] *Wis. Hist. Colls.*, III, 439–40; Burlington *Saturday Evening Post*, Dec. 20, 1913 and Jan. 31, 1914.

of pinelands[1] from which their own employees logged the timber. Their own rafting crews and their own lake vessels carried the sawed lumber to market. They maintained retail lumberyards in which their product was sorted, seasoned, and distributed. They operated flour mills where they ground the meal for their crews; blacksmith and machine shops in which they manufactured and repaired their tools; general merchandise stores in which they sold to their operatives and to others the clothing, food, and supplies that they required; while some even went so far as to maintain farms upon which they produced the pork, wheat, and fodder consumed by their working force.

A conspicuous instance of thorough integration in the lumber industry in Wisconsin was that of Knapp, Stout & Company of Menomonie, said at that time to be the greatest lumber corporation in the world. In 1873 this firm owned 115,000 acres of pinelands on the Chippewa and Menominee rivers, from which it cut and manufactured during the year in its various steam and water-power mills 55,000,000 feet of lumber, 20,000,000 shingles, and 20,000,000 lath and pickets. It maintained a foundry, machine shop, and blacksmith shop, a grain warehouse of 40,000 bushels capacity, and a gristmill in which its yearly requirements of flour were ground. It owned six large farms in Dunn and Barron counties, containing 6,000 or 7,000 acres of improved land, upon which were raised its supplies of wheat and pork. It conducted general merchandise stores the annual sales of

[1] For data relating to the concentration of ownership of pinelands in Wisconsin see Oshkosh *Journal*, Nov. 6, 1869; Chippewa *Union and Times*, Sept. 21, 1867; Wisconsin *Assembly Journal*, 1871, app., 71.

which amounted to $750,000, besides large lumberyards at Reed's Landing, Dubuque, and St. Louis. Twelve hundred men, conducting its manifold activities, were upon its pay roll throughout the year.[1]

During the years of expansion from 1863 to 1872 there emerged from the multitude of inconspicuous lumber operators in the northern pineries nearly all of those great lumber princes who, in the succeeding decade, were to dominate the industry and play a conspicuous part in the political life of the State. Isaac Stephenson, Nelson Ludington, Cadwallader C. Washburn, Daniel Wells, Philetus Sawyer, Thaddeus Pound, Daniel Shaw, J. G. Thorpe, J. H. Knapp, A. L. Stout, Alexander Stewart, and numerous others were names which at this time became familiar to most well-informed people in Wisconsin. It was during these years also that Frederick Weyerhaeuser became interested in Chippewa pinelands, and to exploit them organized the first, and for many years the greatest, of the Weyerhaeuser syndicates, the Mississippi River Logging Company. Thus the close of the Civil War marks a new era in the history of Wisconsin lumbering. Though many small operators continued to flourish, and old-time methods were still employed after the war, the industry assumed a new character from the activities of great lumber corporations.

Within the pineries there grew up, as the industry developed, a number of thriving sawmill centers,

[1] *Wis. Lumberman*, October, 1873, 20; *id.*, January, 1874, 197, 201–7, 254; *id.*, May, 1874, 166–69. In the same references may be found excellent accounts of other great lumber corporations in Wisconsin. See also Oshkosh *Northwestern*, Nov. 22, 1866; Eau Claire *Free Press*, June 20, July 11, and Sept. 19, 1867; Chippewa *Herald*, June 18, 1870.

located usually upon the sites of waterfalls. Dependent for the most part upon the forest for their employment, they prospered or declined as the lumber industry rose or fell. Marinette, Oconto, Peshtigo, Wausau, Stevens Point, Grand Rapids, Black River Falls, Eau Claire, and Chippewa Falls were at this time the most prominent of the pinery towns. Oshkosh, at the outlet of the Wolf pinery, was one of the best known of the Badger sawmill centers, its extensive activities having already brought upon it the sobriquet, "The Sawdust City."[1] It differed, however, from the pinery towns in that it maintained besides its sawmills other interests of more or less importance. The same was true of Green Bay, Fond du Lac, and La Crosse. During the years 1863 to 1872 all of these cities evidenced the prosperity of the lumber industry by the rapidity of their development. Their population increased more than 133 per cent during the decade 1860–70, a growth four times as large as that of the State as a whole.[2]

The manufacture of shingles, like the sawing of lumber, underwent a complete transformation during the period of the Civil War. Prior to 1860 the shingle industry was almost wholly in the hands of farmers. The immigrants who settled on the pine-clad farms of northern Wisconsin, and in particular the Germans and Belgians who made their homes in the northeastern counties of the State, were the shingle-makers or "shingle weavers" as they were popularly called. The industry offered them and their large

[1] In 1866 Oshkosh manufactured 85,000,000 feet of lumber and 80,000,000 shingles. It was then probably the greatest lumber-manufacturing center in the State.

[2] Compiled from the U. S. census reports for 1860 and 1870.

families employment during the long winter months, and gave value to pine which was too far inland to be hauled out in the shape of saw logs. "It is not unusual, during the sleighing season," observed the editor of the Green Bay *Advocate* in 1860, "to see caravans of shingle teams coming into Green Bay, equalling in size and quaintness what we hear of those which make annual pilgrimages from Pembina to St. Paul."[1] Manitowoc was the center of the trade, exporting in 1860 approximately 40,000,000 shingles.[2] Along the shores of Green Bay and on the lower Fox and the upper Wisconsin were numerous other markets to which the farmers carried the product of their winter's toil. Altogether approximately 175,000,000 shingles were thus annually manufactured within the State at the beginning of the Civil War.

Machine-sawed shingles were still in the experimental stage in 1860. They were considered inferior to hand-shaved shingles, and commanded a lower price. However, during the Civil War they came more and more into favor in Chicago and distributing centers on the Mississippi River, and before the end of the war had almost entirely superseded the hand-made product. No doubt this development was due in part to the absence of large numbers of the shingle weavers in military service; in part to the same forces which were encouraging factory production in other branches of industry. During the decade 1860–70 shingle mills developed with even greater rapidity

[1] Wis. Agric. Soc., *Trans.*, 1858–59, 405.

[2] Chicago *Tribune*, Jan. 1, 1861. In 1859 Manitowoc shipped to Chicago approximately 55,000,000 shingles.

than sawmills, and the evolution of shingle machinery was almost as surprising.

As a result of such improvements Wisconsin had become the greatest shingle-manufacturing State in the entire Union by the end of the sixties. During the census year 1869, 806,800,000 shingles were produced,[1] of which Brown County, at the foot of Green Bay, alone contributed more than half. The city of Green Bay in the meantime had captured from Manitowoc the supremacy in the shingle commerce. Favored by the richness of her timber supply and the excellence of her marketing facilities, her trade by 1866 amounted to 200,000,000 shingles. Her mayor, Anton Klaus, alone manufactured 100,000,000 in 1869 in the mills under his control. The historic fur-trade city once more assumed commercial importance and for four or five years maintained the distinction of being the greatest primary shingle market in the world.[2]

Other important products of the pine forest were lath, of which the State produced in 1871, 697,142,000, and pickets, of which it manufactured 310,000,000.[3] For the most part these were sawmill by-products, affording a means for the disposal of pine slabs which at an earlier period had uniformly been wasted. As for the hardwood products, the manufacture of oak staves, particularly in the lower Fox Valley, was a growing industry, though at this time still in its infancy.[4] In the lower Fox Valley, also, the manu-

[1] U. S. *Census*, 1870, III, 613.

[2] Milwaukee *Sentinel*, Feb. 8, 1867 and Feb. 12, 1870.

[3] Estimates accompanying a map of Wisconsin for 1872, printed by Silas Farmer & Company at Detroit, Mich., 1872. The U. S. census returns of 1870 for these items are incomplete.

[4] The manufacture of tight barrel staves by machinery began in the lower Fox River Valley during the Civil War. It gave value to the excel-

facture of railroad ties, woodenware, and wagons consumed a limited quantity of hardwoods. Shipbuilding furnished an outlet for ship timbers and boards on the shores of Lake Michigan, Green Bay, the lower Fox, and the upper Mississippi, while the tanning of leather in a few localities along Lake Michigan and the lower Fox gave value to the bark of the otherwise despised hemlock. All in all, however, the manufacture of hardwoods was of comparative insignificance in Wisconsin.

As we turn from the manufacture to the marketing of lumber, a geographical consideration at once becomes important. The pinery streams of northeastern Wisconsin, it will be recalled, were tributary to Lake Michigan, while those of northwestern Wisconsin were tributary to the Mississippi River. The differing conditions of water depth, current, and wind on these two watercourses necessitated in the pineries tributary to each corresponding differences in the methods of marketing their products.

The pineries tributary to Lake Michigan employed as carriers a considerable fleet of vessels, nearly all of the sailing type.[1] Many of these were craft that had outlived their usefulness in the more profitable grain and merchandise trade but were still good for the lumber commerce, inasmuch as pine cargoes were

lent white oak of northeastern Wisconsin, which previously had been little used except for cordwood. Stave mills began to displace shingle mills in Brown County in the early seventies as a result of the rapid exhaustion of the pine of that region. In Wood and Clark counties also the industry grew rapidly with the advent of railroads.

[1] At this time lake vessels could not take on their cargoes in the ordinary manner from docks at Lake Michigan and Green Bay ports, owing to the shallowness of harbors. It was the custom to raft the lumber to the schooners, which were anchored in deep water.

not injured by exposure to water in their leaky bottoms.

During the early sixties an innovation appeared in this mode of carrying that was pregnant with possibilities not only for the lumber but for the grain and flour commerce as well. Worn-out sailing vessels were partially stripped of their rigging and put in charge of powerful steam tugs, by them to be hauled back and forth to market. For all practical purposes this transformed the old hulks into efficient steamers. Usually some of their sails were retained, which could be hoisted to take advantage of particularly favorable winds.

A further development of this practice was the displacement of tugs by propellers of a type known as steam barges. The latter were able not only to drag their "hookers" but to carry enormous cargoes of lumber. In the early seventies it was not unusual to see a steam barge and a consort of four or even more laden tows in tandem formation plowing their steady course to market. The economies of the system brought it rapidly into favor, and before many years the old schooner fleet in the lumber trade depended upon steam rather than sails for its motive power.

In 1862 the activities of the Lake Michigan lumber carriers were supplemented by the extension from Oshkosh to Green Bay of the Chicago & Northwestern Railroad, the first great lumber-carrying railroad to be constructed in Wisconsin. During the years between 1863 and 1870 this line carried to Chicago from the sawmill towns of the Green Bay and Wolf River pineries 1,125,500,000 shingles, 95,160,000 feet of lumber, 13,250,000 lath, and 6,000,000 staves.[1]

[1] Chicago Board of Trade, *Reports*, 1863–70.

Chicago was the chief market of the two northeastern pinery districts. Milwaukee and Racine consumed considerable quantities of lumber and shingles but their receipts did not compare with those of their great southern rival. Chicago was the greatest lumber market in the world. Her receipts from the forests of Michigan and Wisconsin increased fourfold during the decade of the sixties. The output of lumber increased from 262,494,625 feet to 1,018,998,685 feet; of shingles from 127,894,000 to 652,091,000; and of lath from 36,601,000 to 150,000,000.[1] Her five great lumber-carrying railroads and the Illinois & Michigan Canal distributed these vast quantities of pine far and wide over the southern and western plains, where they entered into the fences, barns, and homes of the immigrants who were settling the prairies.

The pinery districts tributary to the Mississippi River followed the picturesque and convenient method of rafting their lumber to market. Indeed, the nature of their streams precluded any other mode of carrying lumber from the mills. The interesting process of constructing a raft need be but briefly described. The boards, as they came from the saws, were piled twelve to twenty courses deep, fastened stoutly together to form so-called "cribs," and top-loaded with bundles of shingles and lath. Six or more cribs fastened end to end formed a "string" or "rapids piece," upon which the hardy raftsmen gaily descended the most dangerous waterfalls, usually with success, sometimes, however, to their sorrow. Where the rivers ran quietly, from two to

[1] *Id.*, 1860–70.

four "pieces," the number varying in individual cases as well as upon different streams, were coupled side by side to form a river raft. Guided fore and aft by ponderous sweeps, but propelled chiefly by the force of the current, such a raft floated down the river, halted now and then to be divided into its constituent parts in order to pass some difficult obstruction, then recoupled to go on as before.[1]

The romance of river rafting is a subject over which the historian would gladly linger. Especially on the wild Wisconsin was the life of the raftsman full of thrilling adventure. The Wisconsin River from Point Bas to Merrill is a succession of dangerous rapids and waterfalls, surging over rocky bottoms at a speed of from ten to twenty miles an hour. To pilot a clumsy "rapids piece" safely over these steep descents of roaring water, where a single slip meant to be dashed to pieces on the rocks below, called for cool daring, strong muscle, and consummate skill. It was hard and rough work, the crew being often immersed to the waist in water whence the chill of ice and snow had not yet departed. When one "rapids piece" was carried safely to a quiet eddy and tied up, the rivermen must trot back—"gigging back" it was popularly called—to repeat the perilous operation, until the whole raft was over the falls. Then there was a brief respite until the next obstruction in the river was reached.

It is little wonder that the men engaged in such work were rough and wild in character. For the most

[1] The methods of constructing rafts and running them to market are described in Wis. Hist. Soc., *Proc.*, 1910, 171–89; *Wis. Hist. Colls.*, III, 435–52; Wis. Agric. Soc., *Trans.*, 1870, 372–74; E. E. Ladu, *Early and Late Mosinee* (Wausau, 1907), 31–35.

part they loved to drink, gamble, and fight, and to the lower river towns, where they were known as "river rats," they were a source of constant terror. Yet they were generous of impulse, courageous, and above all, resourceful. They were among the first to enlist for the war, and on at least one notable occasion they rendered conspicuous service to the cause of the Union. On the famous though disastrous Red River Expedition of 1864 the "pinery boys" of the Twenty-third and the Twenty-ninth Wisconsin regiments, led by Lieut.-Col. Joseph Bailey of Kilbourn, applied to a difficult military problem a homely lumberman's engineering device and thereby saved from destruction a gunboat fleet worth $2,000,000.

Ordinarily lumber rafts from the rivers of Wisconsin arrived without serious mishap at the Mississippi to the satisfaction of all on board, for then the dangerous work of the journey was well over. Before continuing down the Father of Waters a further consolidation of the lumber took place. From eight to eighteen "strings" were combined into a single great hulk known as a Mississippi River fleet, and upon it were erected the cabins of the crew together with a number of rude oars or sweeps on each end. The trip down the Mississippi to the towns where the lumber was sold was usually uneventful, enlivened, however, by drinking and fighting on the part of the uneasy raftsmen.

The average Mississippi River raft became progressively larger as the industry assumed ever greater proportions. Before 1860 it was a large structure that contained more than 500,000 feet of lumber. By 1864 those of average size contained from 600,000 to 1,000,000 feet, with deck loads of a million shingles or lath. In 1870 the great lumber companies of the Chippewa River were sending to market rafts covering from three to four acres of surface and containing from 2,000,000 to 2,600,000 feet of sawed pine.[1]

In 1864 there appeared an innovation in Mississippi River rafting which soon transformed that industry. It consisted in towing, or more correctly speaking, pushing, rafts to market by means of steamboats especially designed for this purpose.[2] Lumber thus transported arrived at its destination in half the time consumed when the current and sweeps provided the sole means of propulsion. In nearly the same ratio the cost of shipment was reduced. For a number of years sweeps were retained at the bow of rafts to guide the lumber on its sinuous river journey. Eventually even these were replaced by steamboats known in the river vernacular as bowboats. Such changes, resulting from the growth of the industry and the high price of labor during the Civil War, proved so successful that by 1873 there were seventy-three steamboats engaged in lumber towing on the upper river.[3]

[1] Chippewa *Herald*, July 16 and Oct. 22, 1870.

[2] The practice originated in local towing on the slack waters of those widenings of the upper Mississippi and St. Croix rivers known as Lakes Pepin and St. Croix. It was customary during the fifties to tow lumber and log rafts on Lake St. Croix from Stillwater to Prescott, permit them to float thence to the head of Lake Pepin, and have them towed again by other boats from the latter point to Reed's Landing. At Reed's Landing, a notable rafting center, they were set afloat for the remainder of the journey down the Mississippi. See Burlington *Sat. Evening Post*, Dec. 20, 1913, Jan. 24, 1914, May 29, 1915, and July 10, 1915; E. W. Durant, "Lumbering and Steamboating on the St. Croix River," in *Minnesota Historical Collections*, X, pt. ii, 663–65.

[3] Wis. Hist. Soc., *Proc.*, 1906, 214; *Wis. Lumberman*, February, 1874, 323.

On the Mississippi there was no great lumber market during our period that could be compared to Chicago. Badger millmen sent rafts to St. Louis as early as 1838, but the Missouri metropolis at the close of the Civil War handled not much more of their product than Iowa and Illinois river towns. Every town or city on the Mississippi River from Prairie du Chien to St. Louis was to some extent a lumber market. Those that were situated on the west bank of the river, in Iowa, and more especially those that had railroad connections with the interior rapidly built up their trade.[1] Iowa river towns received and distributed at this time more than half of the total product of the Wisconsin and Minnesota pineries. In 1869 they received some 450,000,000 feet of lumber of which Dubuque took 81,776,440; Burlington, 60,000,000; and Davenport, 30,000,000.[2] St. Louis, too, by 1869, as a result of the expansion of her railroad lines, was striding swiftly toward the proud position in the lumber trade which she later occupied. Over the railroad lines of these river towns Wisconsin pine found its way as far west as Nebraska and as far south as Missouri.

The tempting trade of the treeless plains west of the Mississippi River was not only a source of competition between the river towns and Chicago but a source of ambitious hope also to the cities of the lower Fox Valley. Oshkosh in particular saw beyond the Mississippi River alluring prospects of a great commerce, the realization of which depended, she

[1] By far the greatest portion of the lumber from the northwestern pineries of Wisconsin was consumed west of the Mississippi River.

[2] St. Louis Union Merchants' Exchange, *Report*, 1869, 72–73.

was sure, on the improvement of the Fox-Wisconsin river route. In the legislature of the State and in the halls of Congress, therefore, Oshkosh became the new champion of this much-discussed and long-delayed enterprise. During the later sixties and early seventies her newspapers never ceased to print glowing predictions of the vast commerce that would follow the opening of the new route to the West, accompanied by demands that the work be at once undertaken.

The Fox-Wisconsin Canal was only one of the many schemes for internal improvement that were being advanced by the lumber interests of the State.[1] Every pinery town in northern Wisconsin had some pet railway project that it was hopefully urging in season and out. While the southern half of the State was groaning under the exactions of overland carriers and demanding legislative relief therefrom, the northern half with equal earnestness was calling for new encouragement to railroad construction and roundly denouncing any movement that would frighten railway capital from the State. Every internal improvement scheme found ready approval in the northern section, and as we shall see in a future chapter this region was ready to forego constitutional safeguards in its zeal for increased transportation.

In spite of all the efforts of northern Wisconsin, however, it was not until near the close of the decade 1860–70 that the first railroads arrived in the heart

[1] The Sturgeon Bay Ship Canal was an improvement of much importance to the lumber interests of northeastern Wisconsin. Its early construction is to be attributed to the influence of prominent lumbermen of this section, notably Isaac Stephenson.

of the pineries. The transformation that these railroads were destined to bring about in the methods of manufacturing and marketing lumber was seen but dimly, therefore, during our period.[1] However, on at least one railroad line significant changes took place. It will be recalled that the Wisconsin River was the least satisfactory rafting stream in the State, and that the pineries upon its headwaters were, as a consequence, unable during the decade of the sixties to maintain their former supremacy. It was in the Wisconsin River district, therefore, that railroad transportation first assumed importance, and it was here that the changes which eventually revolutionized the lumber industry in Wisconsin first appeared.

A striking innovation that arrived as an accompaniment of railroad transportation in the Wisconsin River district was the portable sawmill. This development made feasible the manufacture of lumber in the heart of the forest. However, the change did not noticeably affect the industry until a later period, and to a later period its discussion properly belongs.[2]

Similarly in the transportation of lumber, railroads afforded the pinery streams but little serious competition. The bulky forest product could be carried to market by water at one-tenth the cost of

[1] One of the chief functions of the pinery railroads at this time was to carry supplies to the logging camps and sawmill towns, thus saving the expense of long hauls by wagon. Among the early pinery railroads the Chicago & Northwestern, the Wisconsin Central, the West Wisconsin, the Green Bay & Lake Pepin, and the Wisconsin Valley were most important.

[2] In 1866 a destructive freshet on the Chippewa River carried thousands of logs past all the Chippewa sawmills, strewing them in great quantities upon the lower river bottoms. To manufacture these into lumber several portable sawmills were established by Chippewa River millmen. With such exceptions, however, portable sawmills were unknown in Wisconsin prior to the advent of the railroads.

overland shipment. To be sure, considerable losses of material and labor were involved in the construction of rafts, and the boards arrived at market water-soaked and covered with silt; but in the early days these were less important considerations than the cheapness of transit. Limited quantities of pine were shipped from the forest to Milwaukee and Chicago by way of the Chicago & Northwestern and the several railroads running into the Wisconsin River district. Nine-tenths of all the lumber produced in the State during the seventies, however, found its way to market via the Mississippi River and Lake Michigan.

One of the advantages which Wisconsin sawmill owners hoped to derive from railroad transportation was freedom from the domination of the lumber wholesaler. The latter was at this time an important figure in the economy of the forest industry. He was often its capitalist, loaning to needy millmen, upon the security of the next season's sawing, the money necessary to stock their mills and to pay their operating expenses.[1] He occupied a position of vantage, particularly along the Mississippi River, so long as lumbermen were limited in their transportation entirely to water routes. He knew that a large part of the season's sawing must come down to market on the spring freshets, and that the ordinary millman must sell his product at once in order to secure the means for carrying on the following season's operations. He was thus able to purchase his stock at the low prices incident upon a crowded market, while he could make his sales at leisure.

Wisconsin lumbermen hoped that overland trans-

[1] See Hotchkiss, *Lumber Industry*, 438.

portation would remove this difficulty; that it would enable them to withhold their product from market until prices were favorable. Indeed, by establishing direct relations with retailers they anticipated entirely eliminating the middleman. During the early seventies a few shipments of lumber actually were made directly from manufacturer to retailer, much to the satisfaction of the lumber journals of the day. For the most part, however, conditions remained practically unchanged during the sixties and seventies.

A number of practical considerations served to intrench the wholesaler in his position. Farmers, lacking communication with the pineries, ordinarily purchased their lumber where they sold their produce. Again, the wholesaler at this time was not merely a distributor of lumber. He performed the important service of sorting and seasoning the mill product, a function that the millmen as a rule were obliged to forego because of their financial necessities. The former remained, therefore, throughout our period undisturbed in his sphere.

In lumbering as in agriculture Wisconsin was making great strides during the crucial years of the Civil War. The untimbered states west and southwest of Lake Michigan were filling with settlers, and the marvelous rapidity of their development was the measure of the expansion of the Badger lumber industry. The pineries, which had been exploited in a small way before the outbreak of the war, witnessed at this time an era of remarkable growth, which was to continue until Wisconsin had overtaken Michigan as a lumber producer and had won first place among the lumber states of the Union.

CHAPTER III

LUMBERING

As the lumber industry expanded in Wisconsin there arose within it two conflicting interests whose antagonisms and contentions, resembling nothing so much as the quarrels of rival fur-trade companies in the Northwest at an earlier day, contributed a new chapter of romance to the industrial history of the State. On one hand were arrayed the sawmill interests within the pineries, whose ambition was to manufacture into lumber, without interference, all the pine that was cut from the Wisconsin forests; on the other were the log-driving interests whose function was to supply raw material to the immense mills that lined the Mississippi River and the shores of Green Bay and Lake Winnebago. Nearly every important pinery stream in the State faced this conflict of interests during the period from 1857 to 1873, and the deciding clash in each case came during the decade of the sixties.

Prior to 1860 this question was nowhere regarded as important. Nearly all the logs cut in the northern forests of Wisconsin were manufactured into lumber within the pineries themselves. Perhaps a third of the small annual cut of the St. Croix and the Black was driven down the Mississippi River to supply the sawmills along its banks in Wisconsin, Iowa, and Illinois. On the Chippewa River the quantity of pine thus disposed of was negligible; on the Wisconsin there was practically none. During the closing years of the Civil War, however, the Mississippi River mills began to lay heavier tribute upon the Wisconsin forests. The alarmed sawmill owners of Wisconsin found as a result that they were obliged to pay higher prices for logs. Even more disquieting was the fact that dangerous sawmill competitors were securing a foothold in the very heart of their markets. On the Chippewa, Black, and St. Croix log driving for lower mills assumed particularly menacing proportions, and upon these streams resulting controversies were correspondingly sharp.

The most spectacular clash occurred upon the Chippewa River, and is known as the Beef Slough War. This may be described in some detail, for not only was it typical of the others, but it was representative also of the standard of business ethics of the time. It foreshadowed, moreover, new developments in the lumber industry of the Northwest. Out of it there arose the greatest lumber syndicate of its day, an organization that constituted the beginning of what is now the strongest lumber power on the North American continent.

It so happens that the Chippewa River near its mouth divides into two channels, one of which is for the most part unnavigable and is commonly known as Beef Slough. Beef Slough at that time formed an admirable harbor for the sorting and rafting of such logs as a log-driving company might wish to take down the Mississippi River. The millmen of the Chippewa River appreciated this fact and near the close of the Civil War set about forestalling its use in any such capacity. They purchased the land at its entrance and in 1866 secured from the legislature special logging privileges there,[1] which they had no intention of using but only of holding against possible future users.

Early in 1867 another association, consisting of prominent loggers of Michigan, Fond du Lac, and Oshkosh, who had interests in the sawmills on the Mississippi River, organized a log-driving association known as the Beef Slough Manufacturing, Booming, Log Driving & Transportation Company and applied to the legislature for a charter to erect within Beef Slough the booms and piers necessary for their work. The bill was defeated, and immediately the victorious millmen of Eau Claire and Menomonie sent a crew of some hundreds of their employees with rafts of slabs to close up the entrance to the menacing Slough. The logging company promptly swore out an injunction against the millmen, but not soon enough to prevent the completion of the dam. The next step which it took was more effective, however. Shrewdly dispossessing the millmen of their ownership of the head of the Slough by prevailing upon friendly local authorities to condemn the land for a public highway, they forcibly tore out the offending obstruction. The latter undertaking threatened for a time to lead to a pitched battle between the opposing sawmill and log-driving factions, but fortunately resulted only in a wordy war of rivermen's English.

Such was the status of the controversy when the legislature of 1869 convened. The logging company again made an effort to secure a charter, but its bill was decisively defeated in the Assembly near the

[1] Wisconsin *Private Laws*, 1866, chap. 181.

close of the session. A few days after the vote, however, an innocent-appearing measure was introduced in the Senate providing for the incorporation of the Portage City Gas Light Company. It was less than a week before adjournment. The bill was pushed through the legislature with the rush of business that always attends the close of sessions and was signed by the governor a few hours before the appointed time for adjournment.

Several days after the Portage City bill had thus become law it was learned that hidden away near its close was the following provision: "In all cases where any franchise or privilege has been or shall be granted by law to several persons, the grant shall be deemed several as well as joint, so that one or more may accept and exercise the franchise alone."[1] The logging company had won its fight, for one of its members was a millman who in 1866 had been associated with the Chippewa millmen as an incorporator in their unused charter. It was but a matter of form for him to assign to his new associates the rights and privileges that the secret joker in the Portage City bill had given him. The public chuckled over the sly maneuver, while the two belligerents prepared for a renewal of hostilities.

Within a few months the season for the log drive from the pineries was at hand. The logging company served notice upon the millmen along the Chippewa to pass unmolested all logs bearing the Beef Slough mark. This the sawmill owners were not only unwilling but unable to do, for only two of them possessed the necessary assorting facilities. Moreover,

[1] *Id.*, 1868, chap. 331.

they were unwilling to agree upon a system of log exchanges such as had heretofore governed operations on the river. Here was a deadlock in which force again proved to be the only arbiter. The Beef Slough log drivers, numbering seventy-five rough, belligerent fellows, were not loth on their way down from the pineries to cut open whatever sawmill reservoirs they found containing any of their logs, taking from these not only their own logs but large quantities of others. In Eau Claire County there awaited them the opposing army of the sawmill owners, numbering some 200 equally rough and determined men led by the county sheriff. As the two forces approached the excitement and danger of a bloody clash increased. Fortunately, however, an open battle was averted. The sawmill army was too overwhelming to be resisted, and the leaders of the drive were obliged to submit to arrest. A settlement and an armed truce were eventually effected and the drivers continued on their way.[1]

For several years after 1868 the disputes and contentions of the log-driving and sawmill interests of the Chippewa River continued. In 1870 the Beef Slough Company contrived to secure from the legislature a confirmation and extension of its charter, but by this time its stormy life had brought it to bankruptcy. Its improvements were leased at the close of 1870 to an association of Mississippi River sawmill owners, among whom the leading spirit was Frederick Weyerhaeuser, the present lumber king of America. Early in 1871 this association organized

[1] See Eau Claire *Free Press* and Chippewa *Union and Times* for April and May, 1868.

the Mississippi River Logging Company, which soon became the greatest lumber syndicate of its time.

In the meantime the growth of the log traffic was surpassing even the gloomiest predictions of the Wisconsin sawmill owners. The quantity of logs received and rafted at Beef Slough increased from a meager 12,000,000 feet in 1868 to 274,367,900 feet in 1873.[1] On the Black the traffic rose abruptly from 6,000,000 feet in 1864 to 46,557,700 feet in 1865 and 195,398,830 feet in 1873.[2] "In a few years," complained the sawmill owners of Black River Falls in a remonstrance to the legislature, "the wealthiest portion of the [Black River] pineries will present nothing but a vast and gloomy wilderness of pine stumps."[3]

Log rafting on the Mississippi was revolutionized during the later sixties when the old method of floating the rafts to market was abandoned for the more expeditious system of steamboat towing. This innovation, successfully tried for the first time in 1865, was but an adaptation of the similar departure of the year before in the marketing of sawed lumber. It proved an important factor in the swift growth of the log-driving industry from 1863 to 1872.[4]

[1] Hotchkiss, *Lumber Industry*, 635–36; Wis. *Assem. Jour.*, 1872, app., 105–36; Eau Claire *Free Press*, May 28, 1868.

[2] Hotchkiss, *Lumber Industry*, 501. The log-driving company on the Black River, which was known as the Black River Improvement Association, was incorporated in 1864. For its early history see Usher, *Wisconsin*, I, 182–84.

[3] Wis. *Assem. Jour.*, 1867, 1266–1272. The sawmill owners at Black River Falls made a determined effort in 1867 to secure a repeal of the charter of the log-driving association responsible for these increases but failed.

[4] The methods employed in towing fleets of logs down the lower Wolf River to Oshkosh, Fond du Lac, and other cities on Lake Winnebago differed somewhat from those employed on the Mississippi River. For a complete description of these see *History of Oshkosh* (Oshkosh, 1867),

In the construction of log rafts, however, the wasteful methods of the earlier period persisted. It was the practice at that time to bind the logs together by pinning them to long, stout poles, a process which involved boring two large augur holes into both ends of every piece of timber in the raft. Not only was this costly on account of wasted lumber but it was also a waste of labor, yet it was not until the later seventies that the modern "brailed" raft came into use, whereby the pine was merely surrounded and held in place by a boom or chain of logs and a network of skillfully arranged ropes.

Wisconsin lumbermen came into frequent collision with other interests in the State in their efforts to maintain unobstructed the navigation of their lumbering streams. They resisted vigorously, but without success, the bridging of the Mississippi by the east and west railroads seeking to enter Minnesota and Iowa. The construction of dams for water-power purposes on navigable streams led to many controversies and sometimes to the exercise of direct force. Particularly was this true on the Wisconsin River, where raft running was at best extremely difficult.[1] The most notable contest of this kind was one which arose out of the rivalries of two sawmill communities on the Chippewa River, a contest which in its various forms extended over a period of fifteen years.

74. In 1873 the rafting of logs on Lake Michigan was begun, about 2,000,000 feet being transported thus from Ludington, Mich., to Chicago.

[1] The conflict of interest on the Wisconsin River centered about the erection of a dam for manufacturing purposes at the Kilbourn Dells. The controversy had its origin as far back as 1855 when the Wisconsin River Hydraulic Company was incorporated. During the sixties the contest several times found its way into the legislature, and in the early seventies was carried to the courts.

The immediate cause of the Chippewa Dells controversy, as it was called, was a project for erecting in the Chippewa River, at a point just above Eau Claire, a comprehensive system of dams, piers, and booms, for the purpose of holding and assorting logs. Such a harbor the millmen of Eau Claire asserted was indispensable to their prosperity. Not only would it prevent serious losses of their logs in the annual spring freshets, but it would obviate the necessity for the vexatious system of log exchanges hitherto in general use. On the other hand, the millmen of Chippewa Falls, a few miles above Eau Claire, saw in the project only a selfish scheme to build up the industry of the lower town at their expense. The Dells improvement they maintained would not only put an end to their prosperity but would destroy the free navigation of the Chippewa River, an objection that could not be urged against an improvement of their own which they proposed to make above Chippewa Falls.[1]

As early as 1860 a bill passed both houses of the Wisconsin legislature authorizing the construction of the proposed dam above Eau Claire at the Chippewa Dells. However, Thaddeus Pound, a prominent Chippewa Falls lumberman, who was then enrolling clerk of the Assembly, prevailed upon Governor Randall to veto it on the ground that it contained no provision for locks. In 1867 the fight was renewed, but again the Eau Claire project was defeated. In 1870 a bill was a third time introduced, and a third

[1] The Chippewa Falls project, known as the Eagle Rapids Flooding Dam, was constructed in 1872–73 with a storage capacity of 100,000,000 feet of logs.

time defeated, after a bitter contest in which both sides charged that money had been improperly used.

Nothing daunted by these repeated defeats, the Eau Claire faction returned to the conflict in 1871 with a new bill, carefully drawn and strongly supported. The battle which now ensued was one such as the State had not witnessed since the memorable days of the railroad land-grant controversies. Though the dispute was purely local, the press of the State warmly took sides. Powerful lobbies composed of the shrewdest politicians and keenest legal talent of Wisconsin were maintained at great expense in Madison by both contestants. Rumors of corruption were soon busily flying about the capitol. An investigation was held, during the course of which a sponsor of the disputed bill frankly confessed to attempting to bribe a needy assemblyman.[1] Notwithstanding this offense his name was retained by the Assembly as a beneficiary of the measure. The Senate was even more brazen. It sent to decisive defeat a resolution to strike out the offender's name, after which it permitted the bill to pass.[2]

The measure was sent for signature to Governor Fairchild. He was convinced that the narrow majorities by which it had been carried in both houses had been secured dishonestly. In a ringing message he rebuked the legislature for its apparent acquiescence in corruption and returned the measure with his veto.[3] The friends of the bill endeavored to repass it but failed. A second investigation more thorough

[1] Wis. *Assem. Jour.*, 1871, 710, 801–20, 1000–1002.

[2] *Ibid.*, 836–38, 1000–1002; Wisconsin *Senate Journal*, 1871, 711–12.

[3] Wis. *Assem. Jour.*, 1871, 1000–1002.

than the first was now held. During its course legislators told of having rolls of greenbacks slipped into their pockets, of receiving offers of bribes varying from $100 to $1,000, of being urged in a friendly spirit by fellow-members and others not to be punctilious, but to share in the general and profitable grafting. Some acknowledged having accepted from the contestants loans of considerable sums of money. Among the men who had given such loans were State officials occupying positions of high trust. Though the investigation failed to prove direct bribe taking against any of the legislators, it revealed a moral tone about the capitol that was far from gratifying.[1]

The subsequent history of the Dells controversy was less sensational. It centered about the efforts of the city of Eau Claire to secure as a municipality the privileges which had so long been denied to its lumbermen as individuals. Eventually in 1875 the coveted legislative sanction for the improvement was secured in the form of an amendment to the city charter of Eau Claire.[2] The long-drawn struggle was, however, far from ended. It was now merely transferred from the legislature to the courts.

While these picturesque controversies were absorbing the attention of the people of Wisconsin other problems of far greater importance received but scant consideration. The swift forest destruction that accompanied the expansion of the lumber industry gave concern only to a few obscure idealists.[3]

[1] Wis. *Sen. Jour.*, 1872, app., 135–443.

[2] Wis. *Gen. Laws*, 1875, chap. 333.

[3] In 1867 the State legislature, under the inspiration of Wisconsin's notable scholar, Increase A. Lapham, instituted an inquiry into the evil effects of forest destruction upon the climate and stream flow of the State.

The enormous waste that was going on in logging, sawing, and marketing lumber was likewise regarded as of little moment. Every step in the transformation of the pine tree into the sawed board was marked by improvidence. The log choppers cut the tree high, wasting long stumps, while the sawyers in dividing the fallen pine into logs wasted many feet of clear timber at the tops. Young growth was given scant consideration, while windfalls that were not in prime condition were left to rot. It has been estimated that as a result of careless logging and fires not more than 40 per cent of the magnificent forest that once clothed northern Wisconsin ever reached the sawmill.[1]

In the sawmill the waste continued. Toward the close of the Civil War a few of the larger concerns in Wisconsin attempted to make some use of their waste products, manufacturing lath and pickets from slabs, cutting shingles from culls, and consuming at least a portion of their sawdust and refuse for fuel.[2] But nearly all merely dumped their refuse into a near-by river or destroyed it on the ever-blazing slab pile. Every rise of the pinery streams brought down enormous quantities of sawmill débris, commonly known as "flood trash," while in many a prosperous city of northern Wisconsin it is today possible to point out business blocks built upon the sites of former swamps that were filled with sawmill refuse.

The report submitted by the committee of investigation led to the passage of a law to encourage tree planting, which was, however, entirely ineffective. See *Report on the Disastrous Effects of the Destruction of Forest Trees in Wisconsin* (Madison, 1867); Wis. *Gen. Laws*, 1868, chap. 102.

[1] E. M. Griffith, *Report of the State Forester of Wisconsin*, 1907–8, 49.

[2] The manufacture of lath was somewhat unprofitable even in the larger sawmills, hence many of the millmen preferred to destroy their slabs.

Fire was the dread scourge of the lumber industry. Sawmills and sawmill towns, flimsily constructed of inflammable pine and consuming the airy fuel left by their saws, were periodically swept by the flames. It was a rare sawmill that was not burned to the ground and rebuilt at least twice, while only one thing was more astonishing than the frequency with which sawmill towns were either partially or wholly destroyed, and this was the speed with which they rose from their ashes.

Forest fires were an appalling source of loss. As lumbering operations became more extensive and settlements pressed in close behind the danger of forest conflagrations steadily increased. The careless logging methods of the time, still in vogue in some parts of the United States, were an invitation to the flames. The loggers removed only the choicest pine, while on the floor of the forest they left great heaps of branches and tops, known in the vernacular of the trade as "slashings." Such dead material, soon dry as tinder, in a year of drought needed only a spark from some careless hunter's camp or farmer's burning brush pile, or a chance stroke of lightning, to set it off into an all-devouring blaze. It was characteristic of the attitude of the period toward natural resources that forest fires were merely left to exhaust themselves in their own fury, no effort being made to impede or check the course of the flames.

In 1863, a year of scant rainfall, a disastrous fire swept over the forests along the southwestern shore of Lake Superior, in which it was estimated that lumber to the value of $1,000,000 was destroyed.[1]

[1] Estimate by the *Clark County Advocate,* printed in *Wis. State Jour.*, July 21, 1863.

The smoke, sweeping southward more than a hundred miles, was so thick in La Crosse that for several days the sun was totally obscured, and the atmosphere was rendered murky as far southeast as Milwaukee. "It must be a terrible fire," observed the Eau Claire *Free Press*, "that could fill the heavens with smoke at a distance of 75 to 100 miles."[1]

The following year witnessed an even more disastrous conflagration. As a result of an unprecedented drought, by the middle of May fires were running briskly through the forests on the upper Wisconsin and Black rivers. As the season advanced and the heavens brought no relief the whole northern woods seemed suddenly to burst into flame. From the St. Croix, the Chippewa, the Black, the Wisconsin, and the Wolf River pineries, and from Brown, Kewaunee, and Manitowoc counties came accounts of raging seas of smoke and fire. Scores of villages and hamlets were threatened with destruction. Wausau, Two Rivers, and Neillsville fought off the engulfing flames only by the heroic efforts of their entire populations. For six weeks the northern pineries were ablaze, and immense quantities of valuable timber were destroyed. It is significant that although this was one of the greatest general conflagrations that the State had ever known it received scarcely any notice in the newspapers of southern Wisconsin.

The same lack of interest was again evident in 1868 when for the third time within the decade forest fires ran through the northern woods. The pineries on the Chippewa, the Black, the Wisconsin, and the

[1] Excerpt from the Eau Claire *Free Press*, printed in *Wis. State Jour.*, July 27, 1863.

Wolf rivers and the forests in Kewaunee and Door counties were again the scenes of wide devastation, while along the entire line of the Chicago & Northwestern Railroad from Escanaba to Marquette great areas of magnificent forests were aflame.

One of the reasons for public indifference to these costly conflagrations was that they usually involved little loss of life. Such, unhappily, was not the case in the great forest fire that swept over northeastern Wisconsin in 1871, one of the greatest disasters of its kind in the world's history. Following a three month's drought, fires suddenly broke out here and there in all the counties bordering upon both shores of Green Bay. For three weeks they burned unchecked, and the only notice which they at first received in the State press was an occasional complaint from a neighboring city that the atmosphere was polluted with smoke. By October 4 the conflagration had become so widespread that most of the villages and towns in a strip thirty miles wide and extending from Appleton to Menominee, Michigan, were in imminent danger of destruction.[1]

On the night of October 8 a hurricane coming up from the southwest whipped the flames furiously forward. Soon the whole of northeastern Wisconsin was a howling tempest of fire. Like a destroying demon the fiery sheet swept northward, leaving behind a wide swath of ruined villages, forests, and farms. Oconto, Marinette, Brown, Door, Shawano, and Kewaunee counties, and parts of Manitowoc and Outagamie were desolated on that fateful autumn night. More than a thousand persons were

[1] See Green Bay *Gazette* and Milwaukee *Sentinel* for the dates given.

burned to death in the holocaust, almost as many more were painfully wounded, and 3,000 were made destitute.[1]

Public and private timberlands suffered equally in forest conflagrations. Public lands, however, were exposed to another danger, the trespassing of irresponsible loggers. Timber trespass was a difficult problem to deal with. It was sometimes impossible in the forest to tell just where the surveyor's line between public and private lands ran. No doubt some trespassing was thus unintentional, but a far larger part was unmistakably willful. Some loggers did not even pretend to cut on their own lands, and they were encouraged in this forest free-booting by dishonest mill owners who thereby secured cheaper logs. Other loggers purchased what was known as a "big forty," fortified by the possession of which they proceeded to strip half an adjacent township. The most common practice, however, was to purchase from the State its choice pinelands, paying therefor, in accordance with the loose requirements of the day, only a small installment of the purchase price; then quickly to strip the lands of all their valuable pine and when they were denuded allow them to revert to the State.

In 1865 the Wisconsin Commissioners of School

[1] At the village of Peshtigo the fatalities mounted highest, hence the disaster has since been referred to as the "Peshtigo Fire." See for vivid descriptions, proclamation of Governor Fairchild, Oct. 13, 1871, printed in Milwaukee *Sentinel*, Oct. 14, 1871; also Green Bay *Gazette* for October, 1871; Wisconsin *Legislative Manual*, 1872, 470–80. For a lengthier description by an eyewitness see pamphlet of Rev. P. Pernin, *The Finger of God is there! or, Thrilling Episode of a Strange Event Related by an Eyewitness* (Montreal, 1874).

and University Lands reported to Governor Lewis concerning trespassing as follows:

> Quietly but actively trespassers have been stripping off this timber, sometimes merely for their own use, sometimes making small sales, and sometimes carrying on the shameful business so extensively as to cover the rivers with stolen logs, and to grow rich upon their illgotten plunder. Others, equally guilty, purchase the stolen property, and thus support and encourage the iniquity. Important corporations and prominent men in some parts of the State have been for years engaged in the traffic. Public sentiment thus becomes demoralized, and efforts for the detection and punishment of the criminals are thwarted, and even resented as unwarrantable interference with private rights. To a considerable class, including many besides those actually interested, this robbery of the children's inheritance has come by long use to seem excusable and even right.[1]

For many years the State made little effort to discourage such dishonesty. Private landholders employed experienced woodsmen to protect their timber, but as late as 1860 the State left the difficult task of guarding its remote and interminable forests to county sheriffs, constables, and justices of the peace. In 1860 an improvement was secured when the Commissioners of School and University Lands were authorized to maintain four forest rangers in the northern pineries during the logging season.[2] At the same time, however, the penalty for trespassing was greatly reduced. Trespassers detected in their work were given an opportunity to escape prosecution entirely if they agreed to purchase the land from which they had illicitly cut timber, the only penalty inflicted being to add to the purchase price of the land an additional 25 per cent.

[1] Commissioners of School and University Lands of Wisconsin, *Report*, 1865, 9, bound with Wis. *Mess. and Docs.*, 1865. The State lands were chiefly held for educational purposes, hence the reference to children's inheritance.

[2] Wis. *Gen. Laws*, 1860, chap. 277.

This change, inadequate though it was, and often defeated in its purpose by the dishonesty or incapacity of the rangers, was a distinct improvement. In 1864 the law was strengthened by raising the number of foresters to eight and increasing the penalty in the more flagrant cases of trespassing to 50 per cent. In 1865 other improvements were made, but in 1871 the number of rangers was again reduced to four, a misfortune that was only partially offset by doubling the penalty against offenders.[1] Trespassing upon State lands remained during all the rest of the century a vexatious problem, while the punishment meted out to the timber thieves continued until recent years to be merely the requirement upon detection of purchasing the stolen lumber at an enhanced price.

The leniency to timber thieves displayed by the State and Federal governments was largely a matter of necessity. Public sentiment in the affected districts was unsympathetic toward a rigid enforcement of the land laws, a characteristic frontier attitude, and the only hope of arriving at any kind of settlement was by compromise. "Experience has taught us," declared the United States Land Commissioner in 1865, "that when community interests conflict with law and public opinion is in conflict with its enforcement, it becomes virtually inoperative."[2]

The loss suffered by the State through the operations of timber thieves was very large. In 1860 the

[1] *Id.*, 1871, chap. 21.

[2] U. S. Land Office, *Report*, 1865, 26. See also Cyrus Woodman to James Hinman, April 5, 1861, in Cyrus Woodman Manuscripts in Wisconsin Historical Library.

Commissioners of School and University Lands declared: "Of all the causes which have operated to the depletion of the trust funds of the State, it is believed none has worked greater loss than 'skinning' the pine and other timbered lands of the northern portion of the State."[1] The lands held by the State in trust for the St. Croix & Lake Superior Railroad and for the Sturgeon Bay Ship Canal Company, which for some years received even less protection than the school and university lands, were in proportion more extensively plundered. In 1864 the State forest rangers found that nearly 12,000 acres of the pinelands of the State had been trespassed upon, and in the following year nearly 19,000 acres.[2] In 1864, inadequate as their force was, they seized 19,717,200 feet of pine, 2,861 cords of wood, and 40,000 cedar posts, besides considerable other miscellaneous timber, that had been unlawfully cut from State lands.[3] In 1873 a single forester employed to protect the St. Croix & Lake Superior Railroad land grant discovered and seized in one season upon this grant 11,000,000 feet of stolen logs.[4]

It was observed by the Commissioners of School and University Lands that as soon as an active policy of repression against trespassers was inaugurated the number of acres of pinelands sold by the State suddenly jumped upward. More particularly was it noticed that purchasers were willing to pay for lands in full instead of by installments as

[1] Comrs. of School & Univ. Lands, *Report*, 1860, 61.

[2] *Id.*, 1864, 8, 26; *id.*, 1865, 10.

[3] *Id.*, 1864, 8, 26.

[4] Madison *Democrat*, Sept. 29, 1874. See also *Wis. Lumberman*, October, 1874, 140–41.

before. In 1864, when the number of forest rangers was increased from four to eight, the sales of State lands increased one-third, and the lands fully paid for increased from 76,365 acres to 103,238 acres. "We know," declared the Commissioners, "that a substantial portion of this increase is owing to the watchfulness exercised over the public lands, and the enhanced risk of trespassing on them." "Purchasing," they significantly remark, "is more in fashion than in earlier times."[1]

The lumber industry in Wisconsin was seriously embarrassed by scarcity of labor during the last two years of the Civil War. The remoteness of the lumber camps from settlements, the rough and temporary nature of the work, and the unsatisfactory terms of employment were sufficient even in normal times to render the labor problem in the pineries a troublesome one. The Wolf River and Green Bay pineries, being nearer to large centers of population, experienced less difficulty in securing labor than did the pineries in northwestern Wisconsin. Their advantage was reflected in the lower wages that they were accustomed to pay.

In both sections, however, there was an unusual scarcity of labor during the last two years of the war and the years immediately following its close. Wages as a result rose to unprecedented heights. It was customary in 1860 and 1861 to pay workers in lumber camps from $12 to $25 per month and board, varying with different pineries and with the skill of individual workmen.[2] In 1864, according to newspaper reports,

[1] Comrs. of School & Univ. Lands, *Report*, 1864, 8.

[2] *Wis. Lumberman*, December, 1873, 163; Moses M. Strong Manuscripts, 1859, in Wisconsin Historical Library.

the wages of loggers in the northwestern pineries of Wisconsin ranged from $3 to $4 per day including board, while those of the rivermen were even higher. In the La Crosse *Democrat* of May 29, 1865 a correspondent asserted that raft pilots were receiving in several instances as high as $3,000 per year, while ordinary hands were paid $3 a day, with board for the time consumed in going to market by raft and returning by steamer.[1]

Labor conditions in the lumber camps continued throughout our period to be most unsatisfactory. The food of the laborers was coarse and without variety, the lodgings were unsanitary, and drunkenness was universal. Many logging contractors, moreover, were financially irresponsible, and the lumberjacks were often defrauded by them of the wages of an entire season. Among the responsible companies and particularly among the large sawmill corporations "company stores" were the source of much dissatisfaction. The employees, who were compelled to trade at such stores, frequently found when accounts were balanced at the end of the season that they not only had no wages due them, but were actually in debt to the company for supplies, tobacco, and whisky.

The depression which settled upon the Wisconsin lumber industry from 1868 to 1870 led to severe cuts in wages and to a number of labor disputes, notably at Oshkosh, Black River Falls, and Eau Claire. At Black River Falls an association of river drivers appears to have been organized in 1869, which pur-

[1] See also excerpts from pinery newspapers in *Wisconsin Weekly State Journal*, Mar. 28 and April 4, 1865; Milwaukee *Sentinel*, April 10, 1865.

ported to include rivermen in all the pineries of the State, though it never extended its influence beyond the Black River. At Green Bay and Black River Falls the sawmill owners entered into agreements to secure united action in their relations with employees, an unusual procedure at this early day in Wisconsin lumbering. The nature of the industry, however, precluded any effective organization either of employers or employees, and those associations which were formed were uncertain and unstable in character.[1]

In every new country the natural resources closest at hand are the first to be exploited. Particularly is this true if only a small outlay of money is required in the process. The gifts of nature are transformed into capital as rapidly as possible, and the means thus accumulated form the basis for the development of other fields of industry. In Wisconsin lumber was one of the easiest, and therefore one of the first, of the great natural resources to be thus utilized. To the fortunes realized in the hewing and sawing of pine nearly every other industry in the State in part at least owes its present advancement. Unhappily, the lumbermen of Wisconsin in their eagerness to transmute the great northern forests into gold followed in the footsteps of other pioneer exploiters. With reckless disregard for the future they wasted the gift of the ages. Today when northern Wisconsin is stripped of its priceless heritage of forests the State repents its youthful folly.

[1] By the winter of 1873 wages in the pineries had fallen to the level of 1861.

CHAPTER IV

MINING, 1860–70

In nothing did Wisconsin give more convincing proof of her prosperity during the closing years of the Civil War than in the mining boom which at that time marked her industrial life. Enterprises that had been abandoned in despair after the panic of 1857 secured a new lease on life between 1864 and 1867. Fresh undertakings, both legitimate and spurious, attracted speculators and investors. The large number of mining and smelting companies besieging the State legislature for charters in 1864 obliged that body to enact a general law for incorporating such organizations.[1] In the following session applications for special charters still appeared to the number of forty-two. In 1866, when the mining boom had reached its height, nearly double that number were under consideration.[2]

The most substantial of these mining operations centered about the old lead districts of southwestern Wisconsin, comprising roughly the three counties of Grant, Iowa, and Lafayette. Here since the first days of French occupation the heavy deposits of

[1] Wis. *Gen. Laws*, 1864, chap. 166. The hopeful optimism of the period finds expression in the taxing provisions of this law. Although qualified geologists pointed out the extreme improbability of coal ever being found within the limits of the State, due to the completion of its geologic strata before the carboniferous age, this law imposed a tax of ½ cent per ton upon all coal which should in the future be mined in Wisconsin.

[2] Wis. *Assem. Jour.*, 1865; *id.*, 1866; Wis. *Sen. Jour.*, 1865; *id.*, 1866.

galena had been a fruitful source of exploitation. Lying entirely in the "driftless area," with the mineral-bearing rock exposed to easy operation by the individual miner, this region had become one of the first centers of industry and influence in the State. A fortunate accident of geology determined that the organization of our State government, the agitation for State canals, and the building of the first east and west railroads should all find here their initial impulse.[1]

By 1847 the region had reached the height of its development; thereafter it rapidly declined. The most productive shafts had been worked down to the water level, the superior attractiveness of the gold mines of California and the copper mines of Lake Superior were depleting its labor supply, and the more stable returns of a fertile soil were transforming the remaining miners into farmers. From 1850 until comparatively recent times lead mining in the district was for the most part carried on as a winter occupation of the farmers.

The outbreak of the Civil War witnessed a marked change in the older methods of conducting mining operations. In the former period many of the richest shafts had been abandoned at the water level because of the difficulty and expense of draining. In the early sixties, however, eastern capital was introduced to accomplish what had been impossible for individual enterprise. Large corporations bought up all of the promising diggings in abandoned districts, sank level adits or drains to unwater their

[1] O. G. Libby, "Significance of the Lead and Shot Trade," in *Wis. Hist. Colls.*, XIII, 293.

consolidated holdings, and either operated the diggings themselves or leased them to individual miners on tribute.[1] An example of the successful application of capital and modern mining methods to abandoned mines, which received wide notice in the press of southern Wisconsin during the war, was the Champion lode in the New Diggings district. Here in 1862 the running of a level adit half a mile in length was commenced, which, after an expenditure of $70,000 and about three years of labor, drained ground from which during the next four years 5,000,000 pounds of ore were secured.

Not even the introduction of capital, however, nor the unusual prices paid for lead during the years of the war could permanently check the decline of the industry. The diggings were after all considerably worked out, and the favorable market conditions created by the war merely operated to lessen the rate of decline. While the price of pig lead rose from $4.90 per 100 pounds in July, 1861 to $15 in January, 1865, the production of ore in the Wisconsin lead region fell from 17,037,912 pounds in 1862 to 14,337,895 pounds in 1865 and 13,754,159 pounds by the end of the decade.[2]

A new product of the lead mines during the war,

[1] The tribute varied from one-fourth to one-tenth of all the ore raised, depending upon the richness of the vein, the ease of operation, and the market price of the mineral. See the Moses M. Strong Manuscripts and Cyrus Woodman Manuscripts for this period in the Wisconsin Historical Library.

[2] The statistics of prices are from the report of the Aldrich Committee, 52 Cong., 2 sess., *Senate Reports*, III, pt. 2, 192. The price quoted for 1865 is in greenbacks. The statistics of production are from Moses Strong, "Geology and Topography of the Lead Region," in Chamberlin, *Geology of Wisconsin, 1873–79*, II, 742.

however, more than compensated for this decrease in the output of lead. Prior to 1860 the zinc ores occurring associated with galena had been regarded by the miners as a nuisance, and such as had to be raised had either been thrown away or utilized for making roads. About 1860 smithsonite, one of these ores, popularly known among the miners as "drybone" because of its resemblance to partly decayed bone, began to be smelted with success, and thereafter its production rose by leaps and bounds. In 1860, 320,000 pounds were mined; in 1865 this amount had risen to 4,198,200 pounds and in 1872 to 27,021,388 pounds. Shortly after the close of the war, deeper-lying zinc ore known as blende or blackjack, began to be mined successfully and before many years was being raised even more extensively than "drybone." In 1867, 841,310 pounds were mined; a year later this amount had jumped to 3,078,435 pounds and by 1872 to 16,256,970 pounds. Blende proved to be the most abundant mineral in the lead region, and to the present day it is extensively mined.[1]

This rapid development of the zinc industry in southwestern Wisconsin must be attributed in part to the economies of large-scale lead mining, which made possible the raising of hitherto inaccessible ores. Equally important, however, was the introduction of necessary capital for the establishment of zinc smelteries and the application of metallurgical skill to the reduction of the ores. In 1859 the first attempt in the State at manufacturing zinc from "drybone" was made at Mineral Point. The experi-

[1] *Ibid.*

ment proved successful in a small way, and in 1863 or 1864 a firm of eastern capitalists was induced to expend approximately $100,000 in erecting zinc works there on a more extensive scale. The expense of transporting coal from Illinois to Mineral Point eventually proved prohibitive, however, and the undertaking had to be abandoned.

In the meantime two German graduates of the mining academy of Freiburg, E. C. Hegeler and F. W. Matthiessen, who had visited Mineral Point in 1858 in order to satisfy themselves of the feasibility of profitably smelting its zinc ores, had been favorably impressed and had established a modest smeltery at La Salle, Illinois, where coal was abundant and fire clay near at hand. A number of years were spent in adapting European methods to new materials and new conditions. This was interrupted temporarily in 1861 by the depression which followed the outbreak of the war. The increased demand during the war for zinc to be used in the manufacture of arms and cartridges presented the enterprising firm its opportunity, and by the close of the war it had built up one of the largest zinc manufacturing establishments in the world.

While the smelting of zinc was in an experimental stage the raw ore could be secured for the cost of hauling from the refuse heaps of the mines and the furnaces. Due to the success of the La Salle works, however, its value rose by the end of the war to $10 or $15 a ton, and by the end of the decade, it was one of the most important mineral products of the lead region.

Iron mining during the war was in its infancy. The great mines of the Lake Superior region completely overshadowed those in Wisconsin, attracting thither whatever capital was available for such investment. The Iron Ridge in Dodge County and Ironton in Sauk County were the only localities in the State in which any iron ore was mined. The annual output of the two districts during the early sixties probably never exceeded 7,500 tons.

Beginning with 1870, however, as the result of the erection of a great rolling mill in Milwaukee, the industry assumed new importance. In that year the product of the Wisconsin mines suddenly jumped to 100,000 tons.[1] The Iron Ridge in particular made rapid progress. Its ores, being hard, were deemed desirable for mixing with the softer mineral of the Lake Superior region, and thus they found a ready market not only in Milwaukee but in Cleveland, Chicago, St. Louis, and Wyandotte. In 1870 practically the entire Wisconsin output originated in the Dodge County mines.[2] In 1872 the rich deposits of the Gogebic Range in northeastern Wisconsin were discovered, but it was not until a later period that there developed in this region the great iron interests for which it has since become famous.

A highly speculative mining interest which created excitement in Wisconsin for several years was petroleum. Previous to 1864 this oil had been advertised in newspapers and sold in drug stores chiefly as a medicine. In the frontier region west of Lake Michigan illumination was still limited chiefly to

[1] The Iron Ridge produced more than 90,000 tons of this amount. It sent to Milwaukee for manufacture and export 78,587 tons of ore and some 6,500 tons of pig iron. Milwaukee Chamber of Commerce, *Report*, 1871, 78: *post*, chap. v.

[2] *Ibid.*

the tallow candle and the lard-oil cup. A few of the more enterprising settlers used the serviceable volatile fluids, which were, however, not only expensive but dangerous. During the height of the Civil War improved methods for refining crude petroleum were discovered, which made possible the use of the oil for illuminating purposes. There followed in 1864 a tremendous boom in the oil fields of Pennsylvania, West Virginia, and Ohio. The entire North turned its eyes to the region of the "gushers." The popular imagination was fired with accounts of fortunes made in a day, and tales of the wealth and extravagance of the "petroleum aristocracy" were upon every tongue.

In 1865 the petroleum fever reached Wisconsin. Early in that year alleged indications of oil were reported from various parts of the State and the reports were readily credited. Feverish excitement in the fortunate districts followed each discovery. Stock companies were organized, derricks and boring apparatus were imported from the East, and operations were commenced in approved eastern fashion. The reputable geologists in the State were unanimous in protesting their unbelief; they explained that the oily blue scum on the surface of the marsh waters, which usually created the excitement, was but the result of decay of organic substances, but speculators refused to be discouraged. In 1865 twenty-four petroleum mining companies were before the legislature seeking special charters, all of which were granted; in 1866 the number had risen to forty-two.[1]

[1] See R. D. Irving, "Mineral Resources," in *History of Dodge County*, 162–72; Wis. *Assem. Jour.*, 1865; *id.*, 1866; Wis. *Sen. Jour.*, 1865; *id.*, 1866.

Probably as many more not substantial enough to secure special incorporation were operating under the general laws. Appleton with a population of 2,700 was supporting in May, 1865 seven petroleum companies in various stages of organization; the village of Sparta with a population of about 1,300 early in 1866 was supporting ten or twelve, all operating in the Kickapoo Valley of Crawford County. In the southern part of Monroe County a community which still bears the name of Oil City suddenly grew up about an oil discovery. In Crawford County another community, consisting of a hastily constructed hotel and a barn, adopted the same ambitious appellation. At Appleton, where the excitement centered about an old well from which it was claimed gas intermittently discharged, a miniature mining rush took place. On April 5, 1865 the editor of the Appleton *Crescent* wrote: "Strangers keep flocking to town. There is a constant stream of visitors to the Northwestern Company's well. House room is becoming so scarce that the newcomers will soon be obliged to bring their tents with them, or 'sleep standing.'" On Feb. 16, 1865 Col. Charles S. Robinson, the intelligent and conservative editor of the Green Bay *Advocate*, who was interested in one of the Appleton petroleum companies wrote: "Who knows but Northern Wisconsin may yet become a place of as much wealth and the scene of as much excitement as the oil regions of Pennsylvania now are."

Coupled with easy optimism in stimulating and maintaining the petroleum fever was the usual admixture of fraud. When expensive boring operations continued month after month without producing the promised gushers and investors began to be discouraged, it frequently occurred that limited quantities of crude oil would be struck opportunely of a quality "equal if not superior to that of the Pennsylvania region." A common device for stirring up interest was the importation of strangers posing as geological experts to examine promising prospects. Of course their reports were invariably favorable. In the Prairie du Chien *Courier* of July 7, 1865 occurs a characteristic report by Prof. L. H. Gano of Chicago upon the lands of the Wisconsin Copper Creek Petroleum and Mining Company. Beginning with an elaborate discussion of the geologic structure of the region, bristling with technical terms but peculiarly devoid of meaning, the author concludes: "I shall feel safe in saying the surface indications and natural developments of these lands are unsurpassed by any oil region in the United States, and I have no hesitation in saying that I sincerely believe that proper developments here will be rewarded by flowing wells, yielding in quantity equal to any heretofore developed elsewhere, the geographical formation taken in connection with the natural developments warrant this conclusion." An examination of the Chicago directory for 1865 discloses the learned Prof. L. H. Gano as plain Louis H. Gano, speculative broker in one of the cheaper Chicago business districts.

The extent to which Wisconsin citizens invested in oil speculation at this time can only be approximated. The opportunities offered were certainly abundant, both in home and in foreign ventures. Stock was thrown upon the market in the smallest possible denominations in order that persons of limited means might not be excluded from the opportunity of winning fortunes. Shares were sold for as low as $5, often at a discount of 50 per cent. On Aug. 20, 1865, when the petroleum craze had not yet run its course in the State, the *Wisconsin Daily Capital* estimated that the people of Madison alone had invested over $200,000 in oil wells.[1] The *Bothwell News Letter* of Canada West in the spring of 1866 reported: "Ten oil companies with an average cash capital of twenty thousand dollars each, have been organized in the city of Fond du Lac, nine of which are operating here at Bothwell, and one in Kentucky. The amount of money invested here, by Fond du Lac men alone, including individual investments, cannot fall far short of $300,000. Pretty heavy that for a city of twelve thousand inhabitants."[2] Citizens of Milwaukee sank $400,000 in such speculations, according to an estimate of O. H. Waldo, a prominent Milwaukee business man. "It took only a few hours," he declared, "to raise $100,000 to sink in oil, and the experiment was repeated three or four times."[3] These estimates were no doubt somewhat exaggerated, yet they serve as an indication of the extent to which the prosperous citizens of the State were investing in home and foreign petroleum enterprises during the boom years of 1865 and 1866.

These years saw also a revival of attempts at copper mining, the lead region, Douglas County, and

[1] The population of the city of Madison at this time was 6,648.

[2] Reprinted in Fond du Lac *Reporter*, Mar. 24, 1866.

[3] Address before the Milwaukee Chamber of Commerce, in Milwaukee *Sentinel*, May 29, 1869. See also Oshkosh *Northwestern*, Mar. 29, 1866, for an estimate of the oil investments of Fond du Lac business men.

the lower Fox Valley being the centers of interest. The meager copper deposits of the lead region near Mineral Point, which in the early forties had produced about a million and a half pounds of ore, induced some futile efforts in 1860 and several equally fruitless attempts in the years from 1863 to 1866. In Douglas County three organized efforts at copper mining were made: one at the so-called Fond du Lac mine, in which, in 1863, a company of prominent Milwaukee business men sank about $14,000; another at the Copper Creek mine, an abandoned prospect of the old American Fur Company, upon which in 1864 and 1865, $30,000 was expended; and a third similarly futile effort in 1865 on the Upper Falls of Black River. In the northeastern portion of the State, particularly in the lower Fox River Valley, the finding of fragments of native copper, carried down by the glaciers from the copper-bearing rocks of the Lake Superior region, periodically stirred up excited interest in copper mining and led the Appleton *Crescent* on Feb. 18, 1865 to assert confidently that "a large portion of our country is underlaid with a rich copper bed almost, if not quite equal to the Lake Superior region."

Peat, a product of hundreds of Wisconsin marshes, attracted new interest. In these deposits, it was boldly asserted, the State possessed a boundless source of future fuel supply. During the years 1866 and 1867 eighteen peat-cutting and manufacturing companies came before the legislature for incorporation, their titles indicating that they intended to operate chiefly in the southern portion of the State. The beds, owned by Col. William B. Slaughter, about seven miles west of Madison, which, according to the *Wisconsin State Journal*, contained upward of 300,000 solid cords of peat,[1] were the subject of much discussion and confident hope in the surrounding region. The cost of cutting and manufacturing, however, was prohibitive. Most of the deposits were of inferior quality, and wood was comparatively cheap and pleasanter to handle. With the passing of the boom years the subject was quietly dropped.

At Milwaukee and a number of other points along the shore of Lake Michigan the stratified beds of clay deposited by the lake at a time when it extended far beyond its present limits furnished material for an excellent cream-colored brick which became widely known throughout the country as "Milwaukee Brick." At the chief point of manufacture in the metropolis of the State from 20,000,000 to 25,000,000 were annually produced during the period of the war, the use of which at home and abroad gave to Milwaukee its title, "The Cream City."

The mining boom that swept over Wisconsin from 1864 to 1867 is interesting chiefly as a chapter of beginnings, though significant also as an indication of the prosperity which the State was enjoying. While the East was suffering a temporary depression from the end of the war to 1867, due to the return of the soldiers from the front, and to the fluctuations in the value of greenbacks, the agricultural West was experiencing little, if any, check, and the farmers of Wisconsin possessed an abundance of money for investment in mining speculations.

[1] *Wis. State Jour.*, Mar. 18, 1865.

CHAPTER V

MANUFACTURING

Wisconsin as a State was well adapted to manufacturing. She possessed natural endowments both numerous and in fortunate combination. Raw materials she had in profusion. Her soil gave her wheat for milling, hogs and cattle for packing, and hides for leather. Her forests offered her lumber, both hard and soft, to be fashioned into furniture, woodenware, and ships. Her mines yielded iron for machinery, implements, and rails. Her clay produced excellent brick. Her numerous streams afforded abundant power for the wheels of factories and mills. She had no coal, but her railroads brought her cheaply the carbon product of Illinois, and her lake vessels freely eked out the profits of grain carrying by transporting at little cost return cargoes of the bituminous output of Pennsylvania and Ohio. Finally, her magnificent system of inland waterways and her developing railroads afforded her manufacturers wide and convenient avenues to the markets of the world.

To a limited extent at the beginning of the Civil War Wisconsin had availed herself of these opportunities. Her lumbering and milling industries were developing; those of tanning, brewing, and brickmaking were under way. However, all were still in their infancy. Wisconsin was too young a community to have built up any extensive manufacturing interests. Of the elements necessary to success on a large scale she lacked two. She had neither large centers of population nor surplus capital. Her greatest city contained less than 50,000 inhabitants; she had besides this no town more imposing in population than 7,500. As for capital, instead of possessing a surplus, her pioneers almost invariably began life in debt.

New countries have ever been compelled, because of lack of labor and capital, to send their raw products to older societies for manufacture. To this necessity Wisconsin yielded only unwillingly. "At present," lamented the State's foremost commercial organization in 1871, "we are sending our hard lumber east to get it back as furniture and agricultural implements, we ship ores to St. Louis and New York, to pay the cost of bringing it back as shot, type, pipe, sheet lead, white lead, paint, etc., we ship away our wool crop and import cloths, carpets, blankets and other fabrics; we give rags for paper, and hides for boots and harness, and iron ore for stoves—and our consumers all the while are paying the double costs of this unnecessary transportation."[1]

The people of Wisconsin were eager to correct this unsatisfactory condition. To establish new home industries and further develop those already in existence were among their most cherished ambitions. All interests in the State were agreed upon the desirability of this program. Farmers longed to see industrial communities grow up in their midst to which they could sell the products of their toil at high prices and without much transportation. Mechanics anticipated finding in new factories and

[1] Milwaukee Chamber of Commerce, *Report*, 1871, 16.

workshops increased opportunities for employment. Consumers promised themselves lower prices when the double cost of transporting raw material to the East and bringing it back in the form of finished commodities had been eliminated.

However, Wisconsin lacked the capital necessary to produce this happy consummation. At every step her progress was thereby blocked. She sought to overcome the difficulty by converting her available resources into cash as rapidly as possible and by inducing older communities in the country to come to her support. Her newspapers and public documents were constantly filled with accounts of the splendid opportunities for industrial investments that her resources held out, coupled with urgent solicitations to moneyed men in the East to come and take advantage of them.[1] The eagerness with which she sought the aid of outsiders was one of the notable characteristics of her economic life. It was in striking contrast to her present spirit of independence. Today, capital, though still everywhere welcomed, is carefully hedged about by legal restrictions designed to protect other interests in society. Fifty years ago the need of Wisconsin was so great that capital was invited hither upon its own terms. Wisconsin, bidding against other communities similarly situated for the golden means of industrial development, gladly and without reservation placed her future in the hands of men with money.

By the beginning of the Civil War the southern half of Wisconsin was sufficiently matured to make

[1] See, for example, the annual messages of the governors in Wis. *Mess. and Docs.*, 1860–70.

real progress in manufacturing. Rival interests, such as speculation in land and railroad building, which had hitherto absorbed most of the surplus capital in the State were eliminated. The best government lands in this region were disposed of; the prairies were under cultivation; the railroad lines most urgently needed were completed. The wealth which southern Wisconsin henceforth accumulated and that which it attracted from the East it was able to invest in growing proportions in industrial enterprises.

Thus during the sixties, especially during the latter half of the decade, Wisconsin established a foothold as a manufacturing community. The number of her factories and mills in this period considerably more than doubled; the hands employed in them increased almost threefold.

"It is undoubtedly true," declared the secretary of the Wisconsin Agricultural Society in 1868, "that in manufactories Wisconsin has made more actual progress since 1860 than in any other one of the several departments of industry (agriculture, lumber, and mining) we have had under consideration; and equally true that, in view of the extraordinary natural facilities she possesses for a successful prosecution of very many important branches of the manufacturing business, she has, as yet, relatively done but little."[1]

The communities in Wisconsin best adapted to the purposes of manufacturing were naturally the first to feel the impulse of this industrial development. Milwaukee, because of her commanding position upon

[1] Wis. Agric. Soc., *Trans.*, 1861–68, 56.

Lake Michigan, her excellent communications with the interior, and her large population, was the leader. Even she, until the outbreak of the Civil War, had been chiefly a city of trade. "The business of a large share of our citizens," observed the Milwaukee *Sentinel* in 1862, "has been to dispose of the manufactures of other people, and to traffic in the rich products of our own broad, fertile prairies. Nor can it be said that we have not as a community flourished almost unprecedentedly under this state of things; but at times when there has been a failure of crops in our State, we have seen the folly of relying for our prosperity upon a trafficking business."[1]

To win freedom from dependence upon trade Milwaukee definitely turned during the later sixties to manufacturing.[2] So rapid was her progress that by 1872 one-third to one-half of her working population was engaged in manufactures, and the products of her factories were worth nearly $20,000,000.[3]

Other cities in Wisconsin felt the same impulse toward manufacturing. Fond du Lac and Oshkosh on Lake Winnebago, enjoying easy access to the pineries of the Wolf River as well as excellent rail and water communications, advanced with a pace second only to that of the Cream City. Racine, Sheboygan, Manitowoc, and Kenosha, lake ports of local prominence, La Crosse on the Mississippi River, and a number of interior railroad towns, notably Madison, Janesville, and Watertown, during

[1] Milwaukee *Sentinel*, May 15, 1862.

[2] The Milwaukee Manufacturers' Association was organized Jan. 9, 1863.

[3] Milwaukee Chamber of Commerce, *Report*, 1872, 22–23. See also Milwaukee *Sentinel*, Dec. 30, 1871.

the later sixties laid the foundations for industries which have since become important not only to the State but to the nation.

A cluster of aspiring cities and villages upon the lower Fox River enjoyed advantages for manufacturing which even at this time, when natural gifts in Wisconsin were so abundant and ready to hand, attracted wide attention. The Fox River from Lake Winnebago to Green Bay, a distance of thirty-five miles, has a fall of approximately 170 feet. It is capable of generating water power not only enormous, but what is vastly more important, steady at all seasons of the year. Its flow is perfectly regulated by Lake Winnebago, a great natural reservoir embracing an area of nearly 350 square miles. Neither flood nor drought, so often the bane of industries dependent on water power, ever causes any considerable fluctuations in the lower Fox. Neenah, Menasha, Appleton, and De Pere, which in 1860, as mere villages of a few thousand inhabitants, centered about the falls of this useful stream, were destined by nature to become flourishing industrial communities.

The prevailing industries of these several cities during the decade of the sixties naturally reflected the advantages and the shortcomings of Wisconsin as a manufacturing state. For the most part they were such as depended for success primarily upon an abundance of raw material. Only in rare instances did they require more than a minimum of capital and skilled labor. The grinding of wheat, the manipulation of lumber, the meat-packing industry, the burning of brick, such were the arts that occupied the mills and factories of the State.

Above: A McCormick reaper, one of many such machines that revolutionized wheat production during and after the war. *Below:* The Hammond tannery at Appleton. Military uses of leather goods made Wisconsin a national center for hide-tanning.

Above: Log drivers on a placid sorting pond in the Chippewa Valley. *Below:* Lumber rafts on the Wisconsin River below the Kilbourn dam.

Above: Massive jam of white pine logs at Chippewa Falls, 1869. *Below:* Chippewa River and waterfront at Eau Claire.

Above: A woolen mill at Sheboygan Falls employing both men and women. *Below:* A cooperage and furniture factory at Arkansaw, Pepin County.

The Milwaukee Chamber of Commerce, chartered in 1858.

Alexander Mitchell, railroad magnate and banker.

John Plankinton, meat packer and businessman.

Above: Great Lakes sailing vessel at a Milwaukee River dock. Such craft transported lumber, grain, and ore in the 1860's. *Below:* View of manufactories on the Fox River at DePere, Brown County, a lumber milling and shipbuilding center.

Above: The Reliance Works of Edward P. Allis. Under the stimulus of war Milwaukee became one of the largest producers of iron manufactures in the country. *Below:* Mississippi River Steamer *Diamond Jo* at a Wisconsin landing. Such passenger ships towed wheat barges to rail heads on the Wisconsin shore.

Wisconsin bank notes in use during the Civil War.

The milling of wheat was the leading industrial interest of Wisconsin. None other except the sawing of lumber approached it in importance. Wheat flour, on the basis of value, in 1860 constituted two-fifths of all the manufactures of Wisconsin; in 1870, when the industries of the State had become somewhat more diversified, the fraction still stood at considerably more than one-fourth. In 1860 the gristmill product sold for twelve times as much as any other commodity except sawed lumber manufactured in the State; in 1870 the proportion stood as eight to one.[1] Truly might it be said of Wisconsin that her manufacturing destinies were bound up in the millstone and the saw.

During the Civil War the flouring industry in Wisconsin made but slow progress. The State sent its enormous crops of wheat to market in the form of the berry rather than in the shape of flour. Why it did so is not entirely clear. No doubt one important reason was the expense of transporting the latter to the seaboard. The cost of shipping wheat, even via the lakes, was at no time much higher relatively than that of sending flour. The difference during the greater part of the Civil War was wholly negligible. Indeed, the Milwaukee Chamber of Commerce and the Chicago Board of Trade during several milling seasons observed that proportionally charges on the manufactured product were actually higher than upon grain. Under such circumstances the East preferred to do its own milling. The flour exports of Wisconsin increased only from 550,000 barrels in 1860 to 625,000 barrels in 1865.[2]

[1] U. S. *Census*, 1860, *Manufactures*, 657–58; *id.*, 1870, III, 583–84.

[2] Milwaukee Chamber of Commerce, *Report*, 1861, 6; *id.*, 1865, 17.

A revival in the industry set in at the close of the war. Carrying rates became favorable, and the flow of water for turning the mill wheels was all that could be desired. "The year 1866," according to the Milwaukee Chamber of Commerce, "was one of the most prosperous periods ever enjoyed by the millers of Wisconsin and other northwestern states, and the impetus thus imparted to the business has resulted not only in a large increase of the flour trade, but also of our milling facilities."[1] By 1868, although Wisconsin's home consumption of flour had increased materially due to her rapidly expanding population, her exports had grown to approximately 875,000 barrels.[2]

The recovery was only temporary. After 1868 until well into the next decade the industry was at a standstill. Though Wisconsin produced continually greater wheat crops, the grain itself rather than its product was sold to consumers in the East. On the whole it may be said that the milling industry made less progress in Wisconsin during the sixties than any other important manufacturing interest of the State.

Prior to the advent of the railroads the flouring industry of Wisconsin was widely dispersed over the State. Every village had its dust-laden miller upon whom the surrounding country depended for its supply of flour. The local gristmills were usually

Statistics in these Chamber of Commerce reports take no account of flour manufactured within the State and sent to market via Chicago. On the other hand they include flour originating in Minnesota and merely marketed by way of Milwaukee. Corrections for these items have been made.

[1] *Id.*, 1866, 10.

[2] *Id.*, 1868, 36.

unpretentious in size and backward in equipment. Most of them were of the familiar water-wheel type, the numerous streams of Wisconsin being especially adapted to their use. Here and there an establishment still drew its motive force as of yore from the wind. A few localities, notably Milwaukee, Janesville, and Watertown, conducted their operations upon a larger scale. They were debarred, however, by lack of transportation facilities from serving more than a restricted area. The country mills had the important advantage of proximity to the standing grain, and on the whole they were successful in answering local requirements.

When during the fifties Wisconsin undertook to manufacture flour for export a tendency toward greater centralization manifested itself. For a time this was barely perceptible; later it became very marked. The chief obstacle to concentration had been overcome; by rail grain could be moved with entire success to localities especially adapted to the purposes of milling. In large centers producers of flour enjoyed numerous advantages over their country brethren. They secured the economies of large-scale production, incidental among which was the cheapness with which they could manufacture flour barrels. They possessed a wider choice of grain for gristing and superior marketing facilities for their finished product. When during the seventies important changes in the flouring process rendered the machinery for mills vastly more complex and expensive than it had ever been before, the movement of the industry to the cities commenced in earnest. Country grist-millers during the decade of the sixties easily held their own; during the seventies they were relegated to custom grinding; during the eighties and nineties they were eliminated entirely. In their place developed the powerful merchant millers, men who were not so much expert artisans as successful salesmen. Today a few immense city establishments grind more and better flour than all the Wisconsin gristmillers together half a century ago.

Of all Wisconsin cities Milwaukee was best fitted to be a flouring center. Her railroads gave her easy access to the wheat fields of the interior. Her chief river, dammed about three miles above its mouth, afforded her millers a fair water power. Her commanding position on Lake Michigan opened to her manufacturers the wide markets of the world. These advantages were partially offset, however, by a serious difficulty. The Milwaukee River, upon which the city depended for motive power, was each year becoming less reliable. The destruction of the forests upon its northern headwaters rendered it increasingly subject to floods and succeeding periods of low levels. Frequently mills were crippled for months by lack of water or by damages sustained in the annual spring freshets.

The industry in the Cream City accurately reflected the general situation in the State. During the course of the war it was practically at a standstill. The 202,810 barrels which represented the city's milling product in 1860 also represented that of 1865.[1] From the latter year to 1868, however, there was a rapid advance. During 1866 new mills, equipped with every modern appliance, rose upon every hand.

[1] Milwaukee Chamber of Commerce, *Report*, 1865, 11.

After a particularly disastrous flood in 1866 nearly all the city establishments abandoned water power and substituted steam. Of the sixty-five run of stone in the several mills of the metropolis in that year only fifteen were still propelled by the current of the river.[1] The flour product of the city rose abruptly from 212,829 barrels in 1865 to 625,000 barrels in 1868, almost a threefold increase in three years.[2] This swift expansion was succeeded by an entire decade of quiescence. That in turn was followed by an era of remarkable growth which during the early nineties placed Milwaukee among the greatest flour-producing communities of the world.

Second only to Milwaukee in the Wisconsin flouring industry were the villages of Neenah and Menasha. Neenah in particular was distinctly a milling center. In 1860 she possessed seven flourishing mills; her neighbor across the Fox River had three. Together the two communities enjoyed a manufacturing capacity of some 800 barrels of flour per day.[3] During the war they made little progress, adding only two new mills to their number. Beginning with 1866, however, they forged rapidly to the front. By 1870 they boasted fifteen mills of which Neenah alone had eleven. With forty-five run of stone, they had a capacity for producing 3,875 barrels of flour every twenty-four hours.[4] Favored by a vast water power and by excellent marketing facilities, the only reason

[1] *Id.*, 1866, 12; Milwaukee *Sentinel*, June 5, Aug. 4, Oct. 3, and Nov. 28, 1866.

[2] Milwaukee Chamber of Commerce, *Report*, 1868, 14.

[3] Menasha and Neenah *Manufacturer*, June 6, 1861; *Wis. Farmer*, 1861, 103; Milwaukee *Sentinel*, Nov. 18, 1863.

[4] *Winnebago County Press*, May 7, 1870.

they failed to overtake Milwaukee in the race for development was that they lacked access to the great grain fields of Minnesota, Iowa, and their own State.

Many other flouring centers of local importance were scattered over the State during the sixties, notable among which were Janesville, Watertown, and Appleton. The region along the line of the old La Crosse & Milwaukee Railroad, rich in water powers, supported scores of small but flourishing mills.[1] These minor centers, though unimportant in themselves, in the aggregate furnished the bulk of the flour manufactures of the State.

The milling process employed in Wisconsin at this time was one of long acceptance in the flouring centers of the nation. It dated back to the preceding century, when that ingenious citizen of Delaware, Oliver Evans, invented the American automatic flour mill, which rendered possible the conversion of grain into flour without the intervention of the human hand.[2] It included a number of improvements made since that time, notable among which were the use of French buhr instead of granite in millstones, the substitution of silk for wool in bolting cloths, and refinements in the processes of cleaning wheat and adjusting milling surfaces.

The principal portion of the mill machinery was the

[1] The distribution of the milling industry in southern Wisconsin during the war was roughly indicated by the amount of flour carried over the several roads leading to Milwaukee. The shipments over the La Crosse & Milwaukee Railroad exceeded those of all others combined. See Milwaukee Chamber of Commerce, *Reports*, 1860–65.

[2] For an excellent account of the inventions and methods of Evans see U. S. *Census*, 1880, III, 561–64. See also *Appleton's Cyclopaedia of American Biography*, II, 383–84.

grinding mechanism. This consisted of two flat, circular stones, the upper of which was delicately balanced to revolve upon the nether. The gristing surfaces of both were grooved or dressed in a manner calculated to give them at once a cutting, squeezing, and crushing action. The "runner," as the upper stone was called, was set closely over the lower, so that in motion nearly its entire weight rested upon the kernels of wheat. Upon the accuracy with which this mechanism was adjusted, as well as the condition of its parts, depended the success of the milling operation.

The manufacture of flour under such circumstances was by no means the complicated art which it is now. The grain fresh from the harvest was first thoroughly cleaned and polished by machinery, then conveyed to the rapidly revolving stones where at a single grinding it was reduced to grist. When sufficiently pulverized it was automatically carried to a sifting or bolting machine where the finer particles became flour, the coarser, middlings, and the husks, bran.

This flat or low-grinding method of manufacturing flour had serious shortcomings. Fundamentally it disregarded the nature of the grain. The wheat berry is composed of three parts, a horny outer husk which in the milling process becomes bran, an inner starchy kernel which is converted into flour, and an oily germ or embryo which enters the discarded middlings. The millstones in the low-grinding process crushed these several parts into one indiscriminate mass, thereby rendering bolting unsatisfactory and seriously injuring the quality of the resultant flour. The system, moreover, entailed the waste of a valuable portion of the wheat. The interior starch kernel, or endosperm as it is called, in its natural state is interlaced with a delicate network of gluten fibrils, denser in the outer than in the inner portions. It is well known that gluten gives to flour its rising power and strength; but it also imparts toughness to the endosperm in the proportion in which it is present.[1] Under the low-milling methods the hard, glutinous, outer parts of the kernel were not pulverized as thoroughly as the soft inner layers and were consequently bolted out as a coarse middlings product.

All these difficulties were magnified in the grinding of spring wheat. The kernel of this grain is exceptionally rich in gluten and therefore hard to reduce to flour. In order to pulverize it satisfactorily and at the same time secure a fair daily output of grist, the miller was compelled to run his stones under great pressure and at high speed. Heat was thereby generated and despite ingenious cooling contrivances the flour became discolored and injured in quality. Winter wheat, which is relatively deficient in gluten, is correspondingly soft in texture. It yielded readily to the action of the stones, and thus it afforded the miller an exceptionally white and desirable product.

In yet another respect under these milling methods did spring wheat prove inferior to the winter variety. Under the great pressure of the stones its husk, which is thin and brittle, splintered and pulverized. The powdered bran thus produced could not be wholly

[1] The most thorough modern discussion of the structure of the wheat berry is to be found in William Jago, *The Technology of Bread Making* (London, 1911).

eliminated from the flour by even the most painstaking sifting. The product was thereby discolored, its quality injured, and its keeping powers lowered. Winter wheat, on the contrary, has a tough, thick husk which under pressure merely flattens. The miller was able to sift it from his grist so completely as to leave no trace of its presence.

By these considerations the distribution of the American flouring industry was dictated at this time. St. Louis, the seat of winter-wheat culture in the West, was the most celebrated milling center on the continent. The Northwest, though possessing the greatest wheat fields in the world, was compelled to content itself with a secondary rank as a producer of flour. The Wisconsin gristmill product, though ranking high in its own class, fell far below the average winter-wheat varieties.[1]

On the continent of Europe the art of milling approached a state of perfection quite unknown in America.[2] Hungary in particular was a center for inventions. The Slavic millers were world famous for their skill. Their flour was universally conceded to be the finest that was made. Their methods were wholly unlike those employed in the United States. Long before the sixties they had abandoned the old low-grinding practice and had developed in its place a remarkable process known as high milling and gradual reduction.

The system which they employed was most elaborate. Instead of being ground at a single oper-

[1] The grade of flour chiefly manufactured in Wisconsin was known as "Extra Spring." Milwaukee Chamber of Commerce, *Reports*, 1860–70.

[2] See articles under heading "Flour" in *Encyclopædia Britannica* (9th and 11th editions).

ation the grain underwent a long series of gradual reductions alternated with careful siftings. In the early stages of the process the millstones were run slowly and set well apart so as merely to open the berry for the removal of "crease dirt," germ, and husk. The inner starch kernel was left for a time in the state of coarse granules, which after each breaking were subjected to thorough sifting and purifying. The miller avoided as far as possible making flour in the first operations. Such as did appear was dirty and was sifted out to be utilized in cheap side products. Only when the starch particles had been freed from their major impurities was the actual task of pulverization begun. The latter was again a process of gradual refinements, with new siftings and purifications at every turn. The method was long and expensive but it produced a beautiful white product, pure, nutritious, and of superior bread-making quality.

The millers of America, quite oblivious of this excellent foreign process, were introduced to it in the early seventies by the enterprise of a prominent citizen of Wisconsin. At Minneapolis, Cadwallader C. Washburn, lumberman, general, and governor of the Badger State, owned a large mill to which, in 1870, came Edward N. LaCroix, a French mechanic, with plans for a remarkable contrivance known as a middlings purifier. The device was by no means original with the Frenchman. It had been patented in France early in the sixties, and its principle had long been applied in the great mills of Hungary. It was, simply described, an arrangement of moving sieves, exposed to the action of traveling brushes or air currents, and was employed in European mills to separate broken starch particles from the bits of bran, dirt, and fluffy fibrils that befouled them after each reduction by the stones. It constituted, in short, the key to the entire high-milling process. LaCroix, who had either heard, or read of it, or seen it in operation prior to his emigration to the New World, labored for nearly a year in modifying and perfecting it; his work was supplemented by that of another of Washburn's employees named Smith. Together the two produced an appliance intricate in arrangement and superior to anything ever known in the Old World.[1]

The success of the invention, if such this adaptation may be called, was instantaneous. No sooner had it reached perfection than the Washburn Mill embraced it and with it the high-milling process, the latter, however, in somewhat less elaborate form than that in vogue in Hungary. With astonishing rapidity other mills in the Northwest followed suit. When in 1873 the mammoth Washburn Mill, the greatest at that time in America, was erected at Minneapolis, it was equipped throughout with machinery adapted to the new methods.[2] By the middle of the seventies the "patent" process, as it was called, had found its way into every important milling center in the Northwest, and "patent" flour was the

[1] For a description of this device see U. S. Patent Office, *Reports*, Index Volume, 1790–1873, under subhead "Middlings purifier"; see also U. S. *Census*, 1880, III, 561–79; C. A. Pillsbury, "American Flour," in C. M. Depew, *One Hundred Years of American Commerce* (New York, 1895), I, 269–70; P. T. Dondlinger, *The Book of Wheat* (New York, 1908), 267–82; W. C. Edgar, *The Story of a Grain of Wheat* (New York, 1903), 149–68.

[2] *Wis. Lumberman*, June, 1874, 284.

acknowledged peer among all the gristmill products of America.

The patent process, thus inaugurated, brought about a revolution in American flour milling such as few industries have ever undergone. Awakened by it to a realization of the superiority of European methods, western millers, during the succeeding decades, scoured the continent of Europe for every possible improvement. Late in the seventies they found in Hungary in successful operation the roller process, in which chilled iron rolls displaced or supplemented millstones so that the gradual reduction methods could be carried to greater refinement. Having adopted and improved upon this they branched out into the new art of tempering or conditioning grain for grinding, in which they likewise became proficient. Today, after the lapse of less than half a century, the American Northwest has become the greatest milling center in the entire world.

Innovations such as these served to reverse the relative positions of spring and winter wheat. The former, rich in gluten, under the new processes produced a stronger and richer flour than the latter, and as early as the middle seventies commanded a higher price in the grain markets of the nation. Minneapolis, the seat of American spring-wheat culture, became the greatest milling center in the world; Milwaukee, somewhat less favorably situated with respect to the western grain fields, during the later eighties and early nineties vied with Superior and St. Louis for second place.

Prominent among the minor industrial pursuits of the State at this time was the manufacture of iron. This was an industry for which Wisconsin was well adapted. Iron ore from the mines of Iron Ridge and the upper peninsula of Michigan could be laid down at her lake ports for but little more than the cost of production.[1] Charcoal could be obtained in unlimited quantities from the boundless forests to the northward. Anthracite coal, which the more modern blast furnaces consumed, could be brought to the State for the bare costs of production and of transportation by grain vessels returning from Buffalo. The farming states to the west and south afforded a wide and ready market for the products of foundries and machine shops.

The smelting of iron ore was a branch of the industry that during this period first secured a substantial foothold in Wisconsin. In 1860 there were only three blast furnaces in operation in the State and all of these were of the old charcoal type. One was at Mayville in Dodge County, one at Ironton in Sauk County, and one was at Black River Falls in Jackson County. In 1865 a fourth was established at Iron Ridge in Dodge County, though in the meantime that at Black River Falls had been abandoned. The real beginnings of the industry dated from 1870 when the Milwaukee Iron Company completed, in connection with its newly constructed rolling mills in the metropolis, a modern blast furnace said to have been the largest in the country.[2] This was followed

[1] Some foreign pig iron of Scotch and Pennsylvania origin was consumed in Wisconsin at this time.

[2] Milwaukee Chamber of Commerce, *Report*, 1869, 10–13; *id.*, 1870, 13–14; Milwaukee *Sentinel*, Dec. 30, 1871 and Jan. 1, 1873. The Northwestern Iron Company at Mayville offered upon the outbreak of the Civil War to undertake the manufacture of shot and shell for the State. "We are making arrangements," its vice-president wrote to Governor Randall on May 20, 1861, "with a gentleman to come here & superintend the manu-

in the succeeding years by the erection of two other such establishments and a number of smaller ones in the lower Fox Valley. By 1873 Wisconsin had nine ore-reducing plants in active operation, of which the three in Milwaukee were modern anthracite burners and the remainder smaller charcoal consumers.[1] The aggregate pig iron output of the State in 1873 was 73,984 tons, of which the quota of Milwaukee was approximately half.[2] Though not a very imposing total, this was a great advance over the 25,000 tons which had constituted the entire product of Wisconsin in 1860.[3]

Milwaukee led the State not only in smelting but also in manufacturing iron.[4] Her most important branch of this industry was the production of railroad rails. She set out upon it in 1868, when the Milwaukee Iron Company erected within her limits one of the greatest rolling mills in the entire country.[5] Her suc-

facture of shot & shell—he having made large quantities at Troy for the Government during the Mexican War & is well known by them. We have some assurance of finding a market east. But my object in writing you is to enquire if this State will have occasion to purchase any, and if so how many, and of what kind & sizes?" Apparently Governor Randall was unable to offer the company encouragement, for the project was presently dropped. See Ms. letter of F. Wilkes to Governor Randall, May 20, 1861, in Wisconsin Historical Library.

[1] A complete enumeration of the early blast furnaces in the State, their production, and something of their history is given in Milwaukee Chamber of Commerce, *Report*, 1864, 35; 1865, 40; 1872, 16–17; 1873, 22–23, 30–31; Chamberlin, *Geology of Wisconsin, 1873–79*, I, 613–14, 625–26.

The ore smelted in the Fox Valley establishments was the product of the mines of Lake Superior; that used in Dodge County originated in the Iron Ridge; that reduced in Milwaukee was a mixture of the two.

[2] Milwaukee Chamber of Commerce, *Report*, 1873, 31.

[3] *Id.*, 1872, 16; Wis. Agric. Soc., *Trans.*, 1860, 59.

[4] For an enumeration of the advantages of Milwaukee for manufacturing iron see Milwaukee Chamber of Commerce, *Report*, 1869, 10–13.

[5] The Milwaukee Iron Company was composed of Detroit, Milwaukee, and Chicago capitalists, notable among whom were E. B. Ward of Detroit,

cess was assured from the beginning. The hard ore of the Iron Ridge mixed in proper proportion with the soft mineral of Lake Superior afforded a product that for rails was unsurpassed—tough, durable, and of excellent wearing surface.[1] The industry grew apace. The first rails rolled in Milwaukee passed through the mills in March, 1868. The total output of that year was 7,011 tons; by 1873 it had reached 34,494 tons.[2] In 1873 the Milwaukee plant was the second largest in the United States. The capital which it represented amounted to $2,250,000, the number of men it employed was 1,000, and the value of its manufactured product was approximately $3,000,000.[3]

The foundries and machine shops of the metropolis likewise developed with rapidity, especially after the close of the Civil War. The foundries were engaged chiefly in the production of locomotive parts, stoves, hollow ware, and miscellaneous castings. The machine shops found employment in the manufacture of steam engines, boilers, machinery, gearing for flour mills and sawmills, and repairs upon railroad stock. In 1867 Milwaukee possessed seventeen establishments devoted exclusively to iron manufactures, the total annual product of which amounted to $1,500,000.[4]

S. Clement of Chicago, and Alexander Mitchell of Milwaukee. The company was incorporated under the laws of Wisconsin in 1866. For a detailed account of its early history and a description of its plant, see Milwaukee Chamber of Commerce, *Reports*, 1866, 3; 1869, 10–13; 1870, 13–14; 1871, 21–22; 1872, 29; 1873, 29; Milwaukee *Sentinel*, Dec. 30, 1871, and Jan. 1, 1873.

[1] Milwaukee Chamber of Commerce, *Reports*, 1866–73; Wis. Agric. Soc., *Trans.*, 1869, 42–44.

[2] Milwaukee Chamber of Commerce, *Report*, 1873, 102.

[3] *Id.*, 1872, 29; Milwaukee *Sentinel*, Dec. 30, 1871 and Jan. 1, 1873.

[4] *Ibid.*, Feb. 1, 1867.

By the close of the decade she had become one of the largest and most important iron-manufacturing centers in the Northwest.[1]

Among the several establishments of the city at this time was one destined to have a great future. This was the Reliance Iron Works of E. P. Allis & Company. During the sixties it consisted of a modest shop engaged chiefly in the production of machinery for flour mills. In 1867 it employed but seventy-five hands, and its total annual product was worth not more than $150,000.[2] Five years later it employed 350 men, and its total annual product amounted to approximately $1,000,000.[3] Today it employs thousands of men and represents one of the greatest manufactories of its kind in the world. In 1872 the press of Milwaukee reported with much gratification that the Reliance Works had received from Japan an order for a portable flour mill.[4] Today the Allis-Chalmers and West Allis Corporation as a matter of course scatter their products to the four corners of the globe.

The manufacture of agricultural machinery and implements was an industry that gave employment to a number of smaller cities and villages in the State. It owed its success chiefly to the abundance of excellent hardwoods that the forests of Wisconsin afforded. Beloit, Janesville, Madison, Whitewater, and La-Crosse were considerable local centers of reaper and mower manufacture. Beloit, Whitewater, and several other cities were prominent in the manufacture of

[1] *Ibid.*, Dec. 30, 1871 and Jan. 1, 1873.

[2] *Ibid.*, Feb. 1, 1867.

[3] *Ibid.*, Jan. 1, 1873 and Dec. 30, 1871.

[4] *Ibid.*, Jan. 1, 1872.

plows. Madison, the seat of sorghum culture in the State, was the center for the production of sorghum mills. At Whitewater the inventor, George Esterly, in 1868 produced 5,000 seeders of his own design; in the village of Horicon, Van Brunt & Company turned out 3,200 similar machines; at Beaver Dam, Rowell & Company added its quota of 3,000.[1]

Racine was a center of threshing-machine manufacture of more than local importance. Her position in the industry she owed chiefly to Jerome I. Case, an industrious easterner who had begun life in Wisconsin in 1842 by threshing grain for the farmers of Racine County. At the beginning of the Civil War the J. I. Case factory was one of the largest in the Northwest; at the close of the decade it was one of the largest in America. Its annual output of threshers, horsepowers, and truck wagons was valued in 1870 at more than $1,000,000, and its machines were to be found scattered over every state and territory west of the Mississippi River.[2]

The Civil War gave a tremendous stimulus to the manufacture of agricultural machinery in Wisconsin. The absence of thousands of men and boys who were fighting the battles of the Union compelled farmers to purchase labor conservers on a scale never before known. Factories were crowded with more orders than they could fill. "The several agricultural shops in this city," reported the La Crosse *Democrat* in 1863, "are driven with work and hardly able to meet the demands on them for threshing machines, reapers, fanning mills, &c. A million more dollars could be profit-

[1] Wis. Agric. Soc., *Trans.*, 1861–68, 53–54.

[2] *Ibid.*; *Western Monthly*, September, 1870, 161–64.

ably invested here in the manufacture of farm tools and labor saving implements of all kinds. There is no end to the demand which increases each year in astonishing ratio."[1] In 1860 the J. I. Case Company at Racine produced 300 threshing machines; in 1865, 500; in 1870, 1,300.[2] At Horicon the Van Brunt Company in 1861 manufactured 60 seeders; in 1863, 700; in 1866, 1,300; in 1869, 3,800.[3] At Madison, E. W. Skinner & Company began the manufacture of sorghum mills in 1861 by making a single mill; in 1863 the number had increased to 100; in 1865 it was 500.[4] In every part of the State the period of the Civil War saw rapid advance in this important branch of manufacture.

Almost equal in importance to the manufacturing of iron were the industries that centered about the utilization of lumber. These constituted distinct interests not to be confused with the rough sawing of the forest product. They consisted in the fashioning of hard and soft wood into articles of commerce as contrasted with the cutting of logs into material for building. They were activities for which no state in the Union was better equipped by natural endowments than Wisconsin.

These interests centered in the lower Fox Valley and along the shore of Lake Michigan. Menasha, Two Rivers, and, after 1868, Peshtigo were the principal abode of woodenware manufactures.[5] Me-

[1] La Crosse *Democrat*, July 28, 1863.

[2] *Wis. Farmer*, October, 1860, 294; Racine *Advocate*, Feb. 8, 1865; Milwaukee *Sentinel*, Feb. 5 and Oct. 1, 1867, and June 27, 1872.

[3] *History of Dodge County, Wisconsin*, 482.

[4] W. J. Park, *History of Madison* (Madison, 1877), 135.

[5] Wis. Agric. Soc., *Trans.*, 1870, 66.

nasha in 1870 had the greatest tub, pail, and churn factory west of the Ohio.[1] It boasted at that time, also, the largest hub and spoke factory in the Northwest.[2] Every city in the lower Fox Valley, and notably Appleton, De Pere, and Menasha, manufactured large quantities of staves and heading. During the later sixties Sheboygan was a growing producer of chairs. Fond du Lac, Racine, and Milwaukee were notable centers of sash, door, and blind manufacture. In 1868 the factory of C. J. L. Meyer at Fond du Lac ranked as the largest in the world, producing 25,000,000 lights of window sash, 80,000 doors, and 62,000 pairs of blinds, valued altogether at nearly $1,000,000.[3] Racine, Milwaukee, and Kenosha were well-known producers of farm and lumber wagons.[4] At Racine the establishment of Fish Brothers was one of the largest of its kind in America, with an output in 1868 of 3,000 wagons, valued at $300,000. Milwaukee was a considerable center of furniture, cabinet, and willow ware manufacture, her output in 1868 amounting in value to approximately $500,000. Fond du Lac was the home of the Chicago & Northwestern Railroad car works, which during the middle sixties turned out annually from 500 to 600 box cars, flat cars, and coaches.[5] La Crosse during the later sixties supported the largest shipyard on the upper Mississippi River, where light-draught packets and barges for the river trade were constructed in con-

[1] Milwaukee *Sentinel*, Dec. 22, 1871; *Winnebago Co. Press*, July 1, 1871.

[2] *Ibid.*, June 18, 1870 and July 1, 1871.

[3] Wis. Agric. Soc., *Trans.*, 1861–68, 54–55.

[4] *Ibid.*, 53; Milwaukee *Sentinel*, Dec. 29, 1868.

[5] *Wis. State Jour.*, Dec. 1, 1865; Green Bay *Advocate*, Dec. 7, 1865.

siderable numbers.[1] Milwaukee, Green Bay, Manitowoc, De Pere, and Peshtigo maintained shipyards of local importance in which schooners and steamers for the lake commerce were built and repaired. Oshkosh during the Civil War took up the construction of grain barges to be used on the Mississippi River. In addition scores of cities and villages in southeastern Wisconsin sustained upon a small scale activities of various kinds, but all of them centered about the manipulation of wood. Thus, during the later sixties, Wisconsin laid the foundations for future prominence in the manufacture of the products of the greatest of her natural resources.

Next in importance to the manufacture of wood was the tanning and utilization of leather. Wisconsin successfully established herself during our period in what has since become one of her most important industries. The lake-shore cities of the State, and especially Milwaukee, were well equipped for its successful prosecution. They had access to abundant supplies of tan bark. They had excellent facilities for collecting hides and pelts from the interior.[2] For their finished products they possessed a wide and convenient market.

As the result of such advantages Milwaukee forged rapidly to the front. In 1860 she had only nine tanneries, of which but two were substantial establishments.[3] By the close of the Civil War she had

[1] La Crosse *Democrat*, July 7, 1863; Wis. Agric. Soc., *Trans.*, 1870, 428.

[2] The number of hides shipped to Milwaukee in 1860 was 85,409; in 1873 it was 203,416. The number of sheep pelts sent to that market in 1860 was too small to be enumerated; in 1873 it was approximately 100,000.

[3] The tanning industry was undergoing rapid changes at this time, machinery being substituted for hand labor in all the larger establishments.

fifteen; by 1872 she had thirty.[1] The capacity of her individual tanneries, moreover, steadily grew. In 1872 those owned by Pfister & Vogel and the Wisconsin Leather Company took rank among the largest in the entire country.[2] The leather output of the metropolis in the meantime rose by leaps and bounds. In 1860 it was 45,000 hides, 18,000 calf and kip skins, and a small quantity of sheep pelts.[3] By the close of the Civil War it was more than twice this amount.[4] By 1872, it had become 158,523 hides, 125,000 sheep pelts, and a proportionate quantity of calf and kip skins.[5] With the total value of these products amounting in 1872 to $2,560,000, Milwaukee could claim the distinction of being the largest tanning center in the West.[6]

Other lake ports of local prominence in the industry were Racine, Two Rivers, and Two Creeks. Racine at the close of the Civil War sustained eight tanneries;

For excellent descriptions of the tanning methods in vogue, see Racine *Advocate*, Feb. 1, 1865; Milwaukee *Sentinel*, Jan. 5, 1865 and May 30, 1872.

[1] Milwaukee Chamber of Commerce, *Report*, 1860, 34–35; Milwaukee *Sentinel*, Jan. 5, 1865, and Dec. 30, 1871.

[2] For a detailed description of these see *ibid.*, Jan. 5, 1865, May 20 and Aug. 27, 1870, Dec. 30, 1871, and May 30, 1872; Milwaukee Chamber of Commerce, *Report*, 1865, 31; 1867, 40; 1869, 63; 1870, 14–15.

[3] Milwaukee *Sentinel*, Jan. 1, 1861; Milwaukee Chamber of Commerce, *Report*, 1860, 34–35.

[4] *Id.*, 1865, 28; *id.*, 1866, 43.

[5] *Id.*, 1872, 80; *id.*, 1871, 21; *id.*, 1873, 86. Hides in process of manufacture became harness, sole, and upper leather; calf and kip skins were converted into finished products of the same name; sheep pelts became linings and bindings.

A considerable portion of the Wisconsin product was consumed at home in the manufacture of boots and shoes. Milwaukee had several large factories, notable among which was that of Bradley & Metcalf. The manufacture of footwear in Wisconsin at this time was carried on chiefly in small shops widely dispersed over the State. See *post*, 170–72.

[6] Milwaukee *Sentinel*, Jan. 1, 1873.

two years later, a dozen.[1] Two Rivers and Two Creeks in the leather industry were really but outposts of Milwaukee.[2] At the first-named village the Wisconsin Leather Company maintained two immense tanneries; Guido Pfister in 1862 built up Two Creeks about one of his great establishments.[3] The single factor dictating their selection for this work was their proximity to the northern supplies of hemlock bark. When near the close of the decade the economies of large-scale production demanded the concentration of the industry in the metropolis the tanneries of these cities were one after another removed, sold, or restricted in their operations.[4]

The pork-packing industry of Wisconsin even more than the tanning of leather was dominated by Milwaukee. The interior of the State slaughtered and salted for eastern export only a few thousand hogs a year. For the most part it contented itself with butchering for local consumption or for the supply of the lumber camps to the northward.

Milwaukee, on the contrary, was a great meat exporter. Drawing her supplies of live and dressed hogs from interior Wisconsin, Iowa, and Minnesota, she sent barreled pork, lard, hams, middles, and shoulders to every part of the East as well as to England.[5]

[1] Racine *Advocate*, Feb. 1, 1865 and Jan. 2, 1867.

[2] During the summer months the leather manufactured here was sent to Milwaukee by the lake route; during the winter it was carried overland by team. When in 1862 the Chicago & Northwestern Railroad was completed to Green Bay, the tannery product was commonly carted to the latter city and thence shipped by rail to Milwaukee.

[3] R. G. Plumb, *History of Manitowoc County* (Manitowoc, 1904), 39–40; Milwaukee *Sentinel*, Aug. 27, 1870.

[4] Milwaukee Chamber of Commerce, *Report*, 1869, 63–64.

[5] For excellent description of the packing process employed in Milwaukee's largest establishment at this time see Milwaukee *Daily Wis.*, Jan. 5, 1865.

Plankinton & Armour, Layton & Company, Van Kirk, McGeoch & Company, and others during the sixties built up packing plants that were counted among the largest in the entire country. In 1869 the Milwaukee & St. Paul Railway Company established within the heart of the city new and capacious Union Stock Yards, equipped with every modern convenience for receiving, feeding, and yarding hogs and cattle.[1] The packers of the metropolis, who in 1860 had cut for salting only 60,129 hogs, in 1866 cut 133,370 and in 1871, 313,118. This was more than a fivefold increase in a period of eleven years.[2] From a position of comparative insignificance in the industry Milwaukee thus rose within a decade to fourth place among all the pork-packing centers of the nation.[3]

Unlike most of the industries of Wisconsin the manufacture of lager beer had its origin chiefly in a social factor. This was the presence of a large German element in the population of the State. The Wisconsin pioneers of Teutonic stock apparently found it impossible to accustom themselves to the beverages usually consumed by Americans, and wherever they congregated in any numbers there lager-beer breweries quickly made their appearance. The pure water obtainable in all parts of the State as well as the excellent grade of hops and barley that

[1] Milwaukee Chamber of Commerce, *Report*, 1869, 25.

[2] *Id.*, 1861, 20; *id.*, 1871, 71–72.

[3] *Id.*, 1872, 21. The beef-packing industry of Milwaukee developed rapidly during the Civil War, then as quickly dwindled to insignificance. The same was true of Chicago. Kansas City during this decade established itself as the great beef market of the West. The number of cattle packed in Milwaukee in 1860 was 7,876; in 1864, 18,978; in 1871, 2,046.

could be grown upon its soil were other, though less important, factors in determining the growth of this interest.

Milwaukee was then as now the chief center of the industry. She owed her position primarily to her supply of excellent water, her easy access to the hop gardens and barley fields of the interior, her commanding marketing facilities, and above all her overwhelming Teutonic population. Her German citizens not only afforded a dependable market for her product but provided the knowledge and skill necessary for the successful prosecution of the industry.[1] The names of the most prominent brewers of Milwaukee during the sixties are sufficient indication that this interest was in no inexperienced hands—Philip Best, Fred Pabst, Charles Melms, Valentine Blatz, Joseph Schlitz, Franz Falk, Fred Miller, Jacob Obermann. These were the men whose native skill in a traditional German industry built up the brewing interests of the metropolis of Wisconsin.[2]

The Civil War powerfully stimulated the brewing industry not only in Wisconsin but in the entire country. This it did directly by initiating notable social changes; indirectly, by discouraging the consumption of other beverages. Prior to 1861 Germans alone were consumers of the amber fluid. Americans looked upon the habit of beer drinking, as upon all foreign customs, with nativistic contempt. The war happily broadened national sympathies and eradi-

[1] For an excellent description of the brewing process see Milwaukee *Sentinel*, Sept. 1, 1866.

[2] For detailed accounts of these men and their breweries see H. L. Conard, *History of Milwaukee* (Chicago, 1895), II, 27–39; F. A. Flower, *History of Milwaukee* (Chicago, 1881), 1456–1470.

cated narrow race prejudices. The despised foreign born demonstrated upon the battle-field their loyalty to the land of their adoption, and Germans in particular won admiration for their response to the call to arms. A grateful nation at first tolerated, then actually adopted, many of the habits and customs of its Teutonic sons. Americans during the sixties made trial of German beer and found it to their liking. They appreciated the fact that it was lighter and less deleterious in its effects than the whisky which had hitherto constituted their favorite drink. Despite the protests and warnings of prohibitionists the Teutonic beverage rapidly gained favor.

To this natural development Congress added the indirect aid of legislative discrimination. Compelled by the heavy burdens of the war enormously to increase the Federal revenues, it proceeded in 1862 to impose a drastic excise tax upon ardent spirits and a less harsh assessment upon beer and ale.[1] The brewers of the country, quick to seize their advantage, in November, 1862 organized a strong National Association,[2] which during the war, and ever since, has been able to persuade the government to retain the principle of favoritism.

German beer, thus protected, soon became the favorite American drink. "The consumption of hops in America," observes the *Wisconsin Farmer* in

[1] U. S. *Statutes at Large*, 37 Cong., 2 sess., chap. 119, July 1, 1862. In 1860 the distilleries of Milwaukee produced 12,000 barrels of high wines. As a result of the high war tax their output by 1865 had fallen to 3,046. In 1868 the Federal tax was reduced from $2 per gallon to about 60 cents per gallon, and by 1870 the high-wine product of the city was 22,867 barrels.

[2] The fourth congress of this organization was held in Milwaukee, Sept. 8, 1864. The discussion was confined exclusively to problems of Federal taxation. See Milwaukee *Sentinel*, Sept. 14, 1864.

1868, "has been vastly on the increase for several years, especially so since the whisky-tax put such an estoppel on the distillery industry. And, moreover, the taste for beer and ale, and the custom and fashion making it 'respectable' to drink it, is largely growing. Statistics show the increase in consumption, one year greater than its predecessor, to have been thirty per centum, for several years past—since war times."[1]

These changes were speedily reflected in the organization of the brewing industry. Prior to the war it had been a widely dispersed village business, local in its market, and serving only an alien element in the population. It now rose to the dignity of a great export interest, centering in a few large cities and ministering to the thirst of every class and condition of American society.

Milwaukee more than any other city in the country made capital of this development. In 1860 the output of her breweries was but 36,000 barrels; in 1865 it had increased to 55,000 barrels; and in 1873, to 260,120 barrels.[2] The growth of her individual establishments was even more surprising. In 1863 the Pabst Brewing Company produced 3,677 barrels; in 1865, 10,908; in 1873, 100,028.[3] The Joseph Schlitz Company in 1862 produced 1,605 barrels; in 1865, 4,400; in 1872, 32,608.[4] By 1872 the Pabst establishment was already the largest in America;[5]

[1] *Wis. Farmer*, 1868, 321.

[2] Milwaukee Chamber of Commerce, *Report*, 1860, 40; *id.*, 1865, 43; *id.*, 1873, 103. The amount of ale manufactured in the city in 1860 was 9,800 barrels; in 1867, 3,000 barrels. See *id.*, 1860, 40; *id.*, 1867, 50; Milwaukee *Sentinel*, Jan. 1, 1861 and Sept. 1, 1866.

[3] Flower, *History of Milwaukee*, 1458.

[4] Conard, *History of Milwaukee*, II, 38; Milwaukee *Sentinel*, Jan. 1, 1873.

[5] *Ibid.*, Dec. 30, 1871. The Pabst concern was then known as the Philip Best Company.

its product was favorably known and consumed in two continents, penetrating even to the famous beer gardens of Bavaria. Milwaukee by 1872 had become the greatest beer-exporting center in the West,[1] a primacy that she now holds with respect to the entire world.

The manufacture of woolen cloth was another industry that made rapid progress in Wisconsin especially after the close of the Civil War. Woolen mills during this period rose upon every hand. Their number in 1859 was 15; in 1865, 19; in 1871, 54.[2] Their combined equipment, measured in sets of manufacturing cards, in 1859 was but 15, in 1871 was 63. The quantity of raw wool converted into cloth and yarn in these establishments rose from a few hundred thousand pounds in 1859 to 1,620,000 pounds in 1871.[3] Nearly one-half the wool product of the State during the later sixties was thus consumed by home manufactures.

In the later sixties Wisconsin gave to civilization one of the most useful of modern inventions. This was the typewriter, perfected and patented in Milwaukee in 1868. C. Latham Sholes, journalist and prominent State politician, was the ingenious inventor. Associated with him were S. W. Soulé, a

[1] The destruction of the breweries of Chicago in the great fire of 1871 was a powerful factor in stimulating the Milwaukee industry.

[2] U. S. *Census*, 1860, *Manufactures*, 658; W. P. Blake, *Reports of the United States Commissioners to the Paris Exposition of 1867* (Washington, 1870), VI, 122; Wis. Agric. Soc., *Trans.*, 1871, 9–10. Lists of the several woolen mills in the State and details as to their operations are given in *id.*, 1869, 45–56; *id.*, 1870, 63–66; *id.*, 1871, 9–10.

[3] *Ibid.* The Wisconsin Woolen Manufacturers' Association was organized at the close of the Civil War. The proceedings of its annual conventions for the years 1868 to 1871 are in Appleton *Crescent*, Mar. 21, 1868; Milwaukee *Sentinel*, April 14, 1870 and April 13, 1871.

printer, and Carlos Glidden, a retired manufacturer. These three men in the winter of 1866–67 caught the suggestion of a writing machine from a paging device that they had for some time been laboring to perfect. Sholes in particular was struck by the idea of producing a mechanical apparatus that would displace the slow and laborious pen; to its materialization he devoted not only his own enthusiastic efforts but those of a skillful German clockmaker of Milwaukee named Mathias Schwalbach. By September, 1867 he and his friends had completed their first workable model. It was a crude affair, roughly resembling in appearance a sewing machine, though with a keyboard like that of a piano.[1] Patents were obtained in the summer of 1868, after which five years were spent in modifying and perfecting the mechanism. Schwalbach in the course of his labors suggested the banked keyboard. The now famous Edison, to whom Sholes went for counsel, contributed his aid.[2] The result was a device embodying in its construction the basic principles of every typewriter that has since come into use.[3]

Sholes, like many other notable inventors, lost the fruits of his great achievement. Little realizing its worth, he sold out his rights to a far-seeing promoter for the paltry sum of $12,000. He died in Milwaukee

[1] U. S. Patent Office, *Report*, 1868, II, 175, 234; IV, 803, 887. For a description of later patents see *Encyclopædia Britannica*.

[2] *System*, X, 230.

[3] This account is gleaned from the Milwaukee *Evening Wisconsin*, Sept. 26, 1883; Milwaukee *Sentinel*, Jan. 12, 1902; Wis. Hist. Soc., *Proc.*, 1901, 164–66; Minnesota Historical Society, *Bulletin*, February, 1916, 264–69; The Sholes & Glidden Typewriter (advertisement published in New York in 1874 or 1875). A sketch of the life of Sholes may be found in *Appletons' Cyclopædia of American Biography*, V, 515.

in 1890, after a long illness, in comparative poverty.

The typewriter in the meantime won rapid acceptance. In March, 1873 James Densmore, the man to whom the inventor had disposed of his patents, entered into a contract with Remington & Sons, proprietors of the celebrated New York Armory, for the manufacture of 25,000 machines. Before many years the Remington machine was known from one end of the land to the other. Today no business office worthy of the name in the entire world is without its complement of typewriters.

During the decade of the sixties the cities of Wisconsin, and especially Milwaukee, laid the foundations for future prominence in the field of manufacturing. Their progress, temporarily retarded by the Civil War, after the return of peace was astonishingly rapid. By 1873 the municipalities of the State no longer depended for a livelihood solely upon trade. Their interests had become diversified; in their own workshops and mills they consumed the raw materials that the State produced. Wisconsin had at length realized her cherished ambition of possessing home manufactures.

CHAPTER VI

LABOR[1]

The Civil War produced no great problem of industrial labor in Wisconsin. Manufacturing in the State in 1861 was in its infancy; wage earners as a class were a negligible factor. Five-sixths of the State's 800,000 inhabitants gained their livelihood by tillage of the soil. There was no city in Wisconsin beside Milwaukee that could boast a population of more than 7,500, and even Milwaukee was more a trading than an industrial center.[2] In a community thus simply organized, labor difficulties could not assume the importance that attended them in the highly complex and inelastic manufacturing communities of the East. Yet even in Wisconsin the changes wrought by the Civil War, and the readjustments that followed, led to organized resistance by wage earners; even in this frontier region there developed a distinct, class-conscious movement of industrial labor—the first in the history of the State.

The close of the year 1860 found the industries of Wisconsin just recovering from the disastrous panic of 1857. An extraordinary wheat crop, the greatest

[1] I am under deep obligation to Prof. John R. Commons of the University of Wisconsin, whose lectures on the American labor movement from 1860 to 1893 furnished the national background for this study; also to Selig Perlman of the Federal Industrial Commission for kind permission to use material relating to the national labor movement during the Civil War, prepared by him while research assistant to Professor Commons.

[2] The population of Milwaukee in 1861 was approximately 50,000.

ever raised in the State, had been harvested, and under its stimulus every interest was springing into new life. But war descended upon the nation, followed by the collapse of Wisconsin's financial system, and once more industry was paralyzed. Not until early in 1863 when the greenback inflation first made itself felt in rising prices, and the maintenance of huge Union armies brought increased employment to northern workshops and mills, was the black cloud of industrial depression again lifted.

Partly as a result of hard times, there was no unusual scarcity of industrial labor in the State during the first two and a half years of the war. The drain of men into the army was comparatively slow, not more than 30,000 being absent in military service at the close of 1863. Of these, moreover, approximately 21,000 were at the time of their enlistment mere youths of twenty-one years or under,[1] and the absence of such of them as came from the cities, where they had not yet fitted themselves into the industrial life of their communities, was not likely to be seriously felt.[2] Whatever lack of labor was produced by enlistments was abundantly compensated for by the same factors that came to the rescue of the farmers. There was some complaint, it is true, during 1863

[1] On Nov. 1, 1863 the number of troops who had enlisted from Wisconsin was 41,775, of whom 24,812 were still in the service. In approximating 30,000 as the number of absentees from the State I have included deaths, desertions, and missing. It is usually estimated that about five-sevenths of the Union soldiers at the time of their enlistment were twenty-one years of age or under.

[2] The enlistment of boys was a more embarrassing matter on the farms than it was in the cities, for agricultural apprenticeship begins early, and at eighteen or nineteen the boy has already become an important factor in the life of the farm. The city mechanic becomes a skilled workman at a much later age.

of lack of labor for railroad construction and for logging operations in the northern lumber camps, but these were exceptional and may be readily explained by the irregularity and uncertainty of the wages paid, the hardness of the fare, and the seasonal character of the employment.[1]

As a corollary of this comparative sufficiency of labor, the industrial workers of the State shared but little in the prosperity that followed 1863. While prices were rising by leaps and bounds, wages advanced with but a laggard step. At the end of 1863 the wholesale price of flour in Milwaukee was $4.80 to $5.60 per barrel as against $3.70 to $3.85 in 1861; potatoes, 40 cents to 45 cents per bushel as against 25 to 30 cents in 1861; mess pork, $16.75 to $17 per barrel as against $9.50 to $10 in 1861; butter 16 to 20 cents per pound as against 6 to 8 cents in 1861; eggs 20 to 22 cents per dozen as against 8 to 10 cents in 1861. Wages of unskilled labor in the meantime advanced only from $1 per day for the season of 1861 to $1.25 for the season of 1863. Prices were rising from 50 to 75 per cent, wages less than half that amount.[2] Well might the editor of the La Crosse

[1] In August, 1863 the contractors for the Milwaukee & St. Paul Railroad were obliged to send to Canada in order to secure a full supply of labor. The road paid its laborers in the autumn of 1863, $1.37½ per day, but in scrip that was not returnable until the next summer, and it had to be exchanged by the laborers at a large discount.

[2] These are the wholesale prices. The records of retail prices are not sufficiently complete for purposes of comparison. Statistics are from the Milwaukee Chamber of Commerce *Reports* and daily market quotations in the Milwaukee press. The western laborer was relatively better off than his brother in the East, for while the wages of both were about the same, the price of food in the West was substantially lower. The advantage is to be accounted for by the closer proximity of the western laborer to free lands.

Democrat declare near the close of 1863, "Mechanics and day laborers, the only classes who are seriously affected by the war, have need to exercise close economy and the nicest calculation."[1]

The years 1864 and 1865 witnessed some slight improvement in the situation. During 1864 Lincoln's calls for troops followed one another with startling rapidity. During the last year and a half of the war Wisconsin sent to the front as large a number of soldiers as during the previous two and a half years. At the same time the expanding industries of the State were demanding more workmen, and from every side rose the complaint of the scarcity of labor. Wages mounted rapidly from $1.25 per day for unskilled labor in the early spring of 1864 to $1.75 per day in the fall, and on a number of railroad enterprises to $2 per day. Prices in the meantime were soaring. At the end of 1864 flour sold at wholesale at $7.75 to $8.25 per barrel; potatoes at 60 to 65 cents per bushel; mess pork at $37 per barrel; butter at 32 to 40 cents per pound; and eggs at 32 to 33 cents per dozen. The advance of wages was again less than the advance of prices, but the rate of loss had been checked.[2]

[1] La Crosse *Democrat*, Oct. 13, 1863.

[2] Wholesale prices during the month of July varied as follows:

	Flour per bbl.	Potatoes per bu.	Mess Pork per bbl.	Butter per lb.	Eggs per doz.
July, 1861	$3 50– $4 15	$0 15–$0 25	....	$0 06–$0 08	$0 06–$0 08
July, 1863	$4 37– $5 75	$0 45–$0 60	$12 00–$13 00	$0 10–$0 15	$0 09–$0 12½
July, 1864	$9 00–$10 00	$0 40–$0 75	$40 00–$42 00	$0 25–$0 33	$0 12–$0 16
July, 1865	$5 00– $6 25	$0 25–$0 60	$30 00–$32 00	$0 10–$0 21	$0 15–$0 20

During the spring of 1865, when it became evident that peace was near at hand, prices rapidly declined, reaching their lowest point in midsummer. Wages in the meantime remained stationary and the war closed with labor in a better position than it had enjoyed for several years. It has been estimated for the North as a whole that during the war prices advanced approximately 100 per cent, while wages rose only 50 to 60 per cent.[1] In Wisconsin labor fared somewhat better, wages having advanced during the war from 60 to 75 per cent. No doubt the proximity of free land, to which labor could readily escape when it felt itself too sorely oppressed, had much to do with this happy fortune. However, in the West as well as the East labor lost in real wages, a misfortune offset only by a somewhat larger opportunity for employment. The fruits of prosperity had passed to the merchant jobbers, who piled up enormous fortunes, the employers, who had enjoyed the benefits of a high war tariff, and the farmers, who had realized upon bountiful crops the unusual prices that the war brought.[2]

The unequal advance of wages and prices during the war, to which unskilled labor could offer but feeble resistance, led skilled labor for the first time in the history of the State to organize generally into trade unions.[3] The movement found expression

[1] Fite, *Social and Industrial Conditions*, chap. 7. I have made liberal use of this valuable work.

[2] J. R. Commons, *History of the American Labor Movement*, Ms.

[3] Some scattering trade unions had been organized prior to the war, among them the Milwaukee Typographical Union No. 23 in 1852 or 1853, the Madison Typographical Union No. 25 in 1857, the Milwaukee Cigarmakers' Union No. 25 in 1860, and the Milwaukee German

chiefly in Milwaukee, where the largest number of wage earners was concentrated. Here during the troubled years between 1863 and 1865 the bricklayers and masons, carpenters and joiners, machinists and blacksmiths, iron molders, custom tailors, and sailors formed protective organizations, while the ship carpenters and caulkers, organized in 1861, and the printers, and the cigar-makers, organized before the war, discarded their former peaceful activities, and adopted more vigorous tactics.[1]

Strikes, hitherto almost unknown in the State, now became a common mode of forcing up wages. The successful organization of a trade union was usually the signal for a strike shortly after. Ordinarily these labor contests, recorded only in the vague recollections of the participants, were in themselves insignificant, involving but a single shop or the crew of a single ship, yet altogether they offer an indication of the social unrest that the high prices of the war had produced.[2] A fair proportion of the total number

Custom Tailors' Union in 1860. These were, however, during their early existence more social than militant in character.

[1] Other trade unions organized in the State during the years from 1863 to 1865 were the Blacksmiths' and Machinists' at Watertown, the Moulders' in Racine, the Carpenters' and Joiners' in Madison, the Custom Shoemakers' in La Crosse, Madison, and Portage, the Custom Tailors' in Madison, and local divisions of the Brotherhood of Locomotive Engineers at Racine and Portage. No doubt many others were organized in various parts of the State, of which, however, no record seems to have been preserved. The labor movement in Wisconsin during this period has been almost entirely ignored in contemporary records. A large portion of the data presented in this chapter has been gleaned from personal interviews with men who were active in the movement.

[2] Of sufficient importance during 1864 and 1865 to receive newspaper mention were the strikes for higher wages of the printers, bricklayers and masons, iron molders, and sailors in Milwaukee, the sawmill operatives in Oshkosh, and the custom shoemakers in La Crosse, Madison, and Portage.

was either wholly or partially successful, for capital was reaping profits so large that it could better afford to yield than to fight. Where the employer, however, offered determined resistance, they uniformly failed; it was an axiom that a strike lasting longer than three days was lost. As a whole it is perhaps safe to say that trade unions were too weak and inexperienced in this frontier community to be able materially to affect wages; while during the war skilled labor fared no better, and in many cases actually worse, than unskilled labor.

In addition to the disparity in the advance of wages and prices, labor nursed during this period a number of other grievances. Prominent among these was irregularity of pay,[1] an evil which had grown to some proportions in the State as a result of the hard times following the panic of 1857. It was a typical frontier difficulty, for the frontier is by definition a region of inadequate capital. The railroads were, as might be expected, particularly delinquent, since with them scarcity of capital was chronic. In other industries labor secured deliverance from this evil during the prosperous years of the war, but railroad employees were still fighting it during the decade of the seventies.[2]

[1] In 1861 Assemblyman J. L. Fobes introduced into the legislature a bill providing for the collection of wages of labor. The subject aroused considerable interest in Milwaukee, where a mass meeting of mechanics and laborers was held on Mar. 11, 1861 to petition the legislature thus to strengthen the lien law. No action was secured, however.

[2] Early in 1865 the blacksmiths and carpenters in the railroad shops of the Milwaukee & St. Paul Railroad, and in 1867 the laborers on the Tomah & St. Croix Railroad were on strike for back pay. As late as 1872 there were numerous strikes for the same reason on railroads under construction in northern Wisconsin. On the Wisconsin Central Rail-

Similar grievances were store pay and scrip pay, inheritances likewise of a previous period of hard times.[1] The employer who paid his labor in store orders was usually himself interested in some way in the concern upon which the orders were given, and realized thus a profit not only on the production, but also on the consumption, of his workmen. The laborers, however, who purchased with store orders, saw in them only another mode of reducing wages, for not only did the storekeeper refuse to sell them such standard commodities as flour and meat, but on all others either gave inferior goods or charged higher prices. The man who "went for his pay with a bag" in every case secured less for his money than his cash-paying neighbor.[2]

The amount of store orders which workmen were required to accept in lieu of wages varied with individual trades and employers. The coopers were nearly always paid in cash, for the millers and packers who employed them were in turn able to command

road near Stevens Point the laborers engaged in a rather serious riot in 1872, tearing up track and seizing a locomotive and twenty-five cars which they proposed to hold until their back pay was turned over to them.

[1] The following, from an editorial of Mark M. Pomeroy in the La-Crosse *Democrat* of Sept. 8, 1863, offers an indication of the nature of the problem in the smaller towns: "The laborer is worthy of his wages, and he is a foolish man to work if he does not receive them—not in cats, dogs, old wagon tires, and water-melon rinds, but in cash or its full equivalent—is foolish to work and live from week to week on promises made to the ear, but broken to the heart. We hope the day will come when mechanics will altogether refuse to work for anything but cash in hand promptly paid." M. M. Pomeroy later became a prominent editor and Greenback politician in the state of New York, being at one time an aspirant for the presidential nomination of the Greenback Labor party.

[2] Shrewd buyers sometimes managed to conceal from the storekeeper the fact that they intended to pay in store orders, but the trick did not often succeed.

cash. In some of the building trades, on the other hand, wage earners received their entire wages in cash only as a special grace on occasions like Thanksgiving, Christmas, and Independence Day.

Scrip pay was a special affliction of railroad labor. The scrip was usually issued payable six months or more after date, and the unfortunate laborer who was under the necessity of immediately converting his wages into cash, could do so only at a large discount. Happily in most trades labor succeeded during the prosperous years which followed 1863, when money was plentiful and profits of employers were large, in shaking off these evils.

The entrance of women into hitherto unoccupied fields gave much concern to organized labor and in particular to the printers of the State. The printing trade early felt a scarcity of labor, for the members of that craft responded with more than usual zeal to the calls for volunteers.[1] Soon after the war began various State exchanges were noticing with favor the increasing employment of women as compositors. Women were admirably suited to enter the occupation, for not only could they quickly become as skillful as men, but they were satisfied with little more than half the wages men demanded. In 1863 Milwaukee Typographical Union No. 23 adopted resolutions protesting against the introduction of female compositors into the office of the Milwaukee *Sentinel*, and, when the proprietors of that paper refused to recede, declared a strike. The controversy

[1] It was estimated in 1865 that the printing offices of the State furnished not less than a regiment of men to the Union cause. In 1864 Milwaukee Typographical Union No. 23 was obliged to disband because of the large number of its members who had enlisted.

aroused wide comment over the State, the press unanimously accepting the *Sentinel's* defense that its course was calculated solely to give employment to women left dependent by the war.[1] The strike was lost, and women continued during the war to occupy a prominent place in the printing offices of the State.

As clerks women invaded a field hitherto left almost exclusively to men. "Within the past few years," declared the Milwaukee *Sentinel* of Mar. 31, 1868, "there has been a decided and strong movement towards the employment of women as clerks in dry goods and fancy stores * * *. The Chicago *Republican* lately said that every young man who sold dry goods, boots, or shoes, hats and caps, etc., behind a counter ought to be ashamed of himself. This is somewhat stronger than we are disposed to put the case; but it is a step in the right direction." In the factories of the State, particularly the woodenware, shingle, and match factories of the Fox River Valley, women likewise found increasing opportunities for employment during the war.

Wages of women were pitifully inadequate, varying during the years of highest prices from $3 to $5 per week. Early in 1864 a communication signed "Many Milwaukee Tailoresses" appeared in the Milwaukee *Sentinel*, in which these unfortunate sweatshop toilers set their grievances before the public. The complaint closed, "Tailoresses who have worked at their trade

[1] The attitude of the press is well reflected in the following extract from the *Dodge County Citizen* of Jan. 15, 1863, which appeared in the *Sentinel* on January 16. "A few weeks ago, the Printers' Union (at the *Sentinel*) struck for higher wages, and the employers, like honorable men, promptly complied. But now the Union has 'struck' *women*—a few women who are nobly bearing the grievances of our national troubles; and the employers, like honorable men, refused *to strike the women* too."

for years, and who own first class sewing machines, can only make twelve common vests per week, or twelve pairs of common pants. * * * Their day may commence at 7 A. M., but it can not close at 6 P. M. It must continue on not unfrequently till the 'wee sma' hours. * * * The maximum of a week's earnings then is: for one dozen vests, $3; for a like number of the ordinary run of winter pants, the same sum—the higher priced pants are only occasionally obtainable, and of these only eight pairs netting $3 per week can be made by one person. Many of us have made twelve pairs of lined pants this winter for $2.64."[1] In Madison the seamstresses faced a similar situation, and found it necessary in the spring of 1864 to organize in order to secure living wages. In 1867 the Milwaukee *Sentinel* estimated that 4,000 girls and young women were employed in the various shops and manufacturing establishments of the city, whose wages ranged "from three to twelve dollars a week—the average being probably five dollars. How do they live on such a pittance? * * * Board alone can hardly be had for less than five dollars a week."[2]

Cheap labor constituted a menace to a number of trades, particularly to the ship carpenters of the lake ports and the Irish deck hands on the Mississippi steamboats. The ship carpenters, whose busy season came during the winter months when navigation was closed, annually found their trade invaded by a horde of hungry house carpenters, thrown out of employment by the suspension of building operations. The intruders were ready to work for anything they

[1] Milwaukee *Sentinel*, Jan. 16, 1864.

[2] *Ibid.*, Aug. 3, 1867.

could get, forcing the ship carpenters in self-defense to adopt the most stringent regulations against non-union labor. In the winter of 1861–62 the Milwaukee Society of Carpenters and Caulkers[1] fought a long, though unsuccessful, strike against the despised "barn-door joiners,"[2] and throughout the period of the war the issue of the closed shop was a source of constant conflict with them.

Up to the close of the war the deck hands on the Mississippi steamboats were almost entirely Irish. Negroes were forbidden to lay hands upon freight, and any effort to employ them was promptly met by throwing the obnoxious blacks overboard. The emancipation of the slaves, however, was the beginning of the end, for it threw upon the market a mass of labor admirably adapted by nature to the irresponsible life of the roustabout. The first evidence of a change on the upper Mississippi occurred in the summer of 1866 when the Northwestern Union Packet Company of La Crosse,[3] whose deck hands were striking for higher wages, brought in from Cincinnati 300 to 400 negroes in their places. Thenceforth the substitution of black for white rousters was rapid, accompanied by a swift decline in wages, and before 1870 negroes were in almost complete possession of the trade.[4]

[1] The Milwaukee Ship Carpenters' and Caulkers' Union was organized in the winter of 1861 as a branch of an organization that seems to have embraced the Great Lakes.

[2] The strike held out for over a month, an unusual duration for a labor contest at this time.

[3] The Northwestern Union Packet Company controlled the steam-packet business on the upper Mississippi in 1866.

[4] In the Milwaukee Coopers' strike of 1872 the millers were reported to be contemplating bringing in Chinese strike breakers. It is doubtful, however, whether the plan was ever seriously considered.

The introduction of machinery seriously affected several trades in the State during the war, though it led to no such direct clashes with labor as occurred in the East. The shoemakers were hardest hit. A series of inventions, stimulated by the war and the huge demands of the Federal government for shoes for its armies, transformed the industry within a period of ten or fifteen years, substituting machinery for the old-time skill of the journeyman.[1] By the end of the war the "Ancient and Honorable Mysterie of Cordwainers" was well on its way to the factory system.[2] The Milwaukee *Sentinel* of April 15, 1869 reports an interview with the foreman of Bradley & Metcalf's boot and shoe manufacturing establishment, already at that time one of the largest in the Northwest, which illustrates the changes going on. "The simple fact proved to be that the division of labor—one single and simple operation being assigned to each class of workmen—and the introduction of machinery,

[1] The inventions which seriously affected the shoemakers began with the introduction of the power pegging machine at Lynn and Philadelphia in 1857. In 1862 the McKay sole sewing machine was invented, which in one hour accomplished the work of a journeyman in eighty, and following that came such a flood of others as induced the Massachusetts commissioner of labor in 1871 to remark that invention seemed to be centering about the shoemaking industry. See *The Knights of St. Crispin, 1867–1874*, University of Wisconsin, *Bulletin*, No. 355 (Madison, 1910).

[2] An interesting transition in the evolution of the factory system in the boot and shoe industry was represented in Milwaukee during the later sixties by an institution familiarly known as "Bradley's Barn." To this frame building, located in the Third Ward, approximately a hundred of Bradley & Metcalf's workmen brought and "worked up" each week the materials handed out to them at the central warehouse. They owned their own simple tools and devices and paid monthly a stipulated rent for the privilege of a working place. A similar institution, in which the employees of Bradley & Metcalf and Atkins, Steele & White were at work, was said to have been located near Fourth and Clybourne streets.

had enabled the manufacturers to substitute unskilled for skilled labor. Mr. Shaw remarked that he could take an unskilled laborer from the street and in two days' time teach him to do some portions of the work as well as a man who had spent years in learning the shoemaker's trade. And he added further that of the 450 men now employed in the establishment, perhaps not more than *ten* were sufficiently skilled to have been of any service ten or fifteen years ago." To meet this unhappy plight and more particularly to protect the vestiges of skill that machinery still left them from the encroachments of "green hands," there was initiated in 1867 what was destined to become the greatest labor organization known up to this time to the American labor movement.

The association of the Knights of St. Crispin was born in the spring of 1867 in the metropolis of Wisconsin. Thither had come at the close of the Civil War Newell Daniels, an intelligent Massachusetts boot-treer, who, appreciating the condition of his trade, had planned before his removal to the West to organize a national union of boot-treers. Early in 1867 he succeeded in interesting six of his fellow-craftsmen in a new plan to organize not only the boot-treers but all the workers of the boot and shoe industry into a great national industrial union. A constitution and a ritual were drafted; one of the charter members, F. W. Wallace, proposed for the title of the organization the picturesque "Knights of St. Crispin," in honor of the shoemakers' patron saint, and on Mar. 1, 1867 the order was launched. Daniels induced the German Custom Shoemakers' Union of Milwaukee to adopt his plan and join the order as Lodge No. 2, after which, with Milwaukee as a base, he began his invasion of the shoemaking centers of the East.[1] His success was almost instantaneous. The form of organization well suited the needs of the industry; its cardinal principle, refusal to teach green hands, was recognized as the only salvation of the craft,[2] and before the end of the decade its membership had jumped to approximately 50,000. In Wisconsin by the end of 1870 eleven new lodges had been organized, at Racine, Waukesha, Janesville, Kenosha, Watertown, Fond du Lac, Green Bay, Sheboygan, La Crosse, Portage, and Oshkosh.[3]

The decline of the organization was as sudden as its rise. Its strikes, which at first were uniformly successful, after 1871 met with a number of crushing defeats, and by the end of 1872 the order was on the verge of dissolution. The only Wisconsin lodge that still sent a delegate to the national convention in that year was the original Lodge No. 1, and even this was obliged to disband during the panic of 1873.

In the coopering industry in Wisconsin machine-made staves for flour barrels first came into general

[1] The German Custom Shoemakers' Union appears to have been organized some time after the close of the war. The custom shoemakers in Milwaukee were almost all German, the factory workers who constituted Lodge No. 1 were predominantly Irish. The data relating to the beginnings of the order I have secured from Daniels' own account in the monthly *Journal of the K. O. S. C.*, January, 1873. For a detailed account of the later history of the Knights of St. Crispin see University of Wisconsin, *Bulletin*, No. 355.

[2] It was hoped that by controlling the skilled operations which machinery had not yet displaced, the members of the craft might still retain possession of the industry.

[3] Of these, however, four (at Waukesha, Kenosha, Sheboygan, and Oshkosh) had by the end of 1872 already been disbanded.

use during the years just preceding the war. With their introduction the most difficult and skilled portion of the slack-barrel cooper's art was displaced, and there remained to the trade only the comparatively simple task of "setting up." The innovation appears not to have been resisted, however, by the coopers of Wisconsin, though indirectly it led to much trouble. The slack-barrel cooper's trade had at its best been a highly seasonal occupation, for barrels were too bulky to be stored, and flour, the one product that made use of slack barrels, was shipped only during a few months in the spring and the fall of the year.[1] Machinery greatly accentuated the evil, for now the preparation of the stock was wholly removed from the trade. The industry became a succession of short periods of rush and long periods of idleness. Each rush was the signal for a strike for increased wages, the Milwaukee coopers succeeding at one time during the later sixties in forcing their piecework rate as high as 25 cents per barrel. The moment the rush was over the millers cut rates to their former level, often as low as 7 or 8 cents.[2] The

[1] Before the war, millers in Milwaukee generally bought their barrels from small coopering establishments scattered over the city. However, the high war taxes on the sale of industrial products (in the case of flour barrels this added 3 per cent to purchase price), led most of the Milwaukee millers to establish cooper shops as departments of their business. Organization of labor in these larger shops was more readily accomplished than had previously been possible.

[2] In 1868, after an unsuccessful strike of the slack-barrel coopers to increase their piecework rates from 15 and 20 cents for flat and round hooped barrels respectively to 20 and 25 cents, a number of the millers agreed to a contract system by which the coopers should be given employment the year round at 12½ cents per barrel. The contract proved unsatisfactory to both parties, the millers finding it almost impossible to secure storage room for the barrels made during the slack season and the coopers revolting at the low prices when the rush season approached.

cooper trade in Milwaukee, where flour milling centered, became during the period of the later sixties and early seventies the most unstable and turbulent in the city.[1]

Advancing prices led, as we have seen, on the one hand to organized efforts to force up wages; on the other they led to coöperative enterprises to reduce cost of living. In the East, where trade unionism was vigorous, the movement toward distributive coöperation was marked; in Wisconsin it was insignificant. In Milwaukee Joseph Bennett, an eloquent English member of the Milwaukee Machinists' and Blacksmiths' Union, who was familiar with the successful Rochdale system in his mother country, preached the principles of coöperation to his fellow-craftsmen so successfully that in 1865 the Union opened a coöperative grocery store, which aroused much favorable interest. It was conducted on too small a scale, however, to succeed, refusing to make deliveries and opening only evenings when the committee of the Union could take charge. After six months the members tired of the experiment and it was abandoned.[2]

I have been told that a similar plan was tried previously, and again after 1868, but was never entirely successful.

[1] The first trade union of slack barrel coopers permanent enough to be termed such was organized in Milwaukee in 1867. During the succeeding three years it led a somewhat precarious existence, the men striking frequently and not always with success. Late in 1870 or early in 1871 it joined the International Coopers' Union (organized May 6, 1870) as No. 1 Wisconsin. In 1872, after a prolonged strike which ended disastrously, it disbanded, but was reorganized in June of the next year. Five other coopers' unions were organized in Wisconsin during 1871, at Watertown, Janesville, Appleton, Racine, and the tight-barrel coopers of Milwaukee.

[2] The enterprising Bay View Lodge of the Sons of Vulcan, organized in 1869, made provision in its act of incorporation (1871) for a coöperative store, but I have found no evidence that such a store was actually undertaken.

Productive coöperation was frequently tried in the State, both during and after the period of rapidly rising prices.[1] The first attempt came early in 1862, when nine members of the Ship Carpenters' and Caulkers' Union of Milwaukee, disheartened by the constant bickering of their organization over the question of nonunion labor, withdrew during the strike of 1861–62 and formed a coöperative shipbuilding association under the title Allan, McClellan & Company. Beginning with limited capital, they contented themselves at first with jobs of repairing, applying only the days when such work was not to be had to the construction of a new ship. They prospered from the beginning but, as was so often the case with successful coöperative enterprises at that time, the more energetic among them bought out the others and thereafter conducted the business on a private basis.[2] The Union in the meantime was nearly wrecked, for the coöperators who had withdrawn were the best workmen and most intelligent leaders in the organization.

Early in 1863 the printers of the Milwaukee *Sentinel*, who were striking against the employment of women as compositors, attempted, when they realized that the strike was about to fail, to establish a paper of

[1] In the East productive coöperation as a movement came at the close of the war. It represented the effort of organized labor to check falling wages and unemployment. In Wisconsin the movement did not attain importance until near the close of the decade, for hard times did not reach the State until that time. The Milwaukee instances which occurred during the war may be regarded as exceptions to the general rule that productive coöperation is a movement accompanying falling wages and unemployment.

[2] The present Milwaukee Dry Dock Company on Jones Island is the successor of Allan, McClellan & Co.

their own.[1] Their capital, however, was insufficient, a difficulty that spelled defeat for many a hurriedly launched coöperative enterprise, and after a struggle of seventeen days they were forced to suspend.[2]

Productive coöperation was stimulated toward the close of the decade by a temporary depression of business in the State. In Milwaukee two attempts were made, one by the journeymen cigar-makers, the other by the journeymen cabinetmakers of the city. That of the cigar-makers, originating in a strike, was abandoned after a year and a half of fair progress because of mutual misunderstanding among the members.[3] That of the cabinetmakers was more successful. The twelve members got on well together, they were wise in drawing to their aid as president and treasurer a well-known business man of Milwaukee, and when after two years they decided to sell out they realized twice the amount of their original investment.[4]

In 1869 twenty-one German Knights of St. Crispin in Milwaukee became infected with the wave of enthusiasm for coöperation which was sweeping over

[1] Three of the early issues of this interesting paper (the Milwaukee *Daily Union*) are in the possession of George Richardson of Milwaukee, one of the leaders in the enterprise, to whom I am indebted for courteous assistance.

[2] The Iron Moulders' Union in Milwaukee at the close of the war was much interested in the discussion of productive coöperation, but nothing definite was attempted.

[3] The moving spirit in this Coöperative Cigar Manufacturing Company was Henry Lecher, still a resident of Milwaukee, to whom I am indebted for courteous assistance.

[4] This coöperative company, known as the Milwaukee Furniture Manufacturing Association, occupied itself chiefly in the manufacture of sashes, doors, and blinds. Its first president was William Frankfurth, a prominent hardware merchant of the city. The company to which it sold out professed also to be coöperative, but was not.

the national order and organized the Milwaukee Boot and Shoe Manufacturing Association. They began with high hopes of success, for they had gathered sufficient capital to be able to purchase a complete set of machinery,[1] and they were the most skilled workers in their craft. They failed, however, after a discouraging struggle of two and a half years. Lack of competent management and a hopeless attempt to compete with factory products when custom orders failed were responsible for their defeat.[2]

On the whole it may be said of productive coöperation in Wisconsin that it proved a failure. Originating usually in a strike,[3] organization was hurried, due regard was not paid to the important matter of selecting members who were both skillful and compatible, and above all capital was insufficient and management usually incompetent. When success was attained productive coöperation failed nevertheless in the sense that it soon ceased to be coöperative. Whether failure or success followed, it always injured the trade union from which the movement sprang,

[1] Stock was limited to $75,000 at $50 per share. The association was reported to have started out with $15,000, but this was an exaggeration.

[2] Other instances of coöperation in Milwaukee during this period were the Carpenters' & Joiners' Building Association, incorporated in 1866, the Badger State Building Association, and the Carpenters' & Housebuilders' Coöperative Company incorporated in 1867. The German Tailors' Union, incorporated in 1871, provided in its articles for coöperation, but I have found no evidence that such was ever attempted.

[3] Coöperation was in some instances purely a strike measure, a club over the heads of refractory employers. Thus the constitution of the Milwaukee Masons' and Bricklayers' Union provided, "In the event a Strike shall be declared, and continue for the space of one week, the Board of Trustees and such additional Members as the Board demands, shall constitute the Board of Building Commissioners, and they shall figure on work, enter into contracts, and furnish bond for the completion of such work as they may obtain."

12

for it drew away the most active and enterprising members of the craft.[1]

The eight-hour philosophy of Ira Steward found many ardent advocates in Wisconsin toward the close of the war. The demand was based not on actual conditions, as was the case in the East where business depression and the return of the soldiers brought on excessive unemployment, but on speculative abstractions. It was the echo, merely, of a real movement in the great industrial centers of the North. In Wisconsin the supporters of the shorter day urged the usual humanitarian considerations; they declared themselves willing to submit to proportionate wage reductions,[2] confident that the withdrawal of so large a supply of labor power from the market would create a demand that would quickly force wages back to their former level. The opposition held up the danger of State interference in the relations between labor and capital; predicted disastrous results to the infant

[1] Trade unions contemplating coöperation found it desirable, in order to acquire legal standing, to incorporate under the laws of the State. They hoped also to secure thereby protection for their funds against dishonest officers. In the East employers vigorously resisted attempts of organized labor to secure legal recognition. In Wisconsin capital was quite indifferent, largely, no doubt, because organized labor here was too weak to constitute a menace. In 1866 the Milwaukee Masons' and Bricklayers' Union, in 1867 the Madison Masons' and Bricklayers' Union, in 1868 the Milwaukee Cigarmakers' and Iron Moulders' unions, in 1869 the Milwaukee Machinists' and Blacksmiths' Union, and in 1871 the Milwaukee Tailors' Union and the Bay View Sons of Vulcan sought and were granted legal recognition.

[2] In the spring of 1867, before the eight-hour law enacted by the State legislature went into operation, the Milwaukee Ship Carpenters' and Caulkers', the Carpenters' and Joiners', and the Machinists' and Blacksmiths' unions adopted resolutions in which they proposed to accept proportionate wage reductions (20 per cent in all these cases). All work over eight hours, however, was to be paid for at the regular overtime rates.

manufacturing interests of Wisconsin; and declared that agriculture, the predominant interest of the State, would suffer at the instance of a mere handful of city laborers. "If labor could secure ten hours' pay for eight hours' work, it would be an injustice to the great overwhelming mass of agricultural labor, which works longer than eight hours a day, for it would raise the price of manufactured products which this class consumes."[1]

As early as 1864 the question was receiving public discussion in Milwaukee. On Sept. 1, 1865 a Labor Reform Association was organized in the city, whose chief object was declared to be agitation for the shorter day. In the November elections of 1865 candidates for the State legislature in several of the larger cities were bidding for the labor vote on this issue, and though the friends of the shorter day were probably in no case sufficiently numerous to be a decisive factor we shall see that the succeeding legislature was not entirely hostile to the movement. During 1866 and the early part of 1867 the General Eight Hour League of Wisconsin,[2] an outgrowth of the Milwaukee Labor Reform Association, spread among the larger towns of the State, where it succeeded in winning a limited support for its program.[3]

[1] Milwaukee *Sentinel*, Jan. 21, 1867.

[2] Early in 1866 the League was reported to be considering establishing an organ of its own in Milwaukee. In 1867 it attempted to secure incorporation under the State laws, but its bill was defeated in the Senate.

[3] In the Milwaukee municipal election of April, 1866 the Eight Hour League placed in the field candidates for the common council in six of the nine wards of the city. For mayor it endorsed the Democratic nominee, John T. Tallmadge, who was known to be friendly to the eight-hour day. None of the candidates except Tallmadge was elected.

In 1866 Assemblyman Orton of Milwaukee[1] introduced in the legislature a bill establishing eight hours as a legal day's labor where no contract existed to the contrary, it being permitted, however, by special agreement to increase the hours to a number not exceeding ten. On Mar. 28, 1866 a substitute measure received a majority in the Assembly, only to be reconsidered and defeated on the following day. "The main object of the bill," shrewdly comments the Madison correspondent of the Milwaukee *Sentinel*, "was to afford those Assemblymen who represent town constituencies an opportunity to blow off a little steam on the subject. It is well known in Milwaukee (and perhaps the same was the case in other localities) that two or three members were helped into their seats by the omnipotent aid of the Eight-pointed star."[2]

By the spring of 1867 public interest in the eight-hour question was at its height. In his annual message of that year Governor Fairchild officially called the attention of the legislature to the matter. "To the men of the West," he declared, "most of whom have at some time been laboring men, surely no argument is needed to show that those who create the wealth of the country should be afforded every possible facility for participating in its enjoyment, and that the non-producers should not enjoy all the luxuries of life, while the producers are awarded only its burdens."

In response to his suggestion three bills were intro-

[1] Charles H. Orton and A. R. R. Butler of the Milwaukee legislative delegation were reported to have won their seats by the aid of the labor vote.

[2] Milwaukee *Sentinel*, Mar. 31, 1866.

duced in the Assembly by members from Milwaukee and Racine, one of which was enacted into law on April 6, 1867. It provided that eight hours should constitute a day's work in all manufacturing establishments in the State except where a contract was agreed upon to the contrary, or where a contract was by the week, month, or year. Women, and children under eighteen, were not to be compelled to labor for longer than eight hours in any one day, and children under fourteen were not to be permitted[1] to labor for longer than ten hours in any one day. Like most of the State eight-hour laws enacted at that time this was obviously not a genuine effort to arrive at an eight-hour day. Only so much of it as applied to children under fourteen years of age appears to have been sincere, and even this was never enforced.

The law was received without enthusiasm by the laboring population of the State. Even in Milwaukee, where agitation had centered, interest was so small that the labor leaders who had planned a demonstration for July 4, when it was to go into operation, were obliged to abandon the idea. The machinists and blacksmiths, who had been its most ardent advocates, now resolved to postpone its adoption. E. P. Allis, a well-known friend of labor, who in 1867 was rapidly forging to the front as a manufacturer of machinery, offered to permit his men to work eight hours for eight hours' pay, but his offer was declined. Of all the trades in Milwaukee only the ship carpenters and caulkers persevered. On July 4 they cele-

[1] Compare "permit" used in this clause with "compel," used in the preceding. The employer who contracted with women or children to labor longer than eight hours per day did not "compel," and therefore did not come within the meaning of the law.

brated the advent of the new law by a procession through the streets of the city, and on the next day, when their employers refused to grant the shorter day, secured it by means of a strike. The reduction of 70 cents per day in their wages, however, soon dampened their enthusiasm, and before the month was over they had returned to ten hours. In summing up the eight-hour movement it may be said that for a time at least it unified the interests of organized labor in the State, though of tangible results it left none.[1]

The temporary industrial depression that struck the East after the close of the war did not reach Wisconsin until three years later.[2] Once arrived, however, it hung on long after the East had recovered; indeed, it was not until the end of 1871 that prosperity returned. During these years of hard times, when strikes failed and unemployment was general,[3] labor

[1] The Milwaukee Stone Cutters' Union in June, 1869 adopted the eight-hour day, one of the last unions of that craft in the country to do so.

[2] During 1865, 1866, and 1867 business in Wisconsin was progressing steadily, wages were good, and unemployment was rare. In Milwaukee three trade unions were organized during these years in addition to those elsewhere mentioned, the Boilermakers', Cabinetmakers', and Stone Cutters'. Of strikes there were four of some importance in Milwaukee, those of the Masons' and Bricklayers', the Printers', and the Coopers' unions.

[3] I have found record of approximately a dozen strikes in various parts of the State during these years, a majority of which were directed against wage reductions or increase of hours. The Chicago *Workingman's Advocate* of June 11, 1870 comments as follows upon the industrial situation in Milwaukee: "From a correspondent we learn that trade matters in Milwaukee are very dull; a large majority of the mechanics of that city are content with the offer of the bosses. Bricklayers who work up to their knees in water are glad to get $3.50 per day, while those who are employed on buildings average only $2.00. The wood-butchers are if possible in a still worse condition, while the plasterers

turned for relief, as it did in the East, to politics. Early in 1869 there was organized at Black River Falls by the State Executive Committee of the National Labor Union, Wisconsin Labor Union No. 1, an organization that differed widely from any the State had hitherto known. Instead of limiting its membership to a particular trade it proposed to welcome workers of every employment and condition;[1] instead of depending upon strikes it proposed to accomplish its ends by uniting the labor vote at the polls. "By the adoption of the principles embodied in the platform of the N. L. U.," wrote the chairman of the State Executive Committee late in 1869, "more will be effected in the establishment of an equitable standard of wages and a fair distribution of what we earn, reasonable hours, and universal emancipation from the power of Capital and Parties, than can ever be accomplished by trade unions as at present organized. Let us all go to work, and organize all kinds of Labor (no matter what the calling or occupation) into one common Labor Union, without prejudice or jealousy, * * * and then our votes will bring about in due time the final result devoutly to be wished for."[2] Four months after this Black River Falls labor union was organized, it issued a call for a

take what's going. Won't some enterprising Milwaukean contract for a load of coolies, as there is no danger of the mechanics of that city objecting to their introduction." In 1872 came a temporary revival of business, accompanied by an epidemic of strikes in every part of the State. At least fifteen occurred in Milwaukee alone, of which those of the coopers, printers, and cigar-makers were long and bitterly fought.

[1] This was the form of organization later adopted by the Knights of Labor. It was well suited to the needs of frontier communities, where there were usually too few mechanics of one trade at work to make possible an organization along trade lines.

[2] Joseph C. Horey in Chicago *Workingman's Advocate*, Dec. 2, 1869.

State convention of various labor associations and friends of labor to meet at Watertown on Sept. 30, 1869, there to organize a State Labor Reform party.

The convention which assembled pursuant to this call held a two-day session at which it adopted a State and a national program embodying the views of the National Labor Congress.[1] The State policy was declared to be:

> 1. To blend and assimilate the interests of the different mechanical trades with all branches of industry.
>
> 2. To establish a uniform price upon all kinds of labor; equal rights to all who toil, be they man, woman, or child—from the commonest day laborer to the best mechanic; from the private soldier to the general in command.
>
> 3. To have the value of all necessary commodities of life produced by labor, measured by the amount of service used in producing them.
>
> 4. To have all manufactured articles stamped and marked, how made and the kind of material of which they are made.
>
> 5. To establish a healthy, friendly, rational intercourse between the different mechanical trades—farmers and miners, and other producers of raw material, upon principles of common sense and justice.
>
> 6. To establish such a system of political and financial laws as will give to all and each the full amount of what is produced by their toil.[2]

With the adoption of this somewhat vague platform the convention adjourned, making no attempt to place in the field any candidates for State office.[3]

[1] For the program of the National Labor Congress see Commons *Hist. of Amer. Labor Movements*, Ms.

[2] Watertown *Democrat*, Oct. 7, 1869.

[3] The convention appears to have been dominated by the Milwaukee delegates. All of the officers elected were Milwaukee men—Thomas C. Tinker, president, representing the Milwaukee Masons' and Bricklayers' Union, August F. Brunnotto, secretary, the Milwaukee Tailors', and Fred Treyser, treasurer, the Milwaukee Typographical Union. Milwaukee was designated as the headquarters of the organization and Watertown as the place for holding conventions. The date for the next annual convention was set for June 28, 1870, but whether it ever assembled can not be determined from any of the Milwaukee or Watertown papers. In 1872 the organization seems to have elected James N. Ruby, representing Wisconsin Labor Union No. 3 of Oshkosh, as its representative

Apparently it was realized that interest in labor reform was too limited to justify an active campaign. In Milwaukee a number of interested trade unions held a joint meeting to receive and ratify the report of their delegates and incidentally to organize a City Labor Reform Assembly,[1] but beyond this the convention appears to have been ignored.

The following year the chairman of the State Executive Committee at Black River Falls, who optimistically estimated the number of members enrolled under the banner of the Labor Reform movement at 5,000, issued a new call for a State nominating convention to be held at La Crosse on September 24. If such a convention ever met it was not noticed by the local papers; at all events no ticket of the new party made its appearance. In the Fourth Ward of Milwaukee in 1869 and in Black River Falls in 1872 local labor tickets were placed in the field, but beyond such local manifestations the political efforts of Wisconsin labor at this time appear to have produced no tangible results.

The history of the Wisconsin labor movement during the years of the war and the years immediately following is thus a record of faint and uncertain beginnings. Wisconsin was still predominantly agri-

to the Ohio convention of the National Labor Reform party, but his name does not appear among the list of delegates who were accredited.

[1] The Milwaukee Labor Reform Assembly (also referred to as City Labor Union) was organized Oct. 8, 1869, the first trade assembly to be organized in the history of the State. At its second meeting on October 20 it appointed committees to organize the various wards in the city into Labor Reform Leagues. The political reforms demanded by workingmen in Milwaukee were the abolition of the caucus system and the opening of the polls on election day from eight o'clock in the morning until eight o'clock at night.

cultural; her industrial population was too limited and scattered to permit of effective organization. The story of this first organizing of the wage-earning class in the State is interesting chiefly as it reflects the more significant movements that were going on in the larger industrial centers of the North.

CHAPTER VII

BANKING

The panic attending the outbreak of the Civil War played havoc with the banking system of Wisconsin. The consequences of a previous decade of reckless financiering were abruptly visited upon the people of the State. For a year and a half Wisconsin expiated old sins by monetary and industrial disaster. She was not alone, however, in these difficulties. The conservative East was almost as sorely tried. In the West, Illinois suffered more keenly even than Wisconsin; Indiana and Missouri endured almost as much.

It was a simple and profitable matter to set up a banking business in Wisconsin prior to the Civil War. An individual invested $25,000 or more in the bonds of some state or of the United States, which he deposited with the bank comptroller. In exchange he received paper currency equal in amount to the market value of his securities. With $25,000 it was possible at the beginning of 1860 to purchase the depreciated bonds of Missouri, for example, to the face value of $31,250. Missouri paid upon these evidences of indebtedness annual interest at the rate of 6 per cent, which upon the sum of $31,250 netted an income of $1,875. The banker having deposited his Missouri securities was presented by the comptroller with $25,000 in bank notes. He was permitted to loan these to clients at an interest rate of 10 per cent, which netted him an additional $2,500. Upon an investment of $25,000 he thus realized a yearly income of $4,375 or 17½ per cent. This business was eminently safe and profitable, and banks of issue naturally were plentiful in Wisconsin.

The Wisconsin code stipulated that the issuing of paper money should be merely an incident of the banker's activity; that his chief function should be to provide discount, deposit, and exchange facilities for commercial operations.[1] This was intended as a measure of safety. It was, however, universally ignored. In 1860 the bulk of Wisconsin's currency was issued by institutions engaged in no other business.[2] The banks located in the small and isolated lumber town of Eau Claire, for example, had on Oct. 1, 1860 a total circulation of $536,764. On the other hand all the powerful commercial banks in the city of Milwaukee had a circulation of only $86,521.[3]

As a further measure of safety the Wisconsin law required banks to possess a working capital of at least $25,000.[4] To legitimate banking this was an obvious necessity. It was essential not only to the ordinary commercial operations of a banking institution but to the prompt redemption of its paper money. However, the law did not specifically direct the State comptroller to inquire whether banks ever had their capital actually paid in, and the require-

[1] Wis. *Gen. Laws*, 1858, chap. 116.

[2] Wisconsin Bank Comptroller, *Reports*, 1857–65. The department held $834,000 worth of Tennessee bonds and $188,000 of Virginia bonds.

[3] *Id.*, 1860, 11–26; Wis. *Assem. Jour.*, 1861, 596–600.

[4] Wisconsin *Revised Statutes*, 1858, chap. 71, sec. 1.

ment was consequently universally ignored.[1] Instead, it was the practice to regard as capital the securities deposited with the comptroller for the protection of outstanding currency. "Banks," declared Governor Randall in his annual message of 1858, "were expected to conduct their business upon their own capital, and give security besides, and such was the view held and acted upon by the Bank Department until a period quite recent. During the past year, however, an entire change seems to have taken place in the practice of the Department in this respect, so that at this time the stocks or collateral deposited, is made to stand for and represent bank capital itself; and very large issues of bills have been credited and put into circulation upon this hypothesis."[2]

A bank whose lack of working capital rendered it unable upon demand to redeem its notes could not easily maintain itself in a commercial center where its paper could be protested and its affairs legally wound up. It was the practice of the wildcat institutions of Wisconsin, therefore, to establish their offices in remote and inaccessible places, in swamps, or in the unknown northern wilderness. One keen financier dodged his note holders by naming his institution "Bank of Green Bay." This title he printed upon his currency, though his actual location was La Crosse. In numerous instances, according to Governor Randall, banks were established at points "unknown to the people of the State or the maps, inaccessible, and beyond the reach of bill-holders, even when known; and not unfrequently the

[1] See Wis. Bank Comptroller, *Report*, 1857, 7.
[2] Wis. *Mess. and Docs.*, 1858, 15.

bills appear to be signed by fictitious names as officers, by minors, or by persons pecuniarily irresponsible."[1]

Dangerous as this condition was, the State moved only half-heartedly to correct it. An adequate remedy would have been a system of central redemption, requiring every bank in the State upon demand to exchange its paper at a central point, such as Milwaukee or Madison, for lawful money of the United States. Such a measure was urgently demanded by the more conservative bankers of the State, but could not be obtained. Instead, the legislature of 1858 enacted a law forbidding banking associations to establish themselves in any township containing less than 200 voters,[2] a loose requirement that offered little real protection. The State comptroller as late as 1861 still found numbers of banks of issue in existence that had not even an office where their bills could be presented for redemption or protested in case of nonpayment.[3] The currency of Wisconsin continued to be for all practical purposes inconvertible.

The most glaring weakness in the banking system of Wisconsin, however, lay in the character of the securities which were required to be deposited with the State. The law called for bonds or stocks of the United States, or of some state, which should "be, or be made to be equal to a stock producing six per cent per annum."[4] The bank comptroller in 1860 observed:

> It is obvious that the safest bonds, viz: of states that are in the most prosperous financial condition, and relatively the least encumbered with

[1] *Ibid.*

[2] Wis. *Gen. Laws*, 1858, chap. 98.

[3] Wis. Bank Comptroller, *Report*, 1861, 7, 114–20; see also Governor Randall's annual message for 1860 in Wis. *Mess. and Docs.*, 1860, 9–10.

[4] Wis. *Rev. Statutes*, 1858, chap. 71, sec. 22.

debt, do not secure the highest rate of interest, and if liberal interest is paid on them they can not be bought at low prices. No banker, therefore, buys U. S., New England or New York bonds as security for his circulation, but mainly such as in fact are more or less depreciated, confiding in his own good luck and in the future development of the resources of States of which he has become the creditor. The law ought not to encourage speculating propensities in any person or persons engaged in banking business and jeopardize the future safety of our circulation. On six, seven and eight per cent paying bonds, the department, under the law, issues circulation up to the whole amount of their market value, on condition that they are below par, or in other words, provided that the ablest financiers of the country deem them unsafe, and are not willing to take them for the price at which they were issued; but bonds, on which those same financiers are willing to pay from one to ten per cent in advance of the sum, for which they were originally issued, in fact such bonds or stocks as would be an eminently safe basis for our circulation, the Comptroller refuses, under the law, to take at market value, discriminating against the best and in favor of the poorest kind of securities. It would seem more reasonable, if the Comptroller had been forbidden to take 6 or 7 per cent bearing stock, which stands below par, at market price, and if he had been ordered to take, at market price, such only as are at or above par. As the law stands we effectually encourage the bankers to buy as security the least safe class of bonds or stocks, and put obstacles in the way of purchasing the best. The banker, for instance, who has deposited Missouri 6 per cent bonds not only expects to earn two per cent per annum [in interest] more on the securities deposited, than he who has secured his circulation with Illinois', Michigan's or Indiana's, but the Missouri man gets circulation for the whole value of his bonds while, for instance, the holder of Illinois and Michigan bonds receives only 100 circulation on bonds he can sell at any time for 105.[1]

Southern states, particularly Missouri, Virginia, Tennessee, North Carolina, and Louisiana, were at this time heavily in debt. Their bonds, which paid high interest, ranged in varying degrees below par. These were the securities that the bankers of Wisconsin deposited with the State, and these formed the basis of Wisconsin's circulation. On Jan. 1, 1860, of the $5,133,565 banking securities deposited with the comptroller, $3,658,000 were in the bonds of the five southern states noted above. Missouri alone

[1] Wis. Bank Comptroller, *Report*, 1860, 7.

furnished $2,049,000 of the total,[1] of which Governor Randall declared in his first message to the legislature, "while a few operators in Wall Street may give them a fictitious value as a banking basis, it is believed that were the demand created for [them by] banking in Illinois and Wisconsin to cease, they would sink at once far below the rates at which they are received on deposit as security for our bank circulation."[2]

The few citizens in Wisconsin who knew of this dangerous situation were lulled into a sense of false security by a provision in the State law requiring each banker to guarantee by personal bondsmen one-fourth of his total outstanding currency.[3] This would, indeed, have furnished a measure of protection if the law had been rigorously enforced. Unfortunately Wisconsin bank comptrollers did not inquire carefully into the character or standing of the bondsmen, and the latter, in times of emergency, frequently turned out to be irresponsible.

Amid these manifold weaknesses there was one important element of strength. This was the Wisconsin Bankers' Association, established in Milwaukee on Sept. 8, 1858, during the height of industrial depression.[4] The purpose for which it was organized was to compel wildcat banks, located in inaccessible places, to redeem their currency at a central seat of exchange. Composed of many of the ablest bankers in Wisconsin, its early policies were shaped to a

[1] Tennessee furnished $750,000, North Carolina, $403,500, Virginia, $240,600, and Louisiana, $153,500.

[2] Wis. *Mess. and Docs.*, 1858, 21.

[3] Wis. *Rev. Statutes*, chap. 71, secs. 33–37.

[4] Milwaukee *Sentinel*, Sept. 9 and 10, 1858. For proceedings which led to the organization of the Association see *ibid.*, Aug. 7, 1857.

considerable degree by Alexander Mitchell, its first president and the greatest pioneer financier in the State. Throughout the critical years of the Civil War it exercised over Wisconsin banks a conservative and salutary influence.

Prior to 1860 the bonds of southern states were not likely to become dangerously impaired in value except during industrial disturbances. They had occasioned bankers in Wisconsin some embarrassment in the panic of 1857, but the losses had not been sufficiently severe to bring discredit upon the State currency, and therefore no public feeling existed against them. In January, 1860, when industrial conditions were again nearly normal, Missouri bonds were worth 80 cents on the dollar; Tennessee, 86; Virginia, 91; North Carolina, 94; and Louisiana, 94.[1]

During the autumn of 1860 the slavery controversy injected a new element of danger into the employment of southern bonds. Lincoln, it was evident, would be elected. The slave states freely threatened in that event to leave the Union. As a result the value of their securities underwent a general decline. The bank comptroller of Wisconsin in 1860 found it necessary to forbid the further deposit of Missouri bonds and to restrict, also, those of Tennessee and Virginia.[2] On October 15, three weeks before the day of election, he was obliged to issue a depreciation levy of 2 per cent against all Missouri securities in his possession.[3] The sectional dispute was merely intensified by the success of the Republican party

[1] See New York daily press for January, 1860.

[2] Wis. Bank Comptroller, *Report*, 1860, 3; Milwaukee Chamber of Commerce, *Report*, 1860, 47.

[3] *Id.*, 1861, 4.

at the polls, and by the end of November, Missouri bonds were worth only 68 cents on the dollar; Tennessee, 74; Virginia, 77; and North Carolina, 79.[1] A second time the comptroller was obliged to issue a depreciation call, and still the decline continued.[2]

The difficulty passed beyond the control of State authorities in the spring of 1861, when secession became an established fact and the hostile sections prepared for war. Early in February the bank comptroller deemed it imperative to issue a third depreciation levy, heavier than any of the preceding, upon southern securities. The State legislature, however, intervened. On February 15 it authorized a postponement of the call, notwithstanding the banking code specifically forbade such delay.[3] "Many well informed citizens," wrote the comptroller, "had declared that a general failure, involving three-fourths of all the banks, was imminent, unless relief in some shape was granted; and there is scarcely any occasion for doubt but at least eighty out of the one hundred and nine then existing banks would have failed, entailing an immense loss on the currency, and probably on the deposits of the people."[4]

No mere temporary forbearance, however, could long hold intact the tottering financial system of the State. On April 2 the comptroller issued the postponed levy and thirteen banks failed to respond.[5] On April 4 the bankers of Chicago threw out the notes of forty of the 109 Wisconsin institutions, and a

[1] New York daily press for period mentioned.

[2] Wis. Bank Comptroller, *Report*, 1861, 4.

[3] Wis. *Sen. Jour.*, 1861, 225.

[4] Wis. Bank Comptroller, *Report*, 1861, 5.

[5] *Ibid.*, 5–6.

number of leading merchants in the Illinois metropolis refused to accept any Wisconsin currency.[1] On the following day the Milwaukee bankers, with the approval of the executive committee of the State Bankers' Association, refused to receive the notes of twenty of the establishments thrown out in Chicago. Approximately $1,000,000 of Wisconsin paper money was thereby completely discredited.[2] On April 13 came the news of the bombardment of Fort Sumter. A week later the bonds of Missouri had fallen to 39½, of Virginia to 36, of Tennessee to 41, and of North Carolina to 45.[3] The currency of the discredited Badger banks went begging about the streets of Milwaukee at 50 cents on the dollar.[4] Never had the State experienced such a collapse as this.

The legislature again interposed, and again the relief which it granted was contrary to the State constitution. On April 17 it passed an act that amounted to suspension of specie payments.[5] Since the basic law of Wisconsin stood in the way of such a change the legislature was compelled to accomplish its object by indirection. It ordered the comptroller to suspend action during the succeeding seven months against institutions that might fail to redeem their bank notes; it prohibited notaries public from pro-

[1] Milwaukee *Sentinel*, April 7, 1861; Green Bay *Advocate*, April 11, 1861. An excellent account is found in Conard, *History of Milwaukee*, 268–69.

[2] Milwaukee *Sentinel*, April 7, 8, and 9, 1861; Milwaukee *Daily Wis.*, April 16, 1861; Wis. Bank Comptroller, *Report*, 1860, 11–26. One of the twenty, the State Stock Bank of Eau Claire, was at first placed on probation, and was published in the discredited list only after it had failed to make good its securities. Three banks had failed previous to April 8, with a total circulation of approximately $250,000.

[3] See financial columns of New York daily press.

[4] See financial columns of Milwaukee daily press.

[5] Wis. *Gen. Laws*, 1861, chap. 308.

testing such money until December 1; and gave banks until that time to answer complaints in any proceedings brought to compel specie payments.

The only practicable test of the solvency of banks in Wisconsin had now disappeared. Confusion and uncertainty intensified the existing crisis. At length the Bankers' Association was compelled to summon a special convention of its members to meet at Milwaukee. The commercial editor of the Milwaukee *Sentinel* on the night of April 25 reported:

> We doubt if such a day as this has ever been witnessed in the money market. Ever since Tuesday it has been known that a convention of bankers would be held here tonight, and it was generally supposed that the meeting would take action in regard to the issues of banks heretofore in good standing. * * * All was feverish excitement, business on Change was brought to a standstill, nobody wanted to touch any currency. * * * Large numbers thronged the stores to purchase, but merchants wanted to do no business, and many went so far as to close their stores entirely. Men rushed about the street to pay some debt, which otherwise they would never have thought of; but every one was willing to trust for anything; in fact, the whole city could have been bought on time, and very long time at that.

As was anticipated, the convention threw out eighteen banks in addition to the twenty-three previously discredited. The paper money of these institutions, amounting to about $800,000, immediately sank from par to 50 cents.[1] Altogether approximately $2,000,000 of Wisconsin's wildcat currency thus dropped into complete discredit at the first sign of the Civil War.

The convention did not permit the weeding out of this unstable money to absorb its entire energy, however. It at once set to work to restore public

[1] Milwaukee *Sentinel*, April 27, 1861, and the succeeding issues. One of the eighteen, the Beloit Savings Bank, had also been in the list thrown out on April 5.

confidence in the remainder. It issued a sweeping statement to the people of Wisconsin, guaranteeing the notes of the seventy banks still in good standing. Each member of the Association agreed to receive these notes at par until the date of the resumption of specie payment seven months hence.[1]

The pledge as a remedy was as dangerous as the crisis which called it forth. The currency of the seventy banks which it underwrote amounted to $2,150,000. More than half of this, if judged by the value of the securities upon which it was based, was worth not even 50 cents on the dollar. The greater part of the remainder ranged in varying degrees from 50 to 80 cents on the dollar. Only $166,220 was fully protected in the bank comptroller's office by par securities as the State law required.[2] However, the people of Wisconsin accepted the guarantee in good faith and the panic quickly subsided.

During the spring of 1861 the securities of seceded southern states continued steadily to decline. On June 3 the comptroller was compelled to issue a fourth levy against them, heavier than any that had preceded.[3] It was no cause for surprise or worry that the forty-one banks already discredited neglected to answer the summons. It was, however, a rude shock

[1] *Ibid.*, April 27, 1861. Fifty-five Wisconsin banks signed the agreement, among them all the Milwaukee banks save one.

[2] These valuations are based upon a statement furnished the State Senate by the bank comptroller on May 22, 1861. See Wis. *Sen. Jour.*, 1861, extra session, 35. The Bank Department held from each bank in addition to marketable securities the personal bonds of stockholders to a total amount of one-fourth its circulation. In almost every case, however, where banks were wound up by the comptroller these bonds proved to be worthless.

[3] Wis. Bank Comptroller, *Report*, 1861, 7.

when eighteen of the seventy institutions vouched for by the convention likewise failed to respond. Even more menacing was the fact that ten of the latter in rapid succession confessed their insolvency by closing their doors.

The guarantors of Wisconsin's currency were dismayed. For every discredited bill of the ten bankrupt banks, $355,000 in all,[1] they were required by the terms of their pledge to exchange dollar for dollar legal money of the United States. The burden thus unexpectedly thrown upon them was doubled, moreover, by bad faith on the part of many interior banks. Contrary to their agreement the latter secretly sorted the paper money that they received, hoarding the best and paying out only the poorest.

The Milwaukee banks, more than any others in the State, were endangered by this situation. Large note-receiving corporations such as railroads, with headquarters in the Cream City, deposited there all the suspicious currency which they gathered and demanded credit for it to its full face value.[2] It was springtime; the farmers were purchasing their supplies; all the doubtful notes in the State swiftly gravitated toward the metropolis. The bankers of Milwaukee faced a dilemma. Either they must permit themselves to be overwhelmed with deposits that upon the resumption of specie payments, if not sooner, would be worth but a fraction of the amount for which they had been received, or they must repudiate their pledge. They preferred the latter alternative.

[1] Compiled from the Wis. Bank Comptroller, *Report*, 1860, and the statement furnished to the Senate by the comptroller, *op. cit.*

[2] Milwaukee *Sentinel*, June 24, 1861.

On June 21 they met and agreed no longer to receive the notes of the ten suspended banks.[1]

The resolution was not published until the close of business on Saturday, June 22. The laboring men of Milwaukee in the meantime had been paid their week's wages largely in the notes of the ten discredited banks. They found when they reached their homes that their bills were no longer receivable except at a ruinous discount. They did not understand that a complicated banking system was responsible for their misfortune. They saw only that they had suddenly lost the fruits of their toil and that somehow the banks were to blame. It was freely charged, moreover, and with apparent truth, that some of the city banks had continued during Saturday to pay out over their counters the notes which they had previously resolved to proscribe.[2] The laborers, and particularly the Germans residing in the northwest section of the city, were ablaze with anger.

Trouble was brewing all day Sunday. On Monday morning an excited crowd assembled on the north side of the metropolis and, preceded by a band, marched to the business center. Arriving at the office of the Wisconsin Marine and Fire Insurance Company, the oldest and most prominent bank in the State, the procession was met by Alexander Mitchell accompanied by the mayor of Milwaukee. The two men attempted to gain a hearing but were hooted down by the now thoroughly lawless mob and Mitchell was forced to beat a hasty retreat. A riot

[1] *Ibid.*

[2] See *ibid.*, June 25–July 5, 1861; Conard, *History of Milwaukee*, 269.

was soon in full progress. The near-by banking offices were gutted, their broken furniture piled high in the adjacent streets and set on fire, and more serious consequences were averted only by the prompt arrival of troops.[1]

For a week Milwaukee remained in a state of feverish excitement. The farmers living in the outlying districts were reported to be aroused and preparing to invade the city for the purpose of wreaking new vengeance on its banks. On July 1 a procession of 500 agriculturists and laboring men, led by a mounted German who flourished a drawn sword "in a highly excited if not graceful manner," paraded the business center of the metropolis.[2] Only the presence of several scowling cannon stationed at the approaches of the banking section, and four companies of troops that had been hurried there, prevented further disturbances. Business in the meantime was prostrate. With the convention pledge repudiated it was impossible to tell from day to day what bank notes would next fall into disrepute.

It so happened that at this time the State government was engaged in an attempt to float a war loan of $1,200,000. The legislature had entrusted the matter to a board of loan commissioners, who in the spring of 1861 had journeyed to New York for that purpose. They had met with a cold reception.

[1] For a description of the riot see Milwaukee daily press for June 25, 1861 and issues immediately following; see also Conard, *History of Milwaukee*, 269. The banks had received sufficient warning to be able to hurry their valuables into vaults. Eventually the city of Milwaukee paid $3,000 to repair the damage done by the mob.

[2] Milwaukee *Sentinel*, July 2, 1861; Milwaukee *Daily Wis.*, July 1, 2, and 12, 1861.

The very best of securities in the panic months that marked the opening of the Civil War found difficult sale in the New York stock exchange. The bonds of the United States, for example, then sold for only 83 cents on the dollar.[1] State bonds, no matter how sound, could scarcely hope to bring as much.

Other difficulties of a local nature impeded the sale of the Wisconsin securities. The question of the constitutionality of the law authorizing the loan raised the issue whether the bonds would be binding against the State. Quite as embarrassing was the evil repute of Wisconsin in the Eastern money markets, the consequence of frequent attempts by her legislatures to relieve her railroad farm mortgagors from the payment of their debts, as well as the almost universal repudiation by cities, towns, and counties in the State of their railroad bond obligations.[2]

Governor Randall was determined, however, to negotiate the loan. To remove the constitutional uncertainty he adopted an unusual course. On June 4, 1861 he sent to the Wisconsin supreme court a communication requesting its views upon this point.[3] Ordinarily a law court will carefully refrain from expressing an opinion concerning a disputed statute until a case involving it is brought up for adjudication. In this crisis, however, the Wisconsin supreme court departed from the precedent. In an open letter to the governor it declared the act constitu-

[1] See open letter of State Treasurer S. D. Hastings entitled *The Specie and Currency Question and the State Treasury*, bound with *Wisconsin Miscellaneous Pamphlets*, X, No. 17, in Wisconsin Historical Library; *Wis. State Jour.*, May 30, 1865.

[2] *Ibid.*; see also *post*, chap. ix.

[3] Milwaukee *Sentinel*, June 8, 1861.

tionally sound and pronounced the bonds issued under it binding contracts with the State.[1] It was not so easy to overcome the other objections to the bonds, however, and the commissioners at length gave up the attempt to negotiate the loan in the East.

In the meantime Governor Randall had received from Alexander Mitchell, the great Milwaukee financier, a novel suggestion. He proposed that the war loan be made to answer the double purpose of raising money for the administration and protecting the currency of the State; that the bankers of Wisconsin be permitted to purchase the bonds upon easy terms, with the understanding that they would deposit them at once in the office of the bank comptroller in exchange for their depreciated Southern securities.[2] The plan had obvious advantages, and the loan commissioners gave it favorable consideration when they returned from their fruitless expedition to the East in the summer of 1861.

Negotiations between the State authorities and a committee composed for the most part of influential bankers of Milwaukee were soon in progress. By a strange coincidence the first formal conference took place on the very day when the Milwaukeeans secretly entered into their resolution to repudiate their convention pledge; the last meeting occurred one day after the memorable bank riot. It was under the shadow of the latter event that an agreement as to the sale of the bonds was eventually concluded.

[1] *Ibid.*

[2] Ms. letter of Alexander Mitchell to Governor Randall, May 18, 1861, in Wisconsin Historical Library.

The terms of the compact thus entered into were favorable to the bankers of the State, and on the whole satisfactory also to the public. The bankers agreed to purchase $800,000 of the Wisconsin bonds, to be paid for nominally at par. Seventy per cent of the purchase price was to be paid at once, of which three-fifths should be in coin or New York exchange and two-fifths in Wisconsin par currency. The remaining 30 per cent should be paid in regular installments within fifteen years. The State was to allow interest at 6 per cent not only upon the portion of the purchase price paid down, but upon that which remained to be paid. The bankers were to deposit the bonds with the comptroller in place of their depreciated securities and jointly agree to maintain at par until December 1 all the Wisconsin paper money then current.[1]

Originally the amount of bonds that the commissioners agreed to sell upon these terms was only $650,000. The sum was increased to $800,000, however, upon the promise of the bankers to take up and redeem at par the currency of the ten institutions rejected from the guaranteed list a few days before.[2]

The result of this transaction was a speedy return of financial tranquillity. Wisconsin bonds were substituted for southern in the comptroller's office as rapidly as was practicable,[3] and by the beginning

[1] The terms of sale were severely criticized by the enemies of the administration and in 1862 were made the subject of a legislative investigation. See Wis. *Assem. Jour.*, 1862, 1361–1536; Wisconsin State Treasurer, *Reports*, 1860–65; *Wis. Weekly State Jour.*, July 9, 1861; *Wis. State Jour.*, May 23, 1865.

[2] *Ibid.*

[3] The bonds of seceded and border states in the hands of the bank comptroller on Jan. 1, 1862 amounted to $469,500, somewhat less than

of September, 1861 the securities of sixty of the seventy current banks of the State were at or above par.[1] The bankers' committee with the aid of the merchants of Milwaukee gathered a fund of $100,000, with which it gradually redeemed the currency of the ten discredited banks.[2] Unhappily this operated chiefly to the advantage of "money shavers," who had purchased the notes from laborers and farmers at merely nominal prices when the panic was at its worst. It has been estimated that the people of Wisconsin lost approximately a million dollars in the financial tangles that marked the spring of 1861.[3]

The history of Wisconsin banking during the remainder of the Civil War was highly creditable, due in large measure to the influence of the State Bankers' Association. When this body assembled in Milwaukee for its third annual convention on Sept. 19, 1861, most of the financial institutions of Wisconsin for the first time in many years were in a thoroughly sound condition. The Association felt sufficiently confident of its strength to adopt a resolution urging every bank in the State to resume specie payments voluntarily on October 15, a month and a half before the date set for redemption by the legislature. As a

one-fifth of the total securities. Of this amount $198,500 was in bonds of seceded states and the remainder in bonds of Missouri and Kentucky.

[1] While the crisis of 1861 was at its height the bank comptroller was directed to publish in the *Wisconsin State Journal* at the beginning of each month a statement showing the condition of all the banks in the State. From these statements, which continued to appear until Feb. 1, 1869, the value of securities has been compiled.

[2] Milwaukee Chamber of Commerce, *Report*, 1861, 33; Milwaukee *Sentinel*, July 1 and 2, 1861; Milwaukee *Daily Wis.*, July 1 and 2, 1861; Wis. Bank Comptroller, *Report*, 1861, 8; Conard, *History of Milwaukee*, 271.

[3] Estimate of State Treasurer S. D. Hastings in *Specie and Currency Question and the State Treasury.*

measure of precaution it decided to discountenance for the time being the organization of any new banks and to permit established institutions to increase their circulation only by special consent of its board of directors.[1] In commenting upon this excellent program of financial regulation the Milwaukee *Sentinel* on September 25 declared: "Although an act of the legislature exempts the banks from the obligation of redemption until Dec. 1st, here we have exchange actually down to par, and the money entering as freely into all business transactions of the State as if the banks redeemed in coin. A parallel for this we do not think can be found in the whole financial history of the West."

It is no easy matter for banks to return to a normal basis of redeeming their paper money after a prolonged period of freedom from that obligation. The public is impatient; as soon as the law has restored the right to exchange suspected notes for specie, people rush to do so. Upon the day set for redemption the doors of the banks are besieged by thousands of clamorous bill holders demanding gold or its equivalent for their paper. Unless the financial institutions are well prepared the stress is likely to force them into bankruptcy.

Such was the danger that on Dec. 1, 1861 awaited the bankers of Wisconsin. They might have avoided it had they followed the recommendation of the Association to return voluntarily to redemption. They had failed to make the effort, however, and the opportunity had passed. It became apparent, moreover, as the time for resumption approached, that

[1] Milwaukee *Sentinel*, Sept. 21, 1861.

some ten or a dozen banks were either indisposed or unable to prepare themselves properly for the crisis. Early in November, as a result, a spirit of nervous uncertainty again manifested itself in Wisconsin.

In Milwaukee on November 11 a rumor spread like wildfire that ten banks were about to be repudiated by the other institutions of the State. The report was entirely unfounded, originating in an unsigned circular distributed about the city apparently by unscrupulous speculators who hoped to buy good money at panic prices. Intense excitement among the laboring population of Milwaukee resulted, which increased when the circular received publication in the Chicago *Tribune* under the caption "More Trouble with Wisconsin Stumptail."[1] It at length became necessary to summon for counsel a special convention of the Bankers' Association.

This body proceeded to its task with characteristic vigor. Ignoring the Milwaukee excitement, it set itself to the important problem of preparing the State banks for the fateful day of resumption. To a committee of its members it delegated full powers to wind up whatever banks refused to make necessary provision for the impending crisis. The circulating currency of such institutions was at once to be retired, dollar for dollar, and whatever deficiency or expense arose in carrying out this program was to be met from the funds of the Association or the

[1] Chicago *Tribune*, Nov. 13, 1861. The Chicago newspapers were ever ready to publish damaging reports concerning Wisconsin currency and Milwaukee newspapers as ready to retaliate in kind. Each of these cities was wont to ascribe its monetary difficulties to the machinations of the other. Illinois suffered more severely than Wisconsin during the monetary crisis of 1861, 89 of her 110 banks going to the wall.

proceeds of an assessment levied upon every bank in the State.[1] Of banking such as this even the conservative East might well have been proud. For a frontier state like Wisconsin it was a truly remarkable achievement.

No less creditable was the manner in which the program was carried into operation. By an arrangement among the bankers of the State the notes of delinquent institutions were sorted out as fast as they came in and sent to the committee of the Association in Milwaukee. Here they were locked up, the committee issuing in exchange certificates of deposit bearing interest at 7 per cent. Four hundred thousand dollars of such money, more than one-sixth of all the current bank notes of Wisconsin, was thus safely stored away when the day of resumption came.[2]

The runs on banks, which accompanied resumption, were severe, in some instances, embarrassing. Their force was broken, however, by an agreement among the members of the Association not to assort against each other until the crisis was over.[3] This action and the careful preparation of the preceding weeks enabled every bank in the State to weather the storm with success. The year closed with public confidence in Wisconsin currency once more restored.

The cost of thus establishing the monetary system

[1] Milwaukee *Sentinel*, Nov. 18, 1861.

[2] *Ibid.*, Nov. 25 and Dec. 15, 1861; J. P. McGregor, "Banking in Wisconsin," in *History of Dodge County, Wisconsin*, 196; Conard, *History of Milwaukee*, 272. As soon as the crisis was over the Bankers' Association forced $200,000 of these doubtful notes into retirement.

[3] The danger of war with England at this time over the "Trent" affair was one factor that prolonged the crisis.

of the State upon a sound basis had been very heavy. Of the 110 banks in good standing at the beginning of the year forty had failed, four were in process of winding up by the Bankers' Association, and one had voluntarily surrendered its charter. Of the $4,580,832 bank notes current on January 1 there remained in circulation at the close of the year but $1,590,691.[1] As a result of this collapse business in Wisconsin, already distracted by the outbreak of the Civil War, received a blow from which it did not recover for almost two years.

The suffering which these difficulties imposed upon the people of Wisconsin stirred into new flame an old though dying prejudice against banks. Wherever losses had been severe, popular resentment found expression in largely attended anti-bank and hard-money meetings. In some localities there was agitation for an unconditional repeal of the entire banking law. The lead region gave vent to its dissatisfaction by actions as well as words. In the summer of 1861 its miners, farmers, and traders agreed no longer to accept in payment of their products anything but actual specie. During the remainder of the year while the State as a whole fretted and fumed over paper money, this mining community transacted its business almost entirely upon a gold basis.[2]

[1] The statistics for the beginning of 1861 are from Governor Randall's annual message in Wis. *Mess. and Docs.*, 1861, 6–7; those for the end of 1861 are from the monthly statement of the bank comptroller in *Wis. State Jour.*, Jan. 3, 1862. The total par currency of Wisconsin on Dec. 31, 1861 was $1,731,587, which included the issue of several banks established during the year.

[2] *Ibid.*, June 4, 1861; Correspondence from May 23 to July 10, 1861 in the Cyrus Woodman Letter-Press Manuscripts, Vol. II, in the Wisconsin Historical Library.

The crash of 1861 was a blessing to Wisconsin in the sense that it forced to immediate correction the manifold weaknesses in the currency code. By an almost unanimous referendum in the fall of 1861 a statute was adopted which assured for the future proper restrictions upon banks of issue. It provided that no bonds except those of the state of Wisconsin or the national government should thenceforth be received as security for paper money. Each bank was required to have in addition to its securities a bona fide cash capital of at least $15,000. The volume of currency which any institution might issue was rigidly limited to three times the amount of its capital actually paid in. Every bank in the State was required to maintain at Milwaukee or Madison an agent authorized at all times to redeem its paper.[1] Thus in law as well as in practice Wisconsin banking was established upon firm ground.

A number of irresponsible bankers in the State rebelled against what they regarded as the unnecessarily stringent requirements of the new law. In the legislative session of 1862 they attempted to secure once more the suspension of specie payments. In justification of their stand they pointed to the fact that New York banks had ceased to redeem late in 1861, that the Federal government had immediately followed suit, and that suspension had thereafter become general throughout the North. They proceeded to draw up and introduce into the legislature a bill, ingeniously worded so as to accomplish their

[1] The law was enacted on April 13, 1861, amended in the extra session of 1861, and submitted to the people of the State for approval at the regular November election. See Wis. *Gen. Laws*, 1861, chap. 242.

ends without openly violating the State constitution. The measure as framed permitted bankers to redeem their notes in drafts on the protested banks of New York City; allowed them one year within which to answer complaints of bill holders; prohibited notaries public from protesting State currency; and impeded in other ways, well known to any representative stay law of the western frontier, the proper enforcement of the banking code.[1] The bill was passed in the Senate despite an opinion of the attorney-general of the State pronouncing it unconstitutional.[2] In the Assembly, however, where the experiences of the preceding year were not yet forgotten, it was decisively defeated.

During 1862 State authorities carefully enforced the new monetary code, and the Bankers' Association continued to exert its influence against undue expansion. The volume of State circulation increased only $697,000, the total being still at the end of the year $2,000,000 short of the amount current on Jan. 1, 1860.[3] "Indeed," complained the commercial editor of the Milwaukee *Sentinel* early in 1862, "if it were not for the fact that large amounts of Eastern and Canadian capital have been invested here in the purchase of produce and provisions, business would be virtually suspended. As it is, our markets are not unfrequently brought to a stand through the difficulty

[1] The bill is printed and vigorously denounced in a minority report of the Assembly committee on banking in Wis. *Assem. Jour.*, 1862, 234–40. In its objects and methods the measure was strikingly similar to the farm-mortgage stay laws which at this time were receiving the attention of the Wisconsin supreme court. See also *ibid.*, 585–87.

[2] For the opinion of the attorney-general see *ibid.*

[3] *Wis. State Jour.*, Jan. 5, 1863.

of raising money even on the best kind of business paper."[1]

In the autumn of 1862 the nation recovered from the industrial prostration of 1861, and during the following year set out upon an era of expansion such as it had never seen before. New enterprises of every kind sprang into vigorous life; old ones became infused with new energy. Increasing business demanded a growing currency, and State banks throughout the North eagerly responded to the opportunity. Under similar circumstances in the preceding decade wildcat inflation had gained an easy entrance into Wisconsin. That the same conditions did not prevail in 1863 was due largely to the influence of the State Bankers' Association.

This organization on Feb. 3, 1863 outlined a monetary program for the State that constituted a remarkable departure in western banking.[2] Reflecting a spirit of conservatism and a willingness to coöperate with legal authorities, it was in striking contrast to the monetary heresies and impatience with government restraint that characterized most frontier finance at this time. The Association agreed to reject the notes of any bank thenceforth established in the State without its consent. It forbade existing institutions to add to their circulation except by permission of its board of directors. Those that attempted to violate this provision were at once to be compelled to wind up their affairs. The directors of the Association were ordered to scrutinize carefully the condition and character of all banks in the State, and if

[1] Milwaukee *Sentinel*, Jan. 27, 1862.
[2] *Ibid.*, Feb. 5, 1863.

any were found to be so unstable as to constitute a menace to the public in time of financial trouble they were to be wound up without delay. If there were still in the State any institutions that had no regular office or that transacted no local business, but were exclusively banks of circulation, they were to be dealt with summarily. Whenever it was deemed advisable for any of these reasons to close a bank the members of the Association were to be informed, and they were to assort and send to Milwaukee whatever paper money of the institution they received, in order that it might be presented for protest all at once.

This vigorous program was carefully enforced, and Wisconsin circulation increased but $131,495 during the entire year 1863.[1] In the meantime the United States government, compelled by its necessities to issue enormous quantities of greenbacks, supplied trade with all the money needed for legitimate expansion. Thus on the one hand industry advanced unrestricted, and on the other the character of Wisconsin's circulation was maintained at a high level.

In the same month that the Wisconsin Bankers' Association adopted its restrictive currency program Congress enacted the National Banking Law.[2] This statute was one of the most notable accomplishments resulting from the Civil War. Undoubtedly it constituted the greatest monetary reform that the country had seen since the days of the United States Bank. It

[1] *Wis. State Jour.*, Jan. 6, 1864.

[2] U. S. *Statutes at Large*, 37 Cong., 3 sess., chap. 58, Feb. 25, 1863; *ibid.*, 38 Cong., 1 sess., chap. 106, June 3, 1864. Compare this account with that of Fite, *Social and Industrial Conditions*, 115–17, in which different conclusions are reached. See also U. S. Secretary of Treasury, *Report*, 1864, 46–55.

substituted a central authority, a uniform security, and a fixed type of national bank note for the multitudinous species of easily counterfeited and but locally accepted state notes, the widely varying forms of state security, and the many conflicting state jurisdictions. It corrected every prominent evil of the old state currency system from which the West, and to a less extent the East, had suffered so long and so grievously.

Important though this measure was, for two years it attracted almost no notice in Wisconsin. Popular attention was directed to southern battle-fields; business men already had a satisfactory national currency in the Federal greenbacks; and confidence in the paper money of the State had been restored. Moreover, the law was merely permissive. It did not undertake to force bankers issuing currency under state charters to come within its provisions, and the inducements it held out proved insufficient to win voluntary converts in large numbers either in Wisconsin or in other parts of the Union. Even when, on June 30, 1864, Congress inaugurated a policy of mild favoritism to national banks[1] it won few proselytes. By the end of 1864 only fifteen Wisconsin institutions had availed themselves of the privilege of national incorporation.[2]

If Wisconsin bankers were unusually reluctant to transfer their allegiance to the national government it was because they labored under special difficulties. The Federal law required institutions seeking national charters to deposit United States bonds exclusively as security for circulation. Wisconsin bankers,

[1] U. S. *Statutes at Large*, 38 Cong., 1 sess., chap. 173, sec. 110, June 30, 1864.
[2] U. S. Secretary of Treasury, *Report*, 1864, 46.

unfortunately, were loaded down with the securities of their own State, purchased during the crisis of 1861. These they could not dispose of except at a heavy loss. The same objections which had prevented their sale in the open market in 1861 still militated against them. The bankers of the State, with their means tied up in unsalable bonds, were thus unable, even had they desired, to fulfill the demands of Federal incorporation.

Congress was determined, however, to establish the national banking system. On Mar. 3, 1865 it passed a law so drastic in its discrimination against the currency of state banks as practically to drive the latter out of existence.[1] Wisconsin bankers were thereby left without a choice. To retire their circulation, dispose of their securities upon the best terms obtainable, and reorganize under national charters was the only course left open to them.

This situation was fraught with peril for bill holders as well as bankers of the State. It was likely that weak institutions, crippled by the losses they would suffer in disposing of their Wisconsin securities in an unfavorable market, would be unable to redeem their paper money, and thus would subject the people of the State to the same bitter experiences that had marked the beginning of the war. To further complicate the difficulty, as the result of the near approach of peace the country was already in a state of depression, with the stock and bond market on the verge of actual panic.

Under such circumstances the mere fear of a crisis was sufficient to precipitate one. A few days

[1] U. S. *Statutes at Large*, 38 Cong., 2 sess., chap. 78, secs. 6 and 7, Mar. 3, 1865.

after the Federal tax measure was passed, two Milwaukee banks, which had already secured national charters, announced to their city associates their determination no longer to receive Wisconsin currency except upon special conditions. The nine remaining city banks, after a day's hesitation, felt compelled to adopt the same course. On March 10 they made public a resolution expressing their hope that the legislature then in session would provide for the safety of the State bonds, but declared themselves unable thenceforth to accept any currency except Federal greenbacks and national bank notes.[1] At once a sharp financial panic swept over the State. The notes of a number of banks ceased for a time to circulate, while even the best were sacrificed to brokers at a discount of 25 to 40 per cent.

The loss again fell largely upon the poorer classes whose needs or fears led them to dispose of their currency to "rag speculators" at ruinous prices.[2] on March 13 the Milwaukee *Sentinel* reported: "The laboring classes, who are not posted in such matters, and who hold small amounts which enter into their daily necessities, have been thronging the banks and broker shops, since the notice, changing and disposing of everything bearing the semblance of Wisconsin money, at any rate which the brokers choose to demand. Advice has been tendered them

[1] Milwaukee *Sentinel*, Mar. 10, 1865.

[2] See proclamation of Mayor Kirby of Milwaukee in *ibid.*, Mar. 13, 1865, warning the public against selling their currency to brokers and money sharpers. See also Appleton *Crescent*, Mar. 18, 1865; La Crosse *Democrat*, Mar. 13, 1865; Oshkosh *Northwestern*, Mar. 16, 1865; *Wis. State Jour.*, Mar. 21, 1865; Green Bay *Advocate*, Mar. 16, 1865; Milwaukee *Sentinel*, Mar. 11 to Mar. 25, 1865.

from every quarter to prevent such sacrifices, but in vain." "We have seen, for several days, in the banks of the city," observed the Green Bay *Advocate* on March 16, "crowds of poor men and women anxiously pressing up to the counters to get something in exchange for their little rolls of Wisconsin money, which they had been hoarding up as safe, and as some believed safer than greenbacks." The Milwaukee *Sentinel* found a touch of grim humor in the situation: "As the most of our retail merchants took the currency at par, it was amusing to see the raids upon the dry goods dealers by the ladies on Saturday afternoon. Husbands were never half so willing to furnish their wives with pocket money, for almost all had some few bank notes in their pockets, which knew not whether their redeemer liveth. Therefore, the way the silks and poplins, jaconets and alpacas, delaines and organdies, gaiters and balmorals had to come down from the shelves was a caution."[1] The excitement ran its course in about a week, after which calmer counsel prevailed and conditions gradually became normal.

The panic, according to the press of Wisconsin, was a wholly unnecessary calamity. The bankers of Milwaukee who had precipitated it were denounced by the entire State.[2] They on their part issued a public statement shifting all responsibility upon the two national institutions of the city.[3] The latter

[1] *Ibid.*, Mar. 14, 1865.

[2] It was charged in some quarters, though apparently without foundation, that the Milwaukee bankers had deliberately brought about the panic in order to force favorable action on the so-called Insurance Act then under consideration by the legislature. See *post*, 218.

[3] Milwaukee *Sentinel*, Mar. 14, 1865.

shortly after came in for a severe arraignment at the hands of the Bankers' Association.[1] It was recognized, however, that unless the legislature at once safeguarded the bonds of the State and the currency predicated upon them a crisis of even larger proportions might at any moment arise.

The legislature moved promptly and effectively. On March 16, while excitement was still at a high pitch, it adopted a sweeping resolution pledging the people of Wisconsin to sustain their bonds unimpaired. As for the currency, it promised that provision would shortly be made to maintain it safe from any loss. "We will not hesitate, if necessary," declared the legislators, "to impose such tax or taxes for that object as shall speedily result in absorbing that currency, and retiring all the State bonds that are likely to be thrown upon the market."[2]

This vigorous legislative pledge was wholly fulfilled. Within a few weeks after it was adopted a law was enacted empowering the State treasurer to accept at par any Wisconsin bank notes that had been current prior to the panic and to issue therefor certificates of deposit bearing interest for the remainder of the year at 7 per cent. The same official was authorized to receive and retire the currency of any Wisconsin bank that failed to redeem it, canceling on the part of the State the bonds that the comptroller held as security.[3]

[1] *Ibid.*, Mar. 18, 1865.

[2] Wis. *Gen. Laws*, 1865, Joint Resolution, No. 7, 688.

[3] *Ibid.*, chap. 282. The act was severely criticized by the opponents of the administration. Under its provisions twenty-one banks assigned their bonds to the state treasurer and had their circulation, amounting to about $600,000, retired by him. According to the bank comptroller these

Quite as effective as this was the program adopted for protecting the State bonds. It consisted in creating a market wherein the latter could be sold at par. This had already been accomplished in part by the legislature of 1864, which had directed the Commissioners of School and University Lands to invest the trust funds of the State in such securities.[1] It was supplemented on April 11, 1865 by a statute directing all insurance companies in Wisconsin to deposit with the State treasurer as surety State bonds to an amount corresponding to their total business for the previous year.[2]

With Wisconsin bonds and currency thus carefully safeguarded the conversion of State into national banking institutions proceeded rapidly and easily. Indeed, by the end of 1865 only nineteen banks still did business under Wisconsin charters.[3] By 1866 the amount of State currency in circulation was so small that the banks were encouraged by the legislature to complete its retirement,[4] and, this having

banks would have been wound up but for this act, and their circulation redeemed at considerably less than par. See Wis. Bank Comptroller, *Report*, 1869, 5–6.

[1] *Id.*, 1864, chap. 217. Ultimately the greater part of the State bonds were absorbed by the Commissioners of School and University Lands.

[2] *Id.*, 1865, chap. 320. Alexander Mitchell is credited with having suggested the measure. The sixty-six insurance companies in the State vigorously fought its passage, protesting that it had no other object than to unload upon them bonds that had been purchased below par and were still worth less than par in the open market. Their position appears to have been well taken. Eventually thirty-one complied with the law, depositing Wisconsin bonds to the amount of $366,000. The remainder gave up their business in the State. In 1866, when the banking crisis was over, the measure was repealed. See letter of S. D. Hastings in *Wis. State Jour.*, May 22, 1865; also *ibid.*, Mar. 30 and 31, and April 4, 1865.

[3] *Ibid.*, Jan. 2, 1866.

[4] Wis. *Gen. Laws*, 1866, chap. 143. After 1867 the State banks remaining in operation devoted themselves exclusively to the business of loans and discounts.

shortly been accomplished, in 1868 the office of bank comptroller was abolished.

Thus came to an end the first era in the history of Wisconsin banking. The experiences of the State during that period had been unusual. From 1852, when the banking code was adopted, until the year of southern secession the bill holders of the Badger banks had not suffered a dollar of direct loss. Wildcat practices had, however, undermined the system, leading to its immediate collapse upon the outbreak of the Civil War. For a time during the summer of 1861 utter confusion prevailed, in which bankers and public suffered alike. The general derangement, however, gave to the Wisconsin Bankers' Association an opportunity to build up and extend its power, and during the critical years of the war this organization exerted in monetary matters a potent influence for intelligent conservatism. Finally, with the close of the war came to an abrupt end the interesting story of the early experiment of Wisconsin with State currency, and her entrance upon the Federal system which has persisted to the present day.

CHAPTER VIII

TRADE

The merchants of Wisconsin were by no means content to rest from their labors when they had gathered for export the surplus products of the granaries, lead mines, and pine forests of the region west of Lake Michigan. Pioneers of whatever vocation needed groceries, clothing, hardware, machinery, and the thousand and one commodities that enter into a general retail and jobbing trade. To distribute among western consumers the merchandise purchased in the East or manufactured at home was an industry in itself. It gave employment to every city and village in the State.

Foremost among the wholesale and jobbing centers of Wisconsin was Milwaukee. Favored by excellent railroad connections, her markets extended not only over Wisconsin but Minnesota, northern Iowa, and northern Illinois. Wherever she drew her exports she also sold her merchandise. Thousands of westward-bound immigrants carried her wares with them. During the sixties and seventies she was one of the greatest outfitting centers in the Northwest.

Not only Milwaukee but every lake port, railroad center, river town, and pinery hamlet in the State in its relations with producers was as eager to sell as to buy. Because of lack of transportation facilities few of them possessed more than a local trade. Green

Bay enjoyed a lucrative commerce by wagon with a wide territory, including the Lake Superior mineral region and pinery districts as far west as the Wisconsin River. She attained also a considerable local prominence as an immigrant outfitting center for northeastern Wisconsin. Eau Claire, at the head of navigation on the Chippewa River, was a well-known lumber-supply town. La Crosse during the later sixties was one of the most prominent steamboat entrepôts on the upper Mississippi, and as an immigrant station for northwestern Wisconsin and eastern Minnesota occupied a position much like that of Green Bay for northeastern Wisconsin. Similarly, as a commissary for the pineries of the Black River, La Crosse followed in the footsteps of Eau Claire. Racine and Kenosha, having railroad connections with the interior, enjoyed something of a jobbing trade in southern Wisconsin and northern Illinois. The reach of all of these cities, however, was small compared with that of the State metropolis.

The extensive trade of interior Wisconsin, Minnesota, and northern Iowa was a prize that brought Milwaukee into keen competition with Chicago, St. Louis, and Dubuque. It led also to vigorous rivalry with the great commercial centers of the East. Country merchants at this time still clung to some extent to the policy of making annual pilgrimages to the seaboard to lay in their season's stock of goods, a practice vigorously assailed by jobbers in the West. Thus on every hand were fought the peaceful skirmishes and battles of trade. Milwaukee modestly laid claim to affording interior purchasers as large a choice of merchandise and as liberal terms of payment as any wholesale center in the entire country, and her board of trade in 1863 boasted that three-fourths of all the goods consumed in the region west and northwest of her passed through her jobbing houses.[1]

The panic of 1857 fairly overwhelmed Wisconsin traders and merchants. During the prosperous years preceding it they had been more than ordinarily reckless in extending credits and assuming liabilities. The crash caught them wholly off their guard. A large number failed outright; hundreds of others warded off bankruptcy only because of the forbearance of creditors. Universal depression followed the year of crisis, during which enterprise of almost every description came to a halt.

Not only was business prostration exceedingly acute in Wisconsin but it endured longer than in other parts of the country. A succession of poor crops followed the fateful autumn of 1857. Farmers, lumbermen, and miners were quite unable to buy supplies. Some purchased but neglected to meet their bills, and merchants as a result sank ever deeper into the mire of indebtedness. Although commercial failures in the North as a whole decreased after 1857, in Wisconsin they became more numerous. The total liabilities of bankrupts for the entire North sank from $265,810,000 in 1857 to $73,600,000 in 1858. In Wisconsin, on the contrary, they rose from $1,625,000 in 1857 to $2,750,000 in 1858.[2] In 1859 they fell to $1,655,000, but in 1860 as a result of banking

[1] Milwaukee Chamber of Commerce, *Report*, 1863, 4.

[2] These figures are from R. G. Dun & Company's Annual Circular published in the leading daily papers of the country at the beginning of each year. See New York *Herald*, Jan. 6, 1860, Jan. 1, 1863, and Jan. 5, 1865.

difficulties and threats of secession they again rose to $2,050,000.[1]

The war cloud burst in 1861. Southern merchants promptly repudiated northern debts amounting to approximately $300,000,000. Uncertainty as to the course of the war, the sudden readjustments that the conflict necessitated in every walk of life, and the collapse of state banking systems throughout the country completed the general derangement. Commercial failures in the northern states in 1861 numbered 5,935; the liabilities which they involved amounted to $178,632,000.[2] Almost as disastrous as the panic of 1857 was that of 1861.

From this second great crisis Wisconsin was not exempt. Any general business disturbance in the North was certain to be felt here. However, the merchants of Wisconsin suffered less than did those in the East. A simple agricultural community, few of her business men excepting her bankers had formed commercial ties with the slaveholding states. The repudiation of Confederate debts and the interruption of southern commerce harmed her only indirectly. The farmers of Wisconsin, moreover, in the preceding autumn had garnered the greatest grain crop in her history; they could again purchase supplies and pay for them. Although the liabilities of bankrupts in the North as a whole in 1861 were three times those of 1860 the losses upon the ledgers of Wisconsin rose only from $2,050,000 to $2,675,000.[3]

Almost immune from the depression of 1861 were

[1] *Ibid.*
[2] *Ibid.*
[3] *Ibid.*

those railroad cities of Wisconsin which at the outbreak of the war gained the diverted commerce of the Mississippi River. Milwaukee between 1860 and 1861 found the number of her commercial failures actually decreasing; their total liabilities fell from $753,321 to $537,204.[1] "While we hear of prostration of business in nearly all other sections of the country," observed the Milwaukee *Sentinel* in the autumn of 1861, "we certainly cannot reasonably complain that any such state of things exists here. Even with the drawback of currency, which, better than that of many other states, is still not as good as specie, business here is decidedly active and good. The heavily loaded trains bringing grain do not return empty, but take goods into the country, corresponding to a great extent with the values they bring in."[2] "The statistics show," boasted the Milwaukee Chamber of Commerce in 1862, "that last year mercantile failures in this city, have been fewer and for a less amount than in any other city in the Union, in proportion to population and business."[3]

From the railroad terminal, La Crosse, at the opposite end of the State came the same report at the close of 1861:

> Notwithstanding the cry of hard times, business in La Crosse has steadily and rapidly improved since last year, when our list [of business firms] was but little over one-half the size as now. Business of all kinds, except shaving notes, is better, and money is more plenty. The merchants of the city show us from their cash sales, that trade is, on an average, fully one hundred per cent better this season than last, while the wholesale trade of the city has wonderfully increased.
>
> * * * * * * * *

[1] *Ibid.*

[2] Milwaukee *Sentinel*, June 4, 1861.

[3] Milwaukee Chamber of Commerce, *Report*, 1862, 5.

> From the freight books at the depot of the La Crosse and Milwaukee Railroad, in this city, we learn by actual figures, that there has arrived here for the merchants of this city, one hundred and sixty-five and a half per cent more goods during the year 1861 than for any previous year.[1]

Fortunately throughout the North recovery from the panic of 1861 was rapid. By the summer of 1862 the nation was ready for a new era of expansion. Greenback money became plentiful, prices rose correspondingly, and tradesmen once more found purchasers for their wares. Losses by bankruptcy in Wisconsin fell in 1862 to one-fifth the amount sustained in 1861, and thereafter practically disappeared.[2] Farmers, lumbermen, and miners, who for five years had bought only the bare necessities of life, unloosed their purse strings for a few of the amenities. Stocks of merchandise rose in value from one day to the next, yet purchasers paid the enhanced prices without a murmur. Never did Wisconsin tradesmen find easier or more lucrative sale for their wares than during the years 1863 to 1867.

Profits of merchants and business men increased with a rapidity that satisfied the most grasping. In Milwaukee between 1863 and 1864 the number of persons whose incomes exceeded $10,000 rose from 44 to 83.[3] Speculation flourished under the stimulus of rising prices. John Plankinton, who in 1864 headed the list of Milwaukee's successful merchants with an income of $104,100, won the largest part of it by fortunate investments in wool.[4] All the les-

[1] La Crosse *Democrat*, Dec. 20, 1861.

[2] New York *Herald*, Jan. 1, 1863, Jan. 1, 1864, and Jan. 5, 1865.

[3] Milwaukee *Sentinel*, Aug. 7, 1865. For the incomes for 1865 see *ibid.*, July 31, 1866.

[4] *Ibid.*

sons of caution that two successive panics had taught were forgotten in the universal spirit of good feeling.

A conspicuous evidence of this prosperity was the renewal of building operations in the cities of Wisconsin. Residences, offices, and stores rose from the ground almost over night. In the smaller towns buildings in process of construction were numbered by the hundred, in Milwaukee by the thousand.[1] Local newspaper items like the following from the La Crosse *Democrat* were of common occurrence: "The growth of our city this season is surprisingly large, and very gratifying. Since the first of April [1862] over *two hundred* buildings, of various kinds have been erected."[2] "On every principal street in the city can be seen signs of building. Huge piles of brick. Men busy dressing out stone. Old wooden tenements walking off lively to make room for more substantial business houses."[3]

Public improvements, though somewhat restricted by the financial burdens of the war, by no means came to an entire halt. Throughout the course of the southern conflict the state government continued to press forward the building of its beautiful new capitol. In numerous localities courthouses, churches, and railroad stations were under construction. Much-needed bridges and miles of new city sidewalks rendered business intercourse more safe and pleasant. Streets, though remaining on the whole very bad, were here and there macadamized or covered with

[1] In 1866 Milwaukee erected 1,233 buildings at a cost of $2,467,500; in 1867, 1,388 at a cost of $3,034, 295; in 1868, 1,293 at a cost of $2,583,710. Milwaukee Chamber of Commerce, *Report*, 1868, 9.

[2] La Crosse *Democrat*, Nov. 18, 1862.

[3] *Ibid.*, Mar. 17, 1863.

the much-discussed Nicholson pavement. Milwaukee raised the grade of a considerable section of her down-town business district and rapidly extended her horse-railway line, begun in 1859. A number of municipalities installed new gas-lighting systems; others enlarged systems already in operation. Thus in public as in private building the State progressed during the war.

In growth of population the cities of Wisconsin entirely outdistanced the remainder of the State. Between 1860 and 1865 the agricultural regions gained in numbers only 8.9 per cent. Many of the southern and eastern counties remained stationary; others actually retrograded. The thirty-three largest cities and villages of Wisconsin, on the other hand, gained in numbers 26.6 per cent. Milwaukee became a community of 55,641 inhabitants, an increase in five years of 23 per cent. The eight largest lumbering cities in the State added 61.5 per cent to their population, a gain seven times as great as that of rural Wisconsin.[1]

This rapid growth of Wisconsin cities continued during the second half of the decade. The relative gain over the agricultural districts, however, was considerably less, owing to the movement of unemployed soldiers to the farms and the increase of foreign immigration. Thus the thirty-three largest municipalities in the State between 1865 and 1870 grew only 5 per cent faster than the agricultural region, which was less than one-third the ratio of the preceding years. Milwaukee reflected her swift

[1] The population statistics in U. S. *Census*, 1860 are incomplete. They are reprinted, however, in correct form in the census for 1870. See *id.*, 1870, I, p. xlvi and 287–95; Wisconsin Secretary of State, *Report*, 1865, 87–133.

development as a manufacturing community by adding 28.3 per cent to her numbers. The lumber towns still led all others in the State in the rapidity of their development, their growth for the five-year period being 35.1 per cent.[1]

That so prolonged and costly a conflict as the Civil War should have come to a close without an immediate commercial revulsion was a remarkable tribute to the economic strength of the North. The eastern states in 1865 did suffer a temporary depression of industry; the Northwest merely paused to take breath, then hurried forward as before. The Green Bay *Advocate* on July 10, 1865 observed: "There has been apprehension among some that the closing up of the war and the consequent fall of prices from war figures, would work wide-spread financial disaster. But this has not proved true. The tense-drawn muscles did indeed relax for a little repose, but have again resumed their wonted vigor."

The same pleasing phenomenon was thus recorded by the Milwaukee Chamber of Commerce:

> Whether we shall escape entirely the prostration and derangement of business usually following protracted and exhausting wars, it may now be too soon to judge. But whatever results may be experienced hereafter in this respect, it is gratifying to know that the general business of the country has thus far suffered no serious consequences, and that our own city in particular has continued steadily progressing in commerce, manufactures and population. * * * Our wholesale merchants and jobbers have rarely enjoyed a more prosperous season, and are now putting forth commendable efforts to extend our commerce to sections with which we have hitherto had but little traffic.[2]

Depression, the inevitable though delayed consequence of the war, at length overtook the Northwest

[1] *Ibid.*

[2] Milwaukee Chamber of Commerce, *Report*, 1865, 3.

in 1867. For four years the tradesmen of Wisconsin labored under difficulties similar to those of 1857. In 1871 conditions gradually improved, and hopeful merchants prophesied a new era of unexampled prosperity. For a time it seemed that the good times had in truth come to stay. They proved, however, to be only transient. Rudely and suddenly in the panic of 1873 they took their departure.

One of the numerous problems besetting tradesmen in the State during the opening years of the Civil War was the unsatisfactory condition of their currency. We have already seen in the preceding chapter the manifold shortcomings of Wisconsin's paper money at that time. So notorious were these that business men in the State during the crash of 1860–61 often found it impossible to pay for purchases made in the East in any other way than to ship thither flour and pork.[1] The wary easterners realized that the western money might depreciate in value even while in transit. In Milwaukee during the first eight months of 1861 the rate of exchange for New York currency was altered more than thirty times. Usually it ranged from 5 to 8 per cent; only once, early in January, did it descend to 3 per cent; during the crisis months, April, June, and July, it rose to 10 and 15 per cent.[2] At home and abroad Wisconsin currency was thus in thorough discredit.

Not only by Badger wildcats but by the even more ferocious species of Illinois and Minnesota were the business men of Wisconsin pursued at this time. Compelled by the exigencies of trade frequently to

[1] Milwaukee *Sentinel*, Jan. 1, 1861.
[2] Milwaukee Chamber of Commerce, *Report*, 1861, 34.

accept money that they knew little or nothing about, they were in a sorry predicament. Ordinarily they could accept with assurance no out-of-state bank bills proffered them, excepting possibly those of New England and New York. Between the paper of their own State and that reaching them from other states there was thus little choice.

Quite aside from questions of the intrinsic merit of paper money was the danger of counterfeits. To issue spurious currency was a highly profitable and comparatively safe procedure. Today paper money throughout the country is of a uniform type, easily recognizable, and difficult to imitate. In 1860 approximately 10,000 varieties of American and Canadian bank notes were in circulation within the Union.[1] For any banker to distinguish the genuine issues of all of these from the clever copies made of them was obviously impossible. Immeasurably greater was the perplexity of the ordinary tradesman.

The best and most widely accepted bank notes were those likeliest to be imitated. The issues of 174 of the 185 banks of Massachusetts, for instance, were beclouded with counterfeits during the war. New York fared almost as badly. Of her 303 banks only 45 escaped the attentions of rogues. Altogether in the North at the beginning of 1863 approximately 7,000 kinds of notes were in circulation. Bearing them company were 5,500 varieties of spurious, altered, and counterfeit bills.[2]

So widespread was this evil that in every part of

[1] J. T. Hodges, *New Bank Note Safe-Guard* (New York, 1860), 1.

[2] This account is taken from Fite, *Social and Industrial Conditions*, 113–16; D. R. Dewey, *Financial History of the United States* (New York, 1915), 322.

the country it was necessary to issue weekly periodicals which had no other function than to describe new and old frauds on the market. In the West these Bank Note Safe Guards or Counterfeit Detectors, as they were called, gained a wide circulation during the war, and their services were constantly supplemented by newspaper notices of warning.

The merchant of Wisconsin who in the course of his business was proffered a bank note was at once confronted with a difficult problem in currency. If the bank issuing the money were unknown to him he must determine as well as possible its character for stability. Then he must fetch his Detector and assure himself that the bill was not altered or a counterfeit. If he accepted the money and offered paper in change, his patron needed to be equally cautious. From beginning to end the system was full of vexation and danger.

Fortunately this problem found solution during the war. In 1862 the Federal government, driven by necessity, began to issue legal tenders. By 1864, when the emissions ceased, it had placed in circulation $431,000,000. Everywhere in the West the greenbacks, as they were called, were accepted without reservation. In Wisconsin where, owing to the restrictive policy of the State bankers local currency was insufficient for business needs, the new currency was eagerly welcomed.

The national banking act of 1863 provided another though a less prolific source of Federal paper money. On the whole the measure did not become effective until the closing year of the Civil War. It was of immense importance to the West, however, for it inaugurated a legislative policy which at length in 1866 brought to an end the hated and outworn system of State currency.[1]

A source of much petty annoyance to the merchants of Wisconsin during the early years of the Civil War was the absence of small change. Gold, never plentiful in the West, disappeared from circulation within a few months after the assault on Fort Sumter. The useful fractional coins followed shortly after. By the summer of 1862 small silver, nickles, and even coppers had entirely deserted the channels of trade.

This predicament was not a new one. On every occasion in the history of the State when paper money showed signs of depreciation silver change at once retired from the avenues of commerce. As recently as the winter of 1860–61 the tradesmen of Wisconsin had suffered from this difficulty. They had then endeavored to escape it by issuing token money, known in the vernacular as shinplasters, a device as old as the problem which it sought to obviate.

Everywhere in the State during the summer and autumn of 1862 substitutes for coins made their appearance. They consisted for the most part of pasteboard tickets, stamped to represent 5, 10, 25, or 50 cents. The better varieties were actual bank checks, though, to be sure, they called for fractional parts of a dollar. Such, however, did not remain in circulation long. The banks speedily tired of the nuisance of redeeming them and forbade their further issue.[2] Municipalities in some parts of Wis-

[1] *Ante*, chap. vii.

[2] See Green Bay *Advocate*, Dec. 17, 1862. The reason given by the Bank of Green Bay for refusing any longer to honor checks for fractional

consin improvised pseudo-mints, though not always with success. By far the largest part of the token money consisted of simple fiats of individual merchants unsecured by anything but a signature.

The abuses to which the system was liable soon became apparent. "Our city," said the Milwaukee *Sentinel* in the middle of 1862, "is flooded with shinplasters issued by irresponsible parties. Five, ten, twenty-five, and fifty cent notes are scattered about in endless profusion. Parties whom no one has ever heard of, or ever seen, take the responsibility of forming banking establishments of their own, and issue bank notes without regard to 'expense' or the price of paper. One-horse auctioneers, butchers, saloon-keepers, bootblacks, loafers, and every one who is without money, goes into this business extensively. Some are too lazy to let us know who they are, and merely sign the initials of their names."[1]

According to the Green Bay *Advocate*, "the plasters are to a great extent, mere due bills issued at every two-penny doggery, and there is no dealer of any kind who has a sign hung out but can do a banking business at his own counter."[2]

More reliable, though less convenient, than shinplasters were government postage stamps. On July 17, 1862 Congress made them legal tender and encouraged their use as a medium of exchange. They were ill adapted to their new employment. "The gummy back, fragile texture, small surface and light weight of the stamps made them the worst circulating

parts of a dollar was that "redeeming the same occupies so much of our time as to seriously interfere with our business."

[1] Milwaukee *Sentinel*, Dec. 17, 1862.

[2] Green Bay *Advocate*, Nov. 27, 1862.

medium ever known in the United States. To hand a * * * stage driver his fare of two 3-cent stamps on a wet day, to buy a newspaper on a windy street corner, to make change hurriedly doing the sums necessary in the denomination of 3 cents (the stamp most frequently employed and the one of which there was the greatest supply) into the convenient decimal system—such matters increased the small vexations of life."[1]

At length, in the autumn of 1862, the national government delivered the people of the North from the abuses of shinplasters and the annoyance of postage stamps. Under a liberal interpretation of the law of that year the Treasury Department issued a special form of postage stamps known as postal currency. Unglued and in the shape of miniature bank notes, the new money appeared in denominations of 5, 10, 25, and 50 cents.[2] So popular did it at once become that the incessant labor of government presses for months could not supply the demand for it.

No sooner did the postal currency become plentiful in Wisconsin than shinplasters of every variety disappeared. An act of Congress pronouncing them unlawful, which had been adopted in the summer of 1862 but had never been enforced, was now vigorously applied. In the winter of 1862–63 merchants in every part of Wisconsin agreed no longer to receive or issue the token money except to redeem such as they themselves had issued.[3] By the summer of 1863 the currency troubles of Wisconsin business men were thus well over.

[1] J. F. Rhodes, *History of United States* (New York, 1893), V, 192.

[2] *Ibid.*, 193–94.

[3] See Milwaukee *Sentinel*, Dec. 17 and Dec. 26, 1862; Green Bay *Advocate*, Feb. 19, 1863; Appleton *Crescent*, Jan. 31, 1863.

Pioneer communities invariably pay higher rates of interest for the use of money than older societies. The reason is obvious. Opening a new country involves risks which capital can be induced to incur only upon the promise of generous compensation. In Wisconsin during the forties money frequently commanded a yearly income of 15, 20, and sometimes 25 per cent. To pay such charges was feasible so long as public lands could be purchased at merely nominal prices and speedily sold again to settlers at a handsome margin. Perhaps in these speculative ventures money secured no more than a just share of the gains. In 1851, however, the State legislature limited to 12 per cent the legal charge that could be imposed as interest in Wisconsin.[1]

By the end of the fifties the southern half of the State had advanced to a position where even 12 per cent constituted a social menace. The most desirable government lands had all passed into private hands, and speculating as a profession had given way to agriculture and trade. The farmer and the merchant, who succeeded the land agent, earned only modest returns upon their investments. It was ruinous for them to attempt to pay capitalists the interest charges that the law allowed. Those who persisted in doing it came to sudden grief in the rigid contraction of values that followed the panic of 1857.

During the hard times that succeeded the industrial crisis the people of Wisconsin came to regard 12 per cent interest as usury.[2] Prices upon commodities of

[1] Wis. *Gen. Laws,* 1851, chap. 172.

[2] See annual messages of Wisconsin governors from 1858 to 1862, published in Wis. *Mess. and Docs.,* 1858–62; also an address by L. P. Harvey in Wis. Agric. Soc., *Trans.,* 1858–59, 431–33.

every description were far below normal; only capital commanded as before $12 or more per year for the use of a hundred. "Interest," declared Governor Randall in 1859, "is the rust that is rapidly consuming our people. It not only eats away our surplus profits, but in a majority of cases, is eating deep into our capital. It is unaffected by poor crops and worse markets. It gathers strength and weight and oppressive power continually, whether we sleep or wake, while we rest as well as while we labor. There must come a bitter end to such a policy."[1]

Further restriction by statute of the charges of money lenders was the simple remedy proposed by the debtors of Wisconsin. This, however, involved objections. Capitalists took exception to it on the ground that the price of money should be regulated not by arbitrary enactments but by the laws of supply and demand. Restrictive legislation, they declared, could only injure the State by driving away the financial means necessary to its development. On the other hand the friends of the plan asserted that the only capital which a restrictive law would banish from Wisconsin was such as the State would be better without. They maintained that it was better for Wisconsin to develop slowly and conservatively than to exhaust herself in enriching usurers and money sharks. To permit unproductive money to earn 12 per cent, they asserted, was actually to retard progress. "The farmer who can only realize two or three per cent, after all his toil and labor, on the value of his farm, must be tempted to sell his land, and stop producing, when he discovers that on the money for

[1] Wis. *Mess. and Docs.*, 1859, 29.

which he sells, he can realize without labor, ten or twelve per cent. Capitalists will not put their money into manufactures, while they can realize without risk ten or twelve per cent for the use of their money."[1] Only by limiting interest, it was urged, to a level below the average profit of productive industry could the State prevail upon money lenders to turn their energies to the actual labors of developing natural resources.

At length in 1860 the people of Wisconsin secured the enactment of a law reducing the legal rate of interest to 10 per cent.[2] This afforded them considerable relief despite the fact that the statute was ignored in times of financial stringency. As a result, during the prosperous years of the war, the interest problem disappeared from public discussion.

Thus Wisconsin business men played their part in the industrial development of the State. In its problems as well as in its triumphs they had their full share. By guiding and directing its economic fortunes they rendered the Badger commonwealth important service during the critical years of the Civil War.

[1] *Id.*, 1861, 17.

[2] Wis. *Gen. Laws*, 1860, chap. 202.

CHAPTER IX

RAILROAD FARM MORTGAGES

The policy of public aid for internal improvements was discredited in many parts of the United States even before Wisconsin aspired to a place in the Union. Not only had it plunged commonwealths and local communities into debt but frequently it had left them with half-finished or otherwise useless enterprises on their hands. Individuals entrusted with public donations had shown themselves careless, even at times corrupt, in their management. Rarely had communities been entirely satisfied with their investments. Frequently their discontent was so great as to render them unwilling to pay debts thus contracted. Many localities repudiated their obligations outright; others contested them in the courts; still others compromised as well as they might. Those that met their payments squarely by increasing their taxes found to their consternation many of their most enterprising citizens emigrating to the unburdened states of the new West.

Numbers of these tax-exiled emigrants settled upon the fertile soil of southern Wisconsin. When the constitution of the new commonwealth was framed in 1848 their first care was to write into it an ironclad prohibition against State aid of any kind, either by subscription or by the loaning of public credit, to any internal improvement.[1] Happy indeed the people that had such a basic law. As a governmental unit, at least, Wisconsin was spared the trials and humiliations that marked the early history of her neighbors.

However, Wisconsin must have railroads. Her citizens clamored for them. Cheap and easy transportation was the goal of their most cherished hopes. In our day rapid transit has come to be taken as a matter of course. Early Wisconsin, however, knew how to appreciate it. Farmers living in the interior were often obliged to cart their wheat forty or fifty miles to market over almost impassable roads and at a cost nearly equaling the price which they received for their grain. Their material progress, to say nothing of their intellectual and spiritual welfare, depended upon securing means of communication with the outside world.

Funds for building railroads, however, were difficult to obtain. A frontier community always lacks ready capital, and Wisconsin was no exception to the general rule. Promoters, moreover, refused to undertake unaided so uncertain a project as building a railroad in a new country. They knew that for many years, while the State was developing and traffic was growing up, they must operate at a loss. They argued that in other parts of the Union states and localities offered aid to such works. Why should Wisconsin be an exception? If its constitution prohibited the central government from extending bounty to railroads, it did not so restrict local com-

[1] "Constitution of Wisconsin," art. 8, sec. 10, in Wis. *Rev. Statutes*, 1858, 40. This prohibition did not extend to land grants donated by Congress to the State for internal improvements.

munities or individuals. Obviously the latter must pledge the support that in other regions was given by state authorities.

Under such pressure individuals and local communities came generously to the support of railroads. Practically every line built in Wisconsin prior to the Civil War had its origin in their encouragement. When, however, the panic of 1857 forced the railroad companies into bankruptcy, the popular suffering that resulted was keener, the losses more directly felt, than in any of the regions where the results of failure were spread over an entire commonwealth.

In the measure that the losses of individuals and localities came close home reluctance to pay them was increased. Wisconsin railroad promoters had, moreover, been more than usually extravagant and corrupt in their management of the funds entrusted to them. It was easy for the Badger farmers and communities to convince themselves that they were justified in disowning their railroad obligations. During the later fifties and early sixties repudiation became almost universal in the State. In the financial circles of the East the name Wisconsin became a term of reproach, synonymous with dishonor and moral turpitude.

Two phases of the problem of railroad indebtedness assumed importance in Wisconsin during the war. One related to the obligations of localities. The other concerned itself with the so-called railroad farm mortgages, a difficulty unique in the history of the United States. For nearly ten years it distracted southern Wisconsin, dominating political parties, compelling the support of legislatures and governors, and threatening the independence of a hostile judiciary.

This embarrassing problem was introduced to Wisconsin by her pioneer railroad company, the Milwaukee & Mississippi. The latter, upon its march across Wisconsin, had scarcely reached Waukesha, less than a score of miles from Milwaukee, when its funds were exhausted and it was casting about for help. On Feb. 28, 1850 its officers called a meeting of stockholders and interested farmers at Waukesha to take counsel. There Joseph Goodrich, a prominent resident of the neighboring town of Milton, advanced the proposal that fastened the mortgage difficulty upon the State.[1]

The plan was a novel one. Farmers along the line of the railroad were to be invited to purchase stock even if they had no money with which to pay for it. Instead of cash they might give their personal notes, secured by mortgages on their farms. These notes, together with the mortgages, were to be payable in ten years. The interest on the mortgages was to be 8 per cent, but the railroad stock was to pay dividends of 10 per cent. To facilitate bookkeeping the railroad officials would merely subtract the interest due on the mortgages from the dividends accruing on the stock and permit the remaining 2 per cent of stock dividends to accumulate upon their books until the time when the notes were paid. The Company was to have the privilege of selling these mortgages as collateral security for its railroad bonds in the eastern

[1] "Reply to Address of the Farmers' General Home League," 43–45, bound with Milwaukee & Mississippi Railroad, *Report*, 1849–61, in Wisconsin Historical Library. See also Milwaukee *Sentinel*, Mar. 1, 1861.

money markets and thus obtain the necessary means for carrying its line to successful completion.

Such a plan appealed to the optimistic mind of the western settler. He was at no time disposed to be overcautious, and this was a period of great prosperity. He calculated that when his note came due the accumulated dividends upon the Company's books would already have paid 20 per cent of it. In addition his stock would by that time undoubtedly be worth far more than the par price which he had paid. It would then become a question for him to decide at leisure whether to sell his railroad securities and with the proceeds cancel his mortgage, or keep the stock as a ground-floor investment.

This plan, perfected and varied in its details, grew rapidly in popular favor. It was quickly adopted by all the railroads in Wisconsin, and from there spread into northern Illinois. Its virtues were not allowed to lose any of their attractiveness by the suave stock agents that the railroad companies employed. Many of the latter were no doubt honest in dangling glittering prospects of gain before the eyes of the credulous farmers. Some of them demonstrated their sincerity by signing their own names to large subscriptions of stock. Joseph Goodrich, who induced his neighbors to mortgage their farms to the extent of $100,000, encumbered his own homestead for $10,000.[1] Deacon E. D. Clinton, one of the most successful of the agents, mortgaged his farm for $5,000 and readily accepted credits upon his railroad certificates in payment of services for two and a half years.[2]

[1] See references cited in preceding note.

[2] See letters of E. D. Clinton justifying his conduct as stock agent,

Many agents, on the other hand, were apparently devoid of conscience or honor. Bent solely upon earning the commissions that the railroad companies allowed them they stopped at no falsehood or misrepresentation, however base, to sell their stock. They called popular meetings for the purpose of "raising wind," which they shrewdly managed so as to stir up enthusiasm and lead on hesitating victims.[1] Over and over again they assured the simple-minded farmers that there was no danger in the mortgage plan. Only profit, they declared, could possibly result from it. Whether they were supported in these tactics by the companies that employed them it is difficult to determine. Certain it is that there was some basis for the charge later made that the entire mortgage scheme was conceived and executed in fraud.

During the years 1850 to 1857, while the first fever of railroad construction was at its height, approximately 6,000 Wisconsin farmers mortgaged their homesteads to the extent of from $4,500,000 to $5,000,000 in order to purchase railroad stock. The La Crosse & Milwaukee Railroad received $1,100,000 of such mortgages, the Milwaukee & Mississippi Railroad, $900,000, the Milwaukee & Horicon, $375,000, the Milwaukee & Superior, $200,000, and numerous other railroads, lesser amounts.[2] So enthusiastic were the settlers of south-

in Hartford *Home League*, Aug. 18, 1860 and Nov. 23, 1861; see also *ibid.*, Sept. 8, 1860.

[1] Practically every issue of the Hartford *Home League* during the first year or two of its existence contains accounts of such procedure.

[2] *Ibid.*, Aug. 11, 1860. This paper in subsequent issues presents detailed statistics of the extent of the farm-mortgage difficulty, giving totals by

ern Wisconsin over their new-found scheme that they were disposed to frown upon the cautious who saw breakers ahead and even to denounce as lacking in public spirit those who refused to subscribe.

Disillusion came only too quickly. The farmers learned that the railroad companies were disposing of their mortgages in the eastern money markets at from 50 to 75 per cent of their face value.[1] They discovered that the interest on the mortgages was not being cancelled and that the eastern holders were threatening foreclosure. Rumors of extravagant and fraudulent construction contracts and stories of corruption, rapidly leading the roads into receivership, leaked out. In 1857 came the crash of the panic and every railroad in the State sank at once into hopeless ruin. The bubble had burst! The farmers of Wisconsin had burdened themselves with debt and as compensation had only the worthless stock of bankrupt corporations.

Examination into the records of the railroad companies revealed a degree of fraud which even the darkest suspicions had not anticipated. The Milwaukee & Superior Railroad which had secured mortgages to the amount of $200,000, the Wisconsin Central with $100,000, the Milwaukee & Beloit with $175,000, and other corporations that had received farm mortgages, to say nothing of municipal and county bonds, had dissipated their entire proceeds without having placed in operation a single mile of

counties and also by railroad lines. The references are too numerous to be offered here. See also Wisconsin Railroad Commission, *Report*, 1874, 250–51; "Annual Message," 1861, 10–11, in Wis. *Mess. and Docs.*, 1861.

[1] New York *Tribune*, July 14, 1860; Hartford *Home League*, Feb. 20, 1864.

road.[1] Even the most stable of the railroad companies, if one may speak of stability where there was so little, had squandered the proceeds of their farm mortgages with a recklessness that bordered on the criminal.[2] "In the history of the financial speculations of this country," declared Governor Randall in 1861, "so bold, open, unblushing frauds, taking in a large body of men, were never perpetrated. There was, and is, no law to punish them; because such rascality could not have been anticipated."[3]

In a bitter editorial of Sept. 8, 1860 the Hartford *Home League*, a weekly paper established in the interests of the farm mortgagors, exposed some of the methods by which these early railroad corporations defrauded the Wisconsin farmers.

> 1st. They took stock of the farmers upon the express condition that the roads should be laid in certain localities, and after the stock was thus obtained, the right of way was altered to suit the private speculations of the directors.
>
> 2nd. They made out false reports and false statements in order to show the road to be in a better condition than it really was, and to induce the farmers from such statements to mortgage their farms for stock.
>
> 3rd. They issued large amounts of bogus and fictitious stock in order to overshadow the Farm Mortgage interest, and perpetuate themselves in office.
>
> 4th. They sold the capital stock of the company at a ruinous discount in order to raise money with which to pay semi-annual dividends that they had declared, falsely representing that the money thus paid out was the legitimate earnings of the road over and above expenses.

[1] *Ibid.*, Aug. 11, 1860 and Oct. 24, 1863. On Nov. 8, 1863 this paper estimated that only half of the mortgages floating about the market at that time were represented by completed lines of road.

[2] The Milwaukee & Superior Railroad, whose affairs were investigated by a legislative committee in 1858, presents an extreme instance of such fraud. See Wis. *Assem. Jour.*, 1858, appendix. See also Hartford *Home League*, 1860–64, especially Dec. 22, 1860; *Reply to Address of Farmers' General Home League.*

[3] "Annual Message," 1861, 11, in Wis. *Mess. and Docs.*, 1861.

5th. They colluded with each other and made contracts with themselves for the building and operating of the road at the most extravagant prices.

6th. They bought up large tracts of real estate, and then altered the line of the road so as to accommodate their own land and enhance the value of their own property.

7th. They continued to take Farm Mortgages when they knew that their corporations were bankrupt.

The farmers of southern Wisconsin, once so enthusiastic over the alluring scheme, now denounced it as a deliberate swindle. Not only they but their most prominent public servants voiced this feeling. "The railroad mortgages," declared Governor Randall in his annual message of 1861, "were conceived in fraud, executed in fraud, and sold or transferred in fraud."[1] It was easy under such circumstances for the pioneers of Wisconsin to satisfy themselves that resistance to the payment of such debts was not only justifiable but even a positive virtue.

It was obvious, however, that individual resistance would be worse than useless. Only by union could they hope to defend their homes against foreclosure. Organized resistance to law was by no means unfamiliar to them. In a somewhat similar predicament it had proved entirely effective. When the first settlers came to southern Wisconsin and Iowa the government lands had not yet been surveyed or opened to public sale. The pioneers had simply squatted upon them without securing a legal title. When later the government threw their improved farms upon the open market they were in danger of losing them to speculators who could bid more than they at the public auctions. To prevent such misfortunes they had organized "squatters' protective

[1] *Ibid.*

associations" or "claims clubs," the function of which was to attend government sales en masse and by intimidation or actual violence silence undesirable bidders. When, as occasionally happened, a "claim jumper" did succeed in ousting the original settler, he was either ostracized or his life in the community was made a burden.[1] Some of the men, who in the thirties and forties were members of such organizations, were in the later fifties and sixties entangled in the farm-mortgage difficulty.

Following the earlier precedent, the endangered farmers throughout southern Wisconsin organized semi-secret clubs known as farm-mortgage leagues. As the time for the foreclosure of the encumbrances drew nearer these associations became more numerous and powerful. A Grand State League and two subsidiary general leagues covering all southern Wisconsin were organized in the summer of 1860, at the regular meetings of which delegates from the several local branches gathered for consultation.[2] Together they published a weekly newspaper[3] edited

[1] University of Wisconsin, *Bulletin*, No. 101, 91–98; see also the various local and county histories of Wisconsin. Iowa conditions are described in B. F. Shambaugh, "Frontier Land Clubs or Claim Associations," in American Historical Association, *Annual Report*, 1900, I, 67–84.

[2] Compiled from references in Hartford *Home League*. See especially earlier numbers.

[3] The Hartford *Home League* was established on Aug. 11, 1860, largely as the result of an unfavorable decision by the Wisconsin supreme court in the important railroad farm-mortgage case of Clark v. Farrington. It ran as a weekly for nearly four years, suspending on Mar. 5, 1864 because of lack of support. In its place a number of independent State papers took up the cause of the mortgagors, the most radical of which were the Madison *Argus and Democrat* and the Beaver Dam *Argus*. The latter on July 20, 1864 constituted itself the official organ of the mortgagors, lengthening its title to the Beaver Dam *Argus and Farm Mortgage League* under which head it was issued until Mar. 10, 1866.

by an able journalist, who later presided over the lower house of the State legislature.[1] In addition to their official organ they had numerous independent weeklies at their command. Though professing to be entirely nonpolitical in character, for nearly a decade they dictated to both political parties in the State and constituted a disturbing factor in every important public question.

The political influence of these organizations was far greater than their numerical strength seemed to indicate. The stern issues of the Civil War were rendering elections in the State extremely close, and politicians in both parties realized that a doubtful contest might at any time be swung by their organized vote. Outside their ranks, moreover, they had numerous supporters. Though they were not strong in the larger cities of Wisconsin, the latter fearing that organized resistance to the payment of lawful debts would destroy the credit of the State, they were upheld almost universally by the country districts. Sympathetic neighbors, citizens of communities oppressed by railroad bonds, and a large number of voters, who were exasperated at the nation-wide notoriety which the legislative scandal

[1] Thompson abandoned the Hartford *Home League* in 1864 to become editor and part proprietor of the more promising Janesville *Gazette*. In 1870 he left the *Gazette* to become editor and part owner of the Milwaukee *Sentinel*, at that time the most influential paper in the State. He was much interested in State politics, having served the railroad farm mortgagors as lobbyist at each of the annual sessions of the legislature during the four years in which he was connected with their cause. In 1868 and 1869 he was sent to the legislature by the assembly district of Janesville, and in 1869 was chosen by the Assembly to preside over its sessions as speaker. He was at various times prominently mentioned for nomination as governor on the Republican ticket, but although ambitious for the honor, he never secured it.

of 1856 had brought upon the State, gave them their coöperation.[1]

It was important for the farm mortgagors to control local officials, such as sheriffs and registers of deeds, upon whom devolved the duty of executing foreclosure judgments. In the region where the mortgage problem was acute none could hope for election to these offices except those whose attitude toward foreclosure was well known. "No man in the vicinity," declared a Green County writer, "has any sight for an office of trust, profit, or honor, in the gift of the people, unless he is known to be 'sound on the goose,' and any attorney who dares to receive their mortgages for collection, has a poor show for anything better than to be 'hanging around loose' somewhere in some out of the way locality where solitude is the chief attraction."[2] Not infrequently successful candidates for local offices were themselves prominent members of the farmer leagues.[3]

For ultimate success, however, the mortgagors realized that they must look primarily to remedial legislation. It was in this conviction that one of their organs, the Beaver Dam *Argus and Farm Mortgage League*, thus advised them on Sept. 21, 1864: "Within a few weeks the nominations by the different parties [for the legislature] will be made, they are beginning to be made already, and consequently now is the time for farmers to have their eyes open. The farm mortgagors should attend primary meetings and conventions of parties, and see to the nominations; be

[1] See Wis. *Assem. Jour.*, 1861, 318; Hartford *Home League*, 1860–64.

[2] *Ibid.*, Sept. 1, 1860.

[3] *Ibid.*, Feb. 23, 1861 and Oct. 6, 1863; Beaver Dam *Argus*, Sept. 21, 1864.

sure that men firmly in their interests are nominated, and when such men are nominated, then they must look to their election." It is impossible at this distance to determine how carefully the mortgagors followed such advice. The enactments of successive legislatures sufficiently tell the story.

For a short time after the panic of 1857 Wisconsin legislatures were called upon to consider State assumption of the entire mortgage debt. The difficulty with this program was that it required a constitutional amendment, and it was soon given up as impossible of attainment. With more vigor and hope of success the mortgagors entered upon a fight to secure from Congress a modification of the railroad land grant of 1856, so that its proceeds might be applied to the cancellation of the farm encumbrances. Congressman John F. Potter,[1] himself a farm mortgagor, was said to favor this step. This measure, too, was beyond the gift of the legislature, and the farmers demanded immediate relief.

The first legislature that came together after the panic of 1857 pointed out the way of escape. It enacted a law establishing the procedure that should govern Wisconsin courts in all future foreclosure suits against railroad farm mortgagors.[2] If the mortgagor could prove to the satisfaction of a court or

[1] Popularly known in the North as "Bowie Knife Potter," because when challenged by Congressman Roger A. Pryor of Virginia to a duel, in the midst of the secession discussion of 1860, he accepted the challenge and in a spirit of grim humor selected for the combat a pair of vicious-looking bowie knives. When the Virginian Congressman thereupon indignantly withdrew, declaring he was not a butcher, Potter was proclaimed throughout the North as the hero of the hour. See Thwaites, *Wisconsin*, 329; see also Hartford *Home League*, Sept. 1, 1860 and Mar. 1, 1862.

[2] Wis. *Gen. Laws*, 1858, chap. 49.

a jury of his peers that he had been induced to sign the contested security by fraudulent representations of the railroad stock agent, the action to foreclose should be discharged and judgment for costs should be assessed against the plaintiff. This would have been legal as well as equitable if in all such actions the plaintiff had been the party guilty of the original frauds. Almost invariably, however, he was an eastern purchaser who could not be presumed to have known when he invested in the mortgage of the methods by which it had been obtained. The law provided, nevertheless, that the defense of fraud should apply especially to such purchasers; in fact it forbade their offering the reply that they were innocent third parties in the transaction.

This unusual measure aroused a storm of protest throughout the East. The Wisconsin legislature was everywhere charged with deliberately releasing its citizens from the payment of their just debts. Even in the commercial centers of Wisconsin the bill met vigorous objection as being discreditable to the State. Despite such opposition, however, and despite the fact that similar legislation had previously been pronounced unconstitutional by the highest tribunal in the State,[1] it was passed, and approved by Governor Randall. It no sooner reached the Wisconsin supreme court in 1860, than it was declared invalid.[2]

The legislature, however, returned to the fray in 1861 with an even more obviously unconstitutional measure popularly known as the farm-mortgage stay

[1] See Fisher v. Otis, 3 *Pinney* 78; Martineau v. McCollum, 3 *Pinney* 455.

[2] Clark v. Farrington, 11 *Wis.* 306; Blunt v. Walker, 11 *Wis.* 334; Cornell v. Hichens, 11 *Wis.* 353.

law.[1] It was drawn by several astute lawyers employed by the Grand State League, and contained twenty-seven elaborate sections. One of the latter reënacted with broader applications the unconstitutional law of 1858. All the others proposed, by one device or another, so to impede, handicap, and tax those suing to foreclose railroad farm mortgages as to render the successful issue of such actions practically impossible.

Once more the angry East stormed and fumed. One writer from New York, after setting forth the discredit that the measure would cast upon Wisconsin and the suffering that it would inflict upon the small holders of railroad mortgages in the East, concludes:

> Besides in these times of secession and reprisal, it might lead to unpleasant reprisals and hostile legislation in other States, which might look towards retaliation. *Already I understand a petition has been forwarded to the Legislature of this State* [*New York*] *by citizens of the State of New York, holders of these bonds, praying that if the act in relation to them now before the Wisconsin legislature should pass, that aggrieved citizens of the State of New York may have right to seize the property of citizens of Wisconsin found within the jurisdiction of the State of New York in satisfaction of their mortgages.*[2]

Protests were again unavailing. In the spring of 1861 the measure was approved by the legislature and signed by Governor Randall. The State had thus deliberately deprived eastern investors of their only means of enforcing payment of the mortgages

[1] Wis. *Gen. Laws*, 1861, chap. 88. See also J. B. Winslow, *Story of a Great Court* (Chicago, 1912), 164–83. This work contains a complete account of the railroad farm-mortgage movement from a legal point of view. I have made liberal use of the valuable data which it contains. See also *Wis. State Jour.*, Mar. 11 and 15, 1861.

[2] Ms. letter of J. Martin to Governor Randall, Mar. 14, 1861, in Wisconsin Historical Library.

they held. Wisconsin stood before all the world at the outbreak of the Civil War as a willful repudiator of her lawful debts. Only the national excitement over the southern conflict prevented her stay law from becoming as notorious in the nation as had been the similar relief laws of Kentucky in 1820.[1] In 1862 the measure was brought upon appeal before the Wisconsin supreme court and was there curtly dismissed as invalid.[2]

Balked in these efforts the legislature of Wisconsin proceeded upon a new tack. In 1862 it adopted a statute authorizing, though not compelling, the several railroad corporations, whose predecessors had received farm mortgages, to reimburse the makers in certain fixed proportions.[3] Needless to say none of the Wisconsin companies availed itself of the provisions of the statute.

Voluntary restitution having thus proved futile, the legislature attempted in a succeeding session to compel the most prominent Wisconsin railroad corporation, the Milwaukee & St. Paul, to retire the mortgages given to the La Crosse & Milwaukee and the Milwaukee & Horicon,[4] two lines which it had taken over. The method by which this was to be done was simple. The railroad company was to pay annually into a State sinking fund 12 per cent of its gross earnings until sufficient means had accumulated to cancel all these farm encumbrances. If the company neglected to comply with the law, the governor was to appoint a receiver to take charge of

[1] Compare W. G. Sumner, *Andrew Jackson* (Boston, 1883), chap. 6.

[2] Oatman v. Bond, 15 *Wis.* 20.

[3] Wis. *Gen. Laws*, 1862, chap. 330.

[4] *Id.*, 1864, chaps. 224 and 332.

its affairs. This legislation, however, was so obviously unconstitutional that the governor of Wisconsin did not even attempt to enforce it.[1]

Notwithstanding these repeated rebuffs, Wisconsin legislatures continued undiscouraged in their efforts to relieve the farm mortgagors. That of 1863 passed a measure which substantially reënacted the fraud defense law of 1858, and in foreclosure suits provided for a jury trial the verdict of which should be conclusive upon the facts involved in each case.[2] In 1864 so much of this law as applied to jury trials was reënacted with greater definiteness and more binding force, it being recognized that in a foreclosure suit of such a character no jury of Wisconsin farmers would decide any issue of fact or law against a distressed neighbor.[3] For a third time, and with still wider application, such a measure was enacted in 1867,[4] though the preceding statute had in the meantime been pronounced unconstitutional by the Wisconsin supreme court.[5]

From 1858 to 1863, with a single exception, every Wisconsin legislature passed one or more measures, fourteen in all, designed to relieve the railroad farm mortgagors.[6] Of these, three were merely special in application, and a fourth was utterly ignored. The

[1] See miscellaneous railroad manuscripts in Wisconsin Historical Library; see also Berlin *Courant*, Dec. 29, 1864.

[2] Wis. *Gen. Laws*, 1863, chap. 305.

[3] *Id.*, 1864, chap. 169.

[4] *Id.*, 1867, chap. 79.

[5] Truman v. McCollum, 20 *Wis.* 360. The law of 1867 was pronounced unconstitutional in Callanan v. Judd, 23 *Wis.* 343.

[6] Most of these have already been cited in the text. Of the others the more important were Wis. *Gen. Laws*, 1859, chap. 149; 1860, chap. 231; 1863, chap. 123; 1864, chap. 241.

remaining ten, the object of which was either to render impossible the foreclosure of the mortgages or to compel the reorganized railroad companies to cancel them, all proved unconstitutional. Practically the entire legislative program of the railroad mortgagors thus ultimately came to naught.

It must not be concluded, however, that these laws were entirely without result. So long as they remained on the statute books, no matter how obviously unconstitutional, they served the purpose of frightening, perplexing, and discouraging eastern mortgage holders, and making them willing to compromise with Wisconsin farmers. On the other hand they earned for the State an unenviable notoriety in the financial circles of the East, which for many years hindered and embarrassed its public and private enterprises.

The governors of Wisconsin, like the legislatures, gave to the railroad mortgagors their sympathy and support. Only in a single instance did the repudiatory enactments of successive legislatures, all clearly unconstitutional, meet the check of the executive veto.[1] Undoubtedly this was due in part to the narrow majorities by which Wisconsin governors were elected during the critical war period. In 1861 Harvey was chosen by a majority of but 8,300 out of a total vote of 100,000; in 1865 Fairchild received a majority of but 9,000 out of a total vote of 105,000.[2]

In the gubernatorial campaign of 1861 the Demo-

[1] Governor Salomon, who came to office not by election but by succession to the deceased Harvey, vetoed a railroad mortgage measure in 1863. It was, however, promptly passed over his head and became Wis. *Gen. Laws*, 1863, chap. 123.

[2] Wis. *Legislative Manual*, 1862, 153; *id.*, 1866, 198.

cratic candidate, Benjamin Ferguson, was himself a railroad mortgagor and, according to the Hartford *Home League*, would never have received the nomination but for this fact.[1] Of the Union candidate the same paper wrote: "We will say here that we have, in our possession, evidence of the most conclusive and satisfactory character, touching the soundness of Mr. Harvey, on the point in question [railroad mortgages], and we had personal cognizance of the fact that our friends in the Republican Convention, had the fullest assurance from the right quarter, before they cast their votes for Mr. Harvey."[2]

In the election of 1863 the Democratic machine committed the error of nominating for its candidate Henry L. Palmer, a man who had served the La Crosse & Milwaukee Railroad as a lawyer during its most corrupt days under Byron Kilbourn. With the exception of the war issue this unfortunate connection, which was promptly uncovered by the Republican press, formed the most prominent text for the campaign. Palmer was denounced by the Hartford *Home League* as the tool of the "corruptionists" and "consolidationists" and the "graduate of the meanest corporation that ever disgraced any state."[3] On the other hand James T. Lewis, the Republican candidate, was warmly commended as the "constant friend and faithful counsellor of the mortgagors,"[4] who if elected would sanction with pleasure anything that could with propriety be done for their relief.

[1] Hartford *Home League*, Nov. 16, 1861.

[2] *Ibid.*, Nov. 2, 1861.

[3] Portage *Register*, Aug. 8 and Sept. 5, 1863. See also Hartford *Home League* for all issues embracing the campaign.

[4] *Ibid.*, Aug. 29, 1863.

On Nov. 4, 1863 Lewis was elected with the unusual majority for that time of 23,363 out of a total vote of 133,820.[1] No doubt recurring confidence in the Republican party as the result of Federal successes at Vicksburg and Gettysburg, as well as the large personal popularity of Lewis in the State, had much to do with this majority. Yet there can hardly be any question that it was due in greater part to the united vote which the farm mortgagors gave him.

Fixed squarely, however, between friendly State authorities and the farmers stood the supreme court of Wisconsin. It availed little that one statute after another was hurried to enactment. One after another this resolute tribunal pronounced them void. The position taken by the court was logical. The railroad companies, it declared, had been given ample legal authority to accept mortgages in payment of stock; they had power to sell or assign these securities to third parties; the sales had been for a valuable consideration and were therefore legal; unless positive proof was presented to the contrary the purchasers must be presumed to have acted without knowledge of the fraud by which the mortgages had originally been obtained; having acted thus, they stood before the law as bona fide and innocent holders; their securities were therefore protected by the constitutional provision which prohibited the State legislature from passing any law impairing the obligation of an existing contract.[2] This stand, however distasteful and disastrous to the farmers of

[1] Wis. *Legislative Manual*, 1864, 182.

[2] Consult Wisconsin *Law Reporter*, especially cases cited elsewhere in this chapter. See also for an excellent account, Winslow, *Story of a Court*, 164–83.

Wisconsin, was undoubtedly correct. To it the supreme bench held unfalteringly. In vain did the lower courts of the State rebel;[1] in vain did the railroad mortgagors thunder invectives; in vain did political disaster threaten this elective tribunal—it remained unshaken.

It was a fairly well-established principle in Wisconsin in 1861 that judges of the supreme court should be elected wholly on the basis of honesty and fitness for office. The impropriety of selecting a magistrate because of his known views on public or private questions likely to come before him for adjudication was generally recognized. The farm mortgagors, however, were in too desperate straits to heed a mere convention. Their only chance for saving their homes lay in reconstructing the supreme court in such a way as to secure from it more favorable interpretation in the future of laws that their legislatures gave them.

Their first attempt to accomplish this end was made in 1861, when Orsamus Cole, one of the three sitting justices, came up for reëlection.[2] It was the practice at this time, though already falling into disuse, for political parties to nominate or indorse judicial candidates. The Republican party, to which Cole owed his original election, was in a quandary. It did not wholly approve his political views, and it desired to placate the farm-mortgage element in its ranks. On the other hand it was unwilling completely to

[1] According to the Hartford *Home League* of June 22, 1861 eight out of the ten circuit courts of the State disagreed with the supreme court in this position.

[2] For a fuller discussion of the judicial campaign here referred to, see Winslow, *Story of a Court*, 164–83.

surrender to the latter. It compromised, therefore, by placing no candidate in nomination, leaving Cole to run as an independent. The mortgagors promptly nominated James H. Knowlton of Janesville, a Republican lawyer of brilliant attainments and considerable prominence, who had won recognition as their greatest legal champion. The Democratic nominee having withdrawn early from the contest, the election was left to be fought out on the farm-mortgage issue.

The campaign was hotly contested. Knowlton was widely denounced as a repudiationist and a candidate willing to run for high judicial office under a pledge. The canvass resulted in a victory for Cole, but by the very narrow majority of 5,000 votes.[1] Although defeated, the farm mortgagors found comfort in one obvious deduction from the results of the campaign. They had demonstrated that they held the balance of political power and that, as long as their organization should be kept up, neither party would dare to ignore their support.[2]

Two years later, in the spring of 1863, the term of Chief-Justice Dixon expired. He had been elected in 1860 when little was known concerning either his own or his opponent's position upon the question of the railroad mortgages. In that contest friends of Dixon had claimed to know that their candidate was not unsympathetic to the stand of the farmers.[3] Many of the latter had undoubtedly voted for him upon this supposition. What was their dismay when

[1] Wis. Secretary of State, *Report*, 1861, 297.
[2] Hartford *Home League*, Aug. 10, 1861.
[3] Winslow, *Story of a Court*, 137–41.

Dixon not only agreed with his associates in the hostile Clark v. Farrington decision shortly after his election, but he himself in no uncertain language wrote a similar verdict in the case of Blunt v. Walker. The mortgagors were furious; they asserted they had been betrayed, and wildly demanded an impeachment. As a result of that treachery, declared the La Crosse *Union:*

> Thousands of little farms, with their white cottages, or more humble cabin—the growing crops—the labor of years—the result of toil—the earnings of honest men, * * * [would all be] swept into the pockets of Railroad owners, as a roulette keeper sweeps the dollars into the bag underneath his table, and turns again to catch new victims. It may be an honor to legalize fraud, but it is not honest, nor is it humanity. There is scarce a county in the State but soon will see going forth from the little homes hallowed by joy and made sacred with grief, leaving a loved fireside wet with tears, a caravan of broken hearts and blasted hopes—wending its way on toward the golden sunset, where fraud, trickery, and dishonesty is not yet in the full tide of successful operation.[1]

When, therefore, Judge Dixon came up for reelection in 1863 the mortgagors to a man were determined that he should be defeated. The Democratic judicial convention, which assembled in Madison early in the spring of 1863, long considered him for nomination. His doubtful political status, however, and the keen opposition of the mortgagors made him unavailable. M. M. Cothren secured the party endorsement by a narrow majority. The Republican caucus after two sittings likewise refused to place Dixon in nomination for much the same reasons as had guided the course of the Democrats. Again the party placed no one in the field, contenting itself with a half-hearted resolution of confidence in

[1] Extract from La Crosse *Union*, printed in Hartford *Home League*, Aug. 11, 1860.

the integrity of the chief-justice. The latter, encouraged by the success of Cole two years before, determined to run independently.

The campaign was marked by even more bitterness than the canvass of 1860. Dixon was ridiculed by the mortgagors as "the boy judge,"[1] the candidate of the foreclosure lawyers, and the tool of corrupt railroads,[2] while Cothren was denounced by his opponents as a Copperhead, a drunkard, a barroom campaigner, and a pledged judicial candidate.[3] The mortgagors, though predominantly Republican and loyal in sentiment, entered the campaign as an organization for the Democrat, the Grand State League having given him its endorsement at its Milwaukee convention in March, 1863.[4] The election was long in doubt, the Democratic press in the meantime jubilantly proclaiming the triumph of its candidate. Indeed, it appeared that Cothren had won, for in the home vote he had received 56,840 votes against 51,948 for Dixon. The returns were still to come from the army, however, and here Cothren's supposed Copperhead leanings affected him disastrously. The military vote turned the election, Judge Dixon winning by a majority of 3,000 votes.[5]

Defeated in their crucial fight to capture the State judiciary the farmers of Wisconsin were confronted with three dismal alternatives. They must pay their

[1] The Wisconsin court, like the judiciaries of most frontier states, was composed of young men. See Winslow, *Story of a Court*, 202–15.

[2] See Hartford *Home League* for the spring of 1863; also Winslow, *Story of a Court*, 202–15.

[3] *Ibid.*; Hartford *Home League* for the spring of 1863.

[4] *Wis. State Jour.*, Feb. 6, 1863 and Mar. 27, 1863.

[5] Wis. Secretary of State, *Report*, 1863, 172.

encumbrances, doubled as they usually were by the neglected interest of ten or twelve years, or submit to foreclosure, or resist the enforcement of the law. Most of them were unable, even if they had been willing, to pay their debts, and numbers of foreclosures took place under the most sorrowful circumstances. Not infrequently families were evicted from their homes after having lost their only bread-winners upon distant southern battle-fields.[1] In a letter to Governor Lewis written just before the close of the Civil War a farmer narrates an instance of this kind which he declares was but one of many in his immediate neighborhood: "An old man, a neighbor of mine, had two boys—his only dependence—killed in the army the past summer. He is now over 60 & nearly past labor. He was sued a few days since on a mortgage given in aid of the La Crosse & Mil. R. R. & he is entirely unable to meet it. Poor old man! He & his old wife must bear it peaceably, & go to the poor-house without a murmur."[2]

There were some instances of resistance to the law, the local farm-mortgage leagues reënacting at foreclosure sales almost the same scenes as had marked the activities of the Wisconsin and Iowa squatters' protective associations twenty years before. The Berlin *Courant* on Dec. 29, 1864 printed the following highly suggestive account of such a proceeding:

A case of attempted sale occurred in the city [Berlin] on Tuesday which shows a spirit on the part of the Leaguers which timid men will not care to brave. A sale had been advertised to come off, and in the interim the

[1] See manuscript letters relating to farm-mortgage movement, in Wisconsin Historical Library; also file of Hartford *Home League*.

[2] Ms. letter of J. A. Roberts to Governor Lewis, Feb. 2, 1865, in Wisconsin Historical Library.

owner of the advertised property [the farm mortgagor] had attempted to compromise, offering what was generally agreed was a liberal sum, to settle. The offer was refused, and the sheriff directed to sell the property. The day of sale came around, and so did the sheriff, and so did a hundred, more or less, stalwart men, who wanted to see fair play. The defendant was anxious that the sale should proceed, but the plaintiff did not appear, and no one could be *induced* to bid on the property in his behalf. As the sheriff could not sell under the circumstances, without violating his instructions, he adjourned the sale till the first day of February next when the dance will begin again. No doubt spectators will be numerous on the occasion, as the interest in the case does not abate in the least.[1]

Another method of discouraging foreclosure proceedings is recounted in the Madison *Argus* of January, 1861. "Some excitement was created in Prairie du Chien on January 9 by a demonstration against a Milwaukee lawyer, Mr. Small, who was in Prairie du Chien preparing some extracts and minutes at the county office to commence foreclosure of some thirty of the farm mortgages. His object being discovered, a large body of men took peaceable possession of him, and shut him up, burned his papers, and kept him close till the next train started, when he was put on board and 'ticketed through to Milwaukee.' "[2] In those cases in which foreclosure sales were successfully effected, the purchasers were likely to find themselves either completely ostracized or roughly hazed.

The limits to which the mortgagors were willing to go in their desperation were set forth in a formal

[1] The situation at Berlin was so threatening that Governor Lewis felt called upon on Jan. 30, 1865 to issue a proclamation, kindly yet firm, warning the mortgagors against resistance to the law. See Milwaukee *Sentinel*, Feb. 1, 1865. The sale eventually came off without disturbance. Complete details may be secured from miscellaneous manuscripts in Wisconsin Historical Library concerning the railroad-mortgage difficulty.

[2] Milwaukee *Sentinel*, Jan. 16, 1861; see also Hartford *Home League*, Jan. 19, 1861.

address sent by their State League to the Milwaukee & Mississippi Railroad Company in the winter of 1860.[1] No Wisconsin document of this entire period, not even those pertaining to the Civil War, surpasses in intense and dramatic human interest this simple statement of her imperiled farmers. Restrained indignation, pathos, defiance, denunciation, spring from every burning sentence. The entire unhappy history of the mortgages passes under review. The agents who induced the farmers to sign them are described—men of winning personality, highly respected in their communities, prominent in their churches, but corrupt at heart. Vividly are pictured the methods they employed, the dazzling promises they held forth, the skill with which they played upon the noblest and the meanest passions of their victims. There follows a recital of the fraud and mismanagement that wrecked the railroads while it enriched their officials and directors. As a result, aged men and widowed mothers were about to lose their homes, the sole accumulation of a hard life. Would not the company come to their rescue, would it not cancel these obligations, would it not restore peace and good feeling along its line? Or would it force law-abiding citizens to desperation, to violence against life and property? They were prepared for either, they would defend their homes against corrupt railroads, greedy eastern speculators, venal courts, and all the world besides.

"But suppose it should result at last that we have no good [legal] defence; or if we have, cannot enforce

[1] *Ibid.*, Dec. 22, 1860. For other addresses of a similar character see *ibid.*, Sept. 22 and Oct. 6, 1860, and Jan. 12, 1861.

it; when you have foiled us in the Courts, and we can make no further struggle there—how are you to dispossess us? Will you *force* us from our homes? When you resort to force, this promise we will keep, though it should be the last:—*We will meet that force in kind.* In doing this, we shall not stop to reckon how much we can bleed and live. With our lives only, will we render up our firesides."

Some violence to railroad property actually followed. Obstructions were placed upon tracks, rails were displaced, and trestlework was injured.[1] In Ozaukee and Washington counties excited Germans set fire to a depot building, destroyed several railroad bridges, cut telegraph poles, and tore up track upon the line of the Milwaukee & St. Paul Railway. The latter corporation found it necessary toward the close of 1865 to abandon its night passenger service between Milwaukee and Portage on account of the danger of such outrages.[2]

Fortunately most of the farmers of Wisconsin were able to adjust their difficulties by other means than open violence. In many cases they came to settlements, favorable on the whole, with eastern holders, who were either too far distant to be able to press their claims vigorously or were discouraged by the successive stay laws of Wisconsin legislatures. Probably not many Wisconsin farmers paid up their

[1] Ms. letter of L. H. Meyers, president of the Milwaukee & Prairie du Chien Railroad, to Governor Harvey, April 3, 1862, in Wisconsin Historical Library; Hartford *Home League*, Feb. 9 and Aug. 10, 1861, and Feb. 15, 1862.

[2] Milwaukee *Sentinel*, Dec. 2, 1865; New York *Times*, Nov. 30, 1865; La Crosse *Democrat*, Dec. 4, 1865; *Wis. State Jour.*, Dec. 5, 1865 and Jan. 9, 1867.

mortgages dollar for dollar. In frequent instances the securities were sent to lawyers in the cities of southern Wisconsin to be cancelled at from 45 to 55 per cent of their face value.[1]

Several prominent railroad companies likewise compromised with their mortgagors upon terms that silenced at least the most active unrest along their lines. The Milwaukee & Mississippi Railroad made particularly gratifying concessions. When it was reorganized in 1861 as the Milwaukee & Prairie du Chien Company the stock held by its mortgagors was exchanged in the ratio of two shares of the new stock for three shares of the old.[2] The former, it is true, was worth but 12 cents on the dollar at the time of the exchange,[3] and many disheartened farmers did not even trouble to make the substitution. In the summer of 1862, however, by virtue of an agreement with a committee of mortgagors, the new company undertook to retire all of its farm encumbrances.[4] The farmers were to surrender the stock which they held, in addition to which such of them as had signed 8 per cent mortgages should pay upon them one-tenth of the principal and such as had signed 10 per cent mortgages should pay one-fourth of the principal. Upon these liberal terms mortgages to the

[1] Milwaukee *Daily Wis.*, Aug. 16, 1860; Hartford *Home League*, Oct. 18, 1862 and Aug. 15, 1863; Milwaukee *Sentinel*, Jan. 22, 1864.

[2] Milwaukee & Prairie du Chien Railway Company, *Report*, 1865, 18–19; "Circular to Stockholders," 2, 3, bound with Milwaukee & Prairie du Chien Railway Company, *Reports*, 1861–66, No. 9; Hartford *Home League*, Nov. 24, 1860 and Nov. 30, 1861.

[3] *Hunt's Merchants' Magazine*, October, 1865, 297; New York *World*, Mar. 4, 1861.

[4] Hartford *Home League*, Sept. 27, 1862. An arrangement of a similar nature was made with the Milwaukee & Watertown Railroad. *Ibid.*, July 18, 1863, and Feb. 20, 1864.

amount of approximately $500,000 were eventually satisfied.[1]

Those farmers who for one reason or another did not take advantage of this arrangement secured even better terms. The shares of the Milwaukee & Prairie du Chien Railroad rose in value by the middle of 1863, under an honest board of directors, to 90 cents on the dollar, and at that rate many were exchanged for farm encumbrances.[2] Altogether about 700 or 800 farmers on this line escaped foreclosure by such settlements.[3]

The settlement on the La Crosse & Milwaukee line was less satisfactory. It consisted in turning over to an association known as the Wisconsin Railroad Farm Mortgage Land Company so much of the railroad grant of 1856 as the La Crosse company had earned by building its road from Portage to Tomah. The lands were to be sold by commissioners of the State, and the proceeds were to be divided among the mortgagors of the La Crosse & Milwaukee Railroad and the Milwaukee & Horicon Railroad.[4] Such an adjustment had been suggested by Governor Randall in 1860 and 1861, and in 1868 Congress was willing to give its consent.[5]

Even in this poor attempt at restitution, misfortune and scandal pursued the farm mortgagors. The meager proceeds of their lands were irregularly,

[1] Janesville *Gazette*, Oct. 3, 1862; New York *Herald*, Nov. 8, 1862.

[2] *Hunt's Merchants' Magazine*, October, 1865, 297; Milwaukee *Daily Wis.*, Sept. 7, 1863; Milwaukee *Sentinel*, Aug. 17, 1863; Hartford *Home League*, Nov. 21, 1863; Janesville *Gazette*, Aug. 9, 1864; Wis. *Gen. Laws*, 1864, chap. 241.

[3] Janesville *Gazette*, Aug. 9, 1864.

[4] Wis. *Private Laws*, 1868, chap. 446.

[5] U. S. *Statutes at Large*, 40 Cong., 2 sess., chap. 267.

if not corruptly, administered by the commissioners to whom they were entrusted. As an example, one of the presidents of the board secured for his son nearly $10,000 in attorney's fees, though he was unable to state under examination the nature of the services for which about $6,000 of this amount had been paid.[1]

Suspicious, also, were the circumstances under which the major portion of the land grant was sold. Approximately two-thirds of it, amounting to about 160,000 acres, had originally been involved in litigation, being claimed not only by the mortgagors but by several railroad corporations. The title of the mortgagors, though contested, was as perfect as any litigated title could well be, and was confirmed to them in 1879 by a unanimous decision of the United States Circuit Court.[2] Upon appeal the case was carried to the supreme court, where it lay for several years.

While pending there, the board of commissioners, at the instance of its president, sold to Philetus Sawyer, who represented the opposing party in the suit, the entire claim of the mortgagors for a sum representing less than a third of the reputed value of the contested lands. The mortgagors should have obtained nearly half a million dollars for this portion of their grant; they actually received but $136,000.[3]

Charges of corruption were at once raised against the transaction, forcing the legislature to appoint

[1] "Report" of Committee of Investigation, in Wis. *Assem. Jour.*, 1883, app. 4, 33–35. See also the books and papers of Wisconsin Railroad Farm Mortgage Land Company in office of Wisconsin secretary of state.

[2] *Ibid.*; Wis. *Assem. Jour.*, 1883, app. 4, 33–35; Madison & Portage Railroad Company v. Wisconsin *et al.*, *Federal Cases*, No. 8938.

[3] See references cited above, note 1.

a committee of investigation. The latter found many evidences of irregular management and severely criticized the sale, but was unable to establish the charges of collusion.[1] To the mortgagors it mattered little whether their loss was due to fraud or to a gross business error. The important fact to them was that they had been deprived of even the pittance that should have come to them.

Altogether the commissioners of the Wisconsin Railroad Farm Mortgage Land Company realized from the sale of lands $280,267, of which they consumed in the way of expenses considerably more than one-seventh. The remainder they distributed to the 1,024 farm mortgagors whose claims, amounting to a total of $1,311,749, they had audited and approved.[2] At the end of 1883 they turned their affairs over to a regular department of the State government, bringing to a close this last unhappy chapter in the history of the railroad farm mortgagors.

By one means or another most of the railroad encumbrances in the State were cancelled before the end of the sixties, and the tension of the problem was relieved. But popular feeling was by no means over. In the course of the difficulty many sturdy Wisconsin pioneers had been evicted from their homesteads, larger numbers had suffered serious losses, and all had for years endured agonies of uncertainty as to their ultimate fate. Nothing could persuade such men that railroad officials were not elementally and thoroughly villainous. Before many years they found

[1] See references cited *ante*, 268, note 1.

[2] Wisconsin Railroad Farm Mortgage Land Company Commissioners, *Substitute Report*, Dec. 1, 1883, 5.

vent for their enmity in the rush of retaliatory legislation that marked the Granger uprising in Wisconsin.

Thus during the period of the Civil War Wisconsin met the problem that had confronted commonwealths elsewhere and at other times in the form of state indebtedness. Her farmers, it is clear, became entangled in the snare chiefly because her basic law estopped promoters from the usual procedure of tapping the public treasury. The framers of the Wisconsin constitution had failed to foresee that a powerful public demand, halted at one obstruction, merely finds other outlets for expression.

To the historian the railroad farm-mortgage uprising is chiefly significant because of the degree to which it typifies the reactions of the pioneer West. In origin, methods, and results it was a characteristic frontier movement. Viewed in the cold light of law it was clearly an attempt at repudiation. It was the revolt of an organized debtor class against an absent creditor class. Southern Wisconsin represented the former—thousands of suffering farmers and their scores of thousands of sympathetic friends. The East represented the latter—thousands of security holders who, in part at least, had invested their money in good faith. The two groups were separated by too great a distance to be able to temper or even to understand the position one of the other. The mortgagors regarded the mortgagees as greedy speculators, who in the hope of winning illicit gain had knowingly and willfully purchased securities tainted with fraud. The easterners, on the other hand, regarded Wisconsin as a community lost to honor, the abode of corrupt politicians, and the home of a degraded people.

CHAPTER X

RAILROAD CONSTRUCTION IN WISCONSIN

At the beginning of the nineteenth century the destinies of the trans-Allegheny region were linked inseparably to the Mississippi River. Upon its ample bosom her farmers sent to market the products of their toil; upon it they depended for their supplies and their connection with the outside world. To it they owed even their intellectual and spiritual progress. Any attempt to limit or restrict its use met with their prompt resentment. Indeed, such prominent and representative westerners as Wilkinson, later commander in chief of the American army, Sevier, who afterward became governor and senator of Tennessee, Robertson, the founder of Cumberland, and Blount, who later served Tennessee as United States senator, would rather have accepted the sovereignty of a foreign power than have permitted the surrender by the American government of the free navigation of the Mississippi River. It is well known that in purchasing Louisiana Jefferson was actuated primarily by the need for securing to the West control of the mouth of the great interior highway.[1]

In 1861 the Confederacy closed this national outlet to northern commerce. It did so only with reluctance. It harbored no resentment against the West; its quarrel was with New England. Indeed, one of the

[1] F. J. Turner, "The Mississippi Valley in American History," in Mississippi Valley Historical Association, *Proceedings*, 1909–10, 159–84.

first measures of the Confederate Congress before the outbreak of hostilities was to promise to the upper valley freedom of navigation of the Mississippi. Some well-informed southerners actually entertained the hope that the Northwest would ultimately join hands with the power that controlled the mouth of the great south-flowing river. It was only when hostilities had formally begun that the Confederacy enforced the blockade at Cairo.

What was the reaction of the Northwest to this hostile blow? Was its commercial life prostrated? Did it consider following the South into secession? Its proud record on the battle-field and in the workshop during four years of bloody war is sufficient answer. The embargo, it is true, seriously embarrassed for a short time the river region between Keokuk and Cairo.[1] In all the region west of Lake Michigan, however, it did not even create a ripple. The press of Wisconsin barely noticed the new order of events, and the vigorous Governor Randall referred to it only in a few brief sentences in his first war message to the legislature.[2]

This strange indifference of Wisconsin, Minnesota, northern Iowa, and northern Illinois to the blockade of the Mississippi has but one explanation. The great river had been superseded by other routes as the carrier of their commerce. The Erie Canal and

[1] Mississippi River towns and Ohio River towns lying in the border region between Union and Confederate territory, particularly Cincinnati and St. Louis, were severely affected by the blockade, for a large part of their wholesale trade had been carried on by river with southern towns. See New York *Tribune*, June 13, 1861; Cincinnati Chamber of Commerce, *Reports*, 1861–65; St. Louis Union Merchants' Exchange, *Reports*, 1861–65.

[2] Special message of May 15, 1861 in Wis. *Mess. and Docs.*, 1862, 33. See also Governor Salomon's annual message of 1863 in *id.*, 1863, p. iii.

the recently completed east and west railroads transported western products to the seaboard more quickly and economically than ever the river had done. The secessionists, who fondly hoped that their control of the southern outlet would force the Northwest to follow them out of the Union, had failed to take cognizance of the fact that during the previous quarter of a century a revolution in transportation had occurred as swift and as tremendous as any the world has ever seen.

On Jan. 24, 1863 the Milwaukee *Sentinel* observed:

> But when it is asserted that the North West will go with the power which holds possession of the mouth of the Mississippi, forsaking her sacred constitutional obligations, it is time to consider what is the actual relative value of the Mississippi as an outlet of our commerce, as compared with the natural and artificial means of communication eastward. We will say nothing now of the utter degradation which would follow the appendage of the free North West as a tail to the Southern Confederacy. We will not urge the strong family ties, which stretch by millions of invisible chords from the East to the West, and whose sundering would cause more lasting woe than all the battles of the present war.
>
> We wish simply to show by cold, undeniable, easily appreciated statistical figures, how insignificant is the value of the lower Mississippi to us of the West, as compared with the communications which terminate at the East.
>
> There is a large portion of the community whose ideas upon this question would have been just, thirty years ago, when the Mississippi was the only outlet for western products. But these thirty years have witnessed the greatest development in the way of artificial communication between the East and West, that was ever known in history.[1]

The Northwest, so the editorial concludes after a striking array of statistics, has no interests in common with the Confederacy. It no longer faces New Orleans; it looks eastward, its outlet is the Erie Canal, and its future lies with New York.

[1] Milwaukee *Sentinel*, Jan. 24, 1863; see also Oshkosh *Northwestern*, Dec. 12, 1860 and Feb. 1, 1861.

The farmers of interior Wisconsin, Minnesota, Iowa, and Illinois were able to make use of the Erie Canal, however, only because they possessed other agents for hauling their products to the shores of Lake Michigan. The latter were the railroads extending westward from Milwaukee and Chicago. To these overland carriers, in the last analysis, Wisconsin and her sister states owed their deliverance from the domination of the southern water route.

The railroads lying west of Lake Michigan differed widely from the eastern trunk lines in the character of the service they performed. They were the grain gatherers of the Northwest. At thousands of minor agricultural depots they picked up small parcels of wheat and corn for transportation to the grain elevators of the lake ports. At the shores of Lake Michigan their labors ceased. Thence to the seaboard their accumulations were transported by the lake carriers or the great eastern trunk lines.

By a coincidence that seems almost providential Wisconsin's important railroads, connecting the Lake and the Mississippi, were completed just in time to be in good running order at the outbreak of the Civil War. Her two chief westward lines, the Milwaukee & Mississippi and the La Crosse & Milwaukee, reached the river in the years 1857 and 1858 respectively. The less important Racine & Mississippi made river connection at Freeport, Illinois, in 1859, completing its own through line in the summer of 1862. When the Civil War began, Wisconsin had in operation some 900 miles of single track, all of which had been constructed during the preceding ten years.[1] It would be

[1] Wisconsin Railroad Commissioner, *Report*, 1889–90, 199.

difficult to exaggerate the extent or the importance of the service which these carriers rendered during the critical years of the Civil War, not only to Wisconsin but to the entire settled region west of the Mississippi.

In the history of the country periods of great prosperity have usually been years of rapid railroad expansion. In Wisconsin, however, the boom years from 1863 to 1868 witnessed practically no progress of this kind. Indeed, less miles of railroad were constructed in the seven years following the outbreak of the war than in the single year preceding the panic of 1857. It is true that railroad building was restricted in other parts of the North during the war, due no doubt to the superior attractiveness of industrial and governmental investments and the high cost of labor and material.[1] In Wisconsin, however, the falling off in construction was unusual and requires further explanation.

The deterrents to railroad construction in the State were local as well as foreign. The northern half of Wisconsin was still a forest wilderness, employing waterways only for the transportation to market of lumber, its single product. This region did not even hold forth a promise of ever being able to sustain a sufficient agricultural population to make railroad investments pay. The southern half of Wisconsin was struggling with an acute problem of railroad indebtedness and as a result of its bitter experiences had become suspicious of all railroad enterprises.

On the other hand, Wisconsin's western neighbors,

[1] See Henry V. Poor, *Manual of Railroads of the United States, 1871–72* (New York, 1871), p. xxiv.

Minnesota and Iowa, held out the most alluring attractions to railroad promoters. They contained a smaller proportion of railroads than the Badger State, and were developing with far greater rapidity. They had several magnificent railroad land grants within their gift which they were eager to bestow upon any responsible taker. Their valuable wheat trade was a final powerful stimulus, the object of keen competition between the railroads of Chicago and Milwaukee.[1]

Especially to the owners of Wisconsin railroad lines did extensions into these new regions appear essential. Southern Wisconsin was becoming increasingly subject to crop shortages, owing to the exhaustion of her soil. The railroads serving this part of Wisconsin repeatedly found themselves without adequate traffic. Necessity itself forced them to seek other sources of freight in the fresh and fertile fields beyond the Mississippi. It was for this reason that, during the years of the war, the owners of the Milwaukee & St. Paul Railway Company took a prominent part in building the Minnesota Central Railroad, and after the return of peace spread their line rapidly over northern Iowa. For the same reason the Milwaukee & Prairie du Chien Company aided in constructing, and eventually took over, the McGregor & Western Railroad. A combination of Chicago and Milwaukee railroad promoters was heavily interested in building the Winona & St. Peter through southern Minnesota, and the Chicago & Northwestern extension across the Michigan peninsula. In 1863 Minnesota had only 31 miles of railroad

[1] See Milwaukee & St. Paul Railway Company, *Reports*, 1860–70; Milwaukee & Prairie du Chien Railway Company, *Reports*, 1861–66.

as compared with 957 in Wisconsin. Nine years later she had approximately 1,900 miles and had almost overtaken her neighbor.[1] It was in these foreign ventures that Wisconsin railroad capital found its outlet during the years 1863 to 1868.

Although railroad construction in Wisconsin was thus practically at a standstill there was no cessation of agitation for new lines. No village or hamlet in the State but had some ambitious railroad project to urge. Local papers and politicians who had an eye to popular favor saw to it that such an issue never slumbered long. Milwaukee was appealed to for railroad connections by every locality within striking distance. The trade that would follow, she was assured, would within a few years repay all her outlay. When she failed to respond she was roundly abused for lack of enterprise and warned that her wide-awake rival to the south would soon seize the opportunity she was neglecting. Although in the seven years following the outbreak of the war only 130 miles of railroad were constructed in the State, thirty-three new railroad companies were incorporated during this period, and these represented only the select few that were mature enough to secure official recognition.[2]

In 1868 railroad building in Wisconsin revived, and thereafter its progress was rapid. Within six years the mileage of the State had more than doubled. In January, 1868 Wisconsin contained but 1,030 miles of railroad, nearly all of which lay within the southern third of its area. By the end of 1873 the

[1] St. Paul Board of Trade, *Report*, 1873, 34.

[2] See Wis. *Private Laws* and Wis. *Gen. Laws* for the years 1861 to 1868.

State contained 2,379 miles, and northern Wisconsin was coming into its own.[1] Into that region three land-grant railroads were being projected, the Wisconsin Central, the West Wisconsin, and the extension of the Chicago & Northwestern from Green Bay to Marinette. Three other lines of notable importance, the Green Bay & Lake Pepin, the Wisconsin Valley, and the Milwaukee & Northern, were at the same time under way. This was as distinctly the period of northern railroad development, as the first period of construction from 1850 to 1860 had been distinctly southern.

The first railroads built in the United States were designed, like the canals which they superseded, to span the land lying between navigable watercourses. It was not expected that they would compete with water routes, but merely serve as feeders to them. The railroads of Wisconsin at the beginning of the Civil War admirably illustrate this general tendency. Wisconsin is a relatively narrow strip of land lying between two great water systems, the Mississippi on the west and Lake Michigan on the east. Her first railroads were constructed primarily with a view to uniting these and serving to carry freight between them. Incidentally, for this reason the general direction of her lines was east and west.

Railroad connection between river and lake had been demanded by the lead miners of southwestern Wisconsin as early as the forties. Lead was thus the first of the economic products of the State actively to raise its voice for overland transportation.[2] By

[1] Wisconsin *Blue Book*, 1911, 660.

[2] See O. G. Libby "Significance of the Lead and Shot Trade in Early Wisconsin History," in *Wis. Hist. Colls.*, XIII, 293–334.

the middle of the fifties the mineral interest of western Wisconsin was decadent. However, a new and more potent force for railroad stimulation had already taken its place. This was the spring wheat of the Wisconsin, Iowa, and Minnesota prairies. Wheat was the power that successfully united the Mississippi River and Lake Michigan.

At the close of the Civil War two new economic forces, lumber and iron, became prominent in northern Wisconsin and upper Michigan. Both clamored for railroad connection with the outside world. The lumbermen and the iron miners required railroads not so much for the shipment of their products to market as for obtaining their supplies. Their demands were reënforced, moreover, by those of the wheat growers of the newly settled northwestern counties of Wisconsin that were pressing to secure direct access to the lake-shore ports. It is doubtful whether, even combined, these forces would have proved sufficient to attract railroad capital. It required the added stimulus of several enormous land grants from the Federal government to accomplish this end, and even with their aid construction lagged until near the close of the decade.

Congress was exceedingly generous to Wisconsin in the quantity of land which it bestowed upon her for the encouragement of her railroad projects. In two magnificent grants, that of June 3, 1856 and that of May 5, 1864, it gave her for this purpose more than 3,750,000 acres, constituting over one-tenth the total land area of the State.[1] None can justly

[1] Wisconsin Railroad Commissioner, *Report*, 1874, pt. 1, 227–43; H. O. Winkler, *A History of the State Lands of Wisconsin* (Ms. thesis, 1912, in the University of Wisconsin Library).

doubt the benevolence that prompted these gifts. The question may, however, properly be raised whether they were wisely given and whether they accomplished the purposes for which they were intended.

No doubt land grants hastened by several years the construction of a few desirable Wisconsin lines. On the other hand, the tardiness with which most of the beneficiaries of such subsidies fulfilled the obligations imposed upon them defeated the object for which they were given. Corporations, at first eager to secure grants, apparently lost all interest in them as soon as they were won. Usually they failed either partially or wholly to take the steps necessary to earn unconditional title. In a number of instances unsubsidized corporations actually penetrated the land-grant regions as soon as did the recipients of public bounty. From the beginning to the end the story of Wisconsin railroad land grants is a dreary recital of time extensions, forfeitures, divisions, and regrants. The energy and patience of successive legislatures and, what was even more deplorable, the honor of at least one of them were dissipated in the process.

The first grant bestowed upon the State provided for one northeastern and one northwestern railroad. This was disposed of by the Wisconsin legislature on Oct. 11, 1856 after a long and exciting contest.[1] So much of the grant as applied to a northeastern railroad was conferred upon the Wisconsin & Lake Superior Railroad; so much as applied to a northwestern railroad was conferred upon the La Crosse

[1] Wis. *Gen. Laws*, 1856, chaps. 122 and 137.

& Milwaukee. The former was but the agent of an association that later developed into the Chicago & Northwestern, and this corporation, having complied with its obligations by constructing a road from Fond du Lac to Marinette, ultimately received patent from the Federal government to 546,446 acres of its grant.[1]

The northwestern portion of the gift contemplated a line extending from Madison or Columbus by way of Portage to St. Croix River or Lake, and thence to the western end of Lake Superior, with a branch jutting off to Bayfield. It was expected that this road would connect at Lake Superior with the projected Northern Pacific, the branch line to Bayfield being the private speculation of a senator from Minnesota. In 1858 a legislative investigation into the circumstances surrounding the bestowal of this grant revealed the astounding and humiliating fact that the La Crosse & Milwaukee Company had secured it only after bribing the governor and practically the entire legislature of the State. The guilty corporation had distributed $355,000 of its bonds among assemblymen, $175,000 among senators, $50,000 to the governor, $16,000 among clerks, and $246,000 among persons in and about the capitol.[2] Wisconsin's shame was cried from one end of the land to the other, while its indignant citizens looked on in helpless rage. Fortunately the La Crosse Company did not long enjoy its ill-gotten gains. Badly managed as well as corrupt, it neglected after securing the grant even to fulfil the requirements

[1] U. S. Land Office, *Report*, 1910, 23.

[2] Wis. *Assem. Jour.*, 1858, appendix; *id.*, 1859, appendix.

imposed by it. When, therefore, its board of directors in 1858 requested the newly elected Governor Randall to certify to the completion of twenty miles of its road, the latter not only refused such a certificate but blocked in the general land office at Washington the patenting of 230,400 acres for which Governor Bashford had previously certified.[1]

The La Crosse & Milwaukee Railroad and its successor, the Milwaukee & St. Paul, repeatedly appealed to Governor Randall and his successors during the Civil War for more generous consideration, protesting against the harshness of their punishment. Popular sentiment, however, was too strong to permit any concession, and in 1868 the Milwaukee & St. Paul, despairing of success, agreed to an act of Congress by which all of that portion of the lands, to which it would have been entitled for constructing sixty-one miles of road from Portage to Tomah, was conferred upon the Wisconsin Railroad Farm Mortgage Land Company. To this corporation 163,159 acres of land were eventually patented and sold for the benefit of Wisconsin's railroad farm mortgagors.[2]

The remainder of the La Crosse & Milwaukee grant was parcelled out by the legislature of Wisconsin during the Civil War to three separate corporations. So much of it as applied to a road from Madison to Portage was in 1861 conferred upon the Sugar River Valley Railroad, which neglected, however, to comply with its requirements and eventually failed, in spite of long litigation, to secure title to any lands. In

[1] *Id.*, 1860, 769–75; A. W. Randall, "Annual Message" for 1859, in Wis. *Mess. and Docs.*, 1859, 16–18.

[2] U. S. Land Office, *Report*, 1910, 23.

1863 that portion which applied to a line from Tomah to Lake St. Croix was conferred upon the newly organized Tomah & Lake St. Croix Railroad, and was ultimately earned, the Federal government having in 1864 almost doubled its value.[1] That portion which applied to a road from St. Croix River or Lake to the western end of Lake Superior, with a branch to Bayfield, had a history which in itself illustrates the entire trend of Wisconsin land-grant transactions.

In 1856 it was secretly transferred by the La Crosse & Milwaukee Company to the St. Croix & Lake Superior Company in return for the support which the latter had given it a few months before in influencing the legislative decision. In the following year the bargain received the formal sanction of the Wisconsin legislature. In 1864 Congress enriched the gift by raising from six to ten miles the radius from which alternate sections of land could be chosen. In spite of all this generosity, however, the St. Croix Company made little effort to earn title, and in 1869, its time limit having expired, the grant reverted to the Federal government. In 1872 Congress was prevailed upon to renew the gift, and it was then conferred upon the Milwaukee & St. Paul Railroad, only to be rejected by the company because of objections to some of the conditions it imposed. Ultimately it was earned by the North Wisconsin Railroad and its successor, the Chicago, St. Paul, Minneapolis & Omaha. It proved to be the richest of any of the railroad land grants of Wisconsin, netting to its beneficiaries a vast domain of 1,288,209 acres of valuable timberland.[2]

[1] *Ibid.*
[2] *Ibid.*

While successive Wisconsin legislatures were thus wearily engaged in donating, dividing, repealing, and reconferring portions of the first great railroad grant of 1856, Congress was preparing to bestow upon the State another grant. The new donation was but one of the many lavish gifts of the Federal government to loyal states during the critical years 1862 to 1864, when more public lands were given away for the encouragement of railroad enterprises than had ever been given before or have ever been given since. The grant comprised "every alternate odd numbered section for ten miles on each side of a railroad located from Portage City, Berlin, Doty's Island, or Fond du Lac in a northwestern direction to Bayfield, and thence to Superior on Lake Superior."[1]

The Wisconsin legislature of 1865 was confronted with the difficult task of disposing of this new bequest. All the cities named in the congressional act were eager to be made the terminal point of the railroad which it contemplated, and to their contentions were added the rivalries of Milwaukee and Chicago. Milwaukee interests favored Fond du Lac, expecting in the event of success to build a line northward connecting with the proposed railroad at the foot of Lake Winnebago. Portage was championed by Chicago which looked forward to a union with the proposed road by way of a line through Genoa and Madison.[2] The legislature seemed to favor Portage but the delegation from that city was divided, a part insisting that in disposing of the lands some provision

[1] U. S. *Statutes*, 38 Cong., 1 sess., chap. 80.

[2] See *Wis. State Jour.;* Portage *Register;* Milwaukee *Sentinel;* and Milwaukee *Daily News*, during legislative sessions of 1865 and 1866.

be made for the relief of Wisconsin's railroad farm mortgagors. The Milwaukee forces shrewdly secured a postponement of the entire question by throwing their strength to this farm-mortgage element.

In 1866 a compromise was effected by incorporating two railroad companies, the first of which was authorized to build a road from Doty's Island to Stevens Point, the second from Portage to Stevens Point, and the two to construct and operate jointly the remainder of the line from Stevens Point to Lake Superior.[1] The bill anticipated a consolidation of the two railroads, which was, in fact, effected three years later. The resulting Portage, Winnebago & Lake Superior Railroad, the name of which was soon changed to the Wisconsin Central Railroad, eventually constructed the necessary track and secured patent in northern Wisconsin to 837,227 acres of valuable timberland.[2]

In southern Wisconsin there was some scattering criticism of the land-grant policy as early even as the sixties. Northern Wisconsin, for the benefit of which the aid was chiefly given, was, however, generally favorable to it.[3] It roundly denounced the antagonism in southern Wisconsin, comparing such an attitude to that of the politician who would "kick away the ladder by which he has climbed up to prominence and fame."[4] Its feeling toward land

[1] Wis. *Private Laws*, 1866, chaps. 314 and 362.

[2] U. S. Land Office, *Report*, 1910, 23.

[3] Wis. *Assem. Jour.*, 1867, 326; Wis. *Sen. Jour.*, 1867, 244; Hartford *Home League*, Nov. 10, 1860. Compare J. G. Thompson, "Wheat Growing in Wisconsin," University of Wisconsin, *Bulletin*, No. 292 (Madison, 1909), 144–45.

[4] There were some exceptions to this rule. In northwestern Wisconsin into which settlement was rushing with great rapidity during the sixties,

grants was strikingly expressed in the Chippewa *Herald* of Nov. 12, 1870:

> What is the public domain good for while it remains public domain? We want cattle—not buffalo. We want sheep—not antelopes. We want emigrants—not Indians. Railroads will not be built through a howling wilderness without aid. Government loses nothing by the aid rendered. It is true, settlers pay more for land, but is there not a large amount of public domain for them to select from? * * * I fear [referring to opposition to land grants] that the same spirit is alive that opposed free schools, free men, and free homesteads.

Northern Wisconsin on the whole considered no sacrifice too great that would bring new railroads. It was willing to go to the same great lengths in its zeal for transportation facilities that had marked southern Wisconsin during the previous period of railroad construction. Towns, cities, and villages all along the lines of projected railroads were ready to plunge themselves into debt in order to encourage construction, although scores of towns, villages, and cities of southern Wisconsin that had adopted the same course during the railroad craze from 1850 to 1860 were now either bankrupt or on the verge of bankruptcy.

It was a fortunate restriction in the Wisconsin constitution which prohibited its legislature from granting aid in any form to internal improvement associations. Undoubtedly the State was saved by it from those embarrassing railroad tangles that marked the early history of Minnesota. Northern Wisconsin, however, in its ardor for overland trans-

the withdrawal of large sections of public lands from entry for the benefit of the "land monopolists" was resented, and the dissatisfaction was increased by the exemption of these lands from taxation and the long delays of the favored railroads in building the promised lines. Chippewa *Herald*, Oct. 29, 1870.

portation was eager to remove this prohibition. In the legislative session of 1867 a joint resolution was introduced calling upon the proper authorities to submit to a vote of the people a constitutional amendment empowering the State to donate $100,000 for every twenty continuous miles of railroad thereafter constructed within Wisconsin.[1] This unusual measure was readily carried, the Senate voting almost unanimously in its favor and the Assembly accepting it by a majority of fifty-six to thirty-three. The northern counties voted solidly for the resolution while the southern counties were divided. The railroad farm mortgagors at first attempted to amend the measure so as to oblige railroads receiving the bounty to discharge their mortgage obligations, but failing in this, they turned solidly to the opposition.[2]

Constitutional procedure made necessary the adoption of the resolution by the following legislature before it could be submitted to a referendum. Fortunately in the legislatures of 1868 and 1869 it was defeated by the votes of southern Wisconsin. We have here, as well as in questions relating to land grants, evidence of an interesting, though not always clearly defined, sectional alignment within the State, the frontier northern areas ranging themselves in favor of railroads and the well-settled southern areas taking their stand against them.

Many and perplexing as were the evils and problems that thus attended the construction of Wisconsin's railroad system, they were a hundred times

[1] Wis. *Gen. Laws*, 1867, Joint Resolution, No. 14.

[2] See index to Wis. *Sen. Jour.*, and Wis. *Assem. Jour.* for 1867 under Resolutions, Joint, No. 16S.

offset by the services which the completed carriers rendered. Undoubtedly it was to overland transportation that the entire region west of Lake Michigan owed its abounding prosperity during the critical years of the Civil War.

The railroads themselves shared generously in this universal affluence. Thanks to the blockade of the Mississippi they enjoyed, uncontested, the rich traffic of the upper valley. New equipments, better roadbeds, and the unification of scattered lines became possible as a result. They gained an advantage over the river route that under ordinary circumstances only the effort of years would have given. The merchants of the upper-river towns learned during the embargo to depend on the speed, certainty, and directness of overland shipment, and when the Mississippi was again opened to commerce it secured only a meager and diminishing fraction of the trade that had once been entirely its own.

CHAPTER XI

RAILROAD CONSOLIDATION

Concentration was one of the striking characteristics of the commercial and industrial life of the United States during the decade of the sixties. In Wisconsin this was particularly true of transportation agents. At no other time in the history of the State has railroad consolidation proceeded so swiftly as during these eventful years. During this period both of the great systems, that we now know as the Chicago, Milwaukee & St. Paul and the Chicago & Northwestern, rose to importance in the transportation world as a result of consolidations.

The experience of the Northwest has been that waves of railroad consolidation follow upon periods of great industrial depression. This is an entirely natural sequence. As a result of hard times newly constructed roads become bankrupt and fall into the hands of their bondholders. The latter, eager to realize upon their property, are ready to sell upon reasonable terms or equally willing to cut competitive expenses by consolidating with rival lines. At the outbreak of the Civil War practically all railroads in Wisconsin were entangled in the crash of the panic of 1857. With scarcely any exception they were bankrupt, isolated, and fragmentary, their lines in the hands of court receivers, and their property for sale under foreclosure proceedings. The unification of these struggling elements into several great railroad systems was the task which the Civil War period inaugurated and partially carried to completion.

The nucleus about which the Wisconsin consolidation movement centered was the old La Crosse & Milwaukee Railroad. This interesting corporation, a part of whose sensational career has already been traced, was in 1859 hopelessly bankrupt. In 1863 its line was sold under foreclosure to its bondholders, who at once organized a new corporation, known as the Milwaukee & St. Paul Railway Company,[1] to operate it. Within a few weeks the latter had reunited the eastern and western divisions of its road, which had been separated during the period of receivership, and, thereafter, despite an almost endless maze of litigation, continued to keep them united except for an interval of two years. In a few months it had come into possession of three other bankrupt lines, the Milwaukee & Western, the Milwaukee & Horicon, and the Ripon & Wolf River, and was making overtures to its chief competitor, the Milwaukee & Prairie du Chien, either to pool earnings or consolidate. Its president, Alexander Mitchell, was president of the recently consolidated Chicago & Milwaukee Railroad, and was in addition actively

[1] The organization of this road led to protracted litigation in which important legal principles concerning the foreclosure of railroad properties and organization of new companies were for the first time laid down. See J. W. Cary, *Organization and History of the Chicago, Milwaukee and St. Paul Railway Company* (Milwaukee, 1893); Wis. Railroad Commission, *Report*, 1874, Official Papers, 78–98; Milwaukee *Sentinel*, Mar. 23, 1863, Feb. 15, 1864, Jan. 4, 9, and 24, 1866, Feb. 10, 1866, Mar. 6, 7, and 14, 1866, Nov. 7, 1866, and Mar. 23, 1868; Milwaukee *Daily Wis.*, June 6 and 13, 1863, and April 4 and 5, 1865; Portage *Register*, May 20, June 17, and July 1, 1865, and Jan. 5, 1866.

interested in the construction of new lines in Minnesota. At the close of the Civil War the Milwaukee & St. Paul was one of the three controlling railway systems in Wisconsin.

The grand coup of the new organization took place in the spring of 1866, being nothing less than the sudden and dramatic absorption of its chief rival, the Milwaukee & Prairie du Chien. For a proper understanding of this interesting event, important not only because of its results but because of the degree to which it typified western railroad and legislative methods, it is necessary to allude briefly to the early history of the Milwaukee & Prairie du Chien Company.

This corporation, like the Milwaukee & St. Paul, was an association of bondholders, organized in 1861 to purchase and operate the line of the bankrupt Milwaukee & Mississippi Railroad. The terms under which the reorganization was affected were somewhat peculiar, though entirely creditable in their spirit to the bondholders. Common stock was to earn no dividends and be entitled to no voice in the election of directors until a mortgage of $2,556,000 had been completely liquidated.

From the beginning the affairs of the new Company were managed conservatively, and the value of its common stock rose from 12 cents on the dollar at the time of reorganization to 90 cents by the middle of 1863.[1] Its securities, it is true, declined heavily during the fall of 1864 and the spring of 1865,[2] but

[1] *Documents Relating to the Organization of the Milwaukee & Prairie du Chien Railway Company* (New York, 1861), bound with Milwaukee & Prairie du Chien Railway Company, *Report*, 1865, 16–24.

[2] *Hunt's Merchants' Magazine*, October, 1865, 297.

this was due to causes which affected adversely all railroad lines in Wisconsin, the failure of the wheat crop of 1864 and the return of peace in 1865. By 1866 the company had received three offers from its rival, the Milwaukee & St. Paul, to consolidate lines or pool earnings. The first of these, made in the summer of 1863, had come to naught.[1] The second, an offer of outright sale in the summer of 1865 by the hard-pressed Milwaukee & St. Paul, it had likewise been obliged to forego.[2] The third, however, a proposal for a system of prorating earnings, suggested in the spring of 1866, it had agreed to[3] and was preparing to try out when several events occurred that necessitated wholly different arrangements.

The first of these was the springing of the notorious "Prairie Dog Corner" on the New York Stock Exchange. "Prairie Dog" is the English version of Prairie du Chien, and the "Prairie Dog Corner" was a speculation in the common stock of the Milwaukee & Prairie du Chien Company. The men engaged in this operation, among whom the brokerage firm of Henry Stimson & Company was the most prominent, had for several months been making their preparations. Quietly, they had bought up, at the low prices prevailing, all of the 29,880 shares of the Prairie du Chien common stock. Many of these they loaned to unsuspecting neighbors, others they scattered about Wall Street subject to short call.

[1] See *post*, 300–304.

[2] Milwaukee & Prairie du Chien Railway Company, *Directors' Proceedings*, June 7 and 9, 1865.

[3] Note that pooling arrangements were at this time entirely lawful. See Milwaukee & Prairie du Chien Railway Company, *Report*, 1866, 7; also Document No. 2242 in the Milwaukee office of the Chicago Milwaukee & St. Paul Railway Company.

On Nov. 6, 1865 they were ready to show their hand. Borrowers were suddenly notified to return their loans, and the firms that had sold short were called upon to deliver. A day of wild sensation followed. Brokers unprepared to deliver rushed to the exchange to buy, only to find that Prairie du Chien common stock was not to be had except at fabulous prices. Stocks which had sold ten days before for $64.50 now commanded $230. According to the New York *Times* it was "the sharpest and beyond all precedent the most sudden corner known to the forty years' history of the New York stock exchange."[1]

It appears that the speculators engaged in this transaction were unaware of the peculiar provision in the Prairie du Chien charter denying common stockholders the right to vote for directors.[2] They were now in the unpleasant predicament of owning a majority interest in a far-off western railroad, yet having no control over its administration. They were, however, resolute men, not to be balked in their purposes by mere legal restrictions. In the spring of 1866 Stimson & Company engaged an astute Madison lawyer to attend the session of the Wisconsin legislature and secure for them an amendment to the charter of the Prairie du Chien Railroad bestowing upon common stockholders the right to a voice in the affairs of that company. Five thousand dollars was to be his reward for securing such an enactment.

[1] For interesting details concerning this corner and the injunction proceedings which grew out of it, see the financial columns of the New York *Herald* and New York *Times* for Nov. 6 to Nov. 20, 1865; also *Hunt's Merchants' Magazine*, December, 1865, 46; Milwaukee & Prairie du Chien Railway Company, *Report*, 1865, 8–9.

[2] *Ibid.*, 16–24.

On March 22 the measure desired by Stimson & Company was introduced with entire candor in the Senate. On the previous day, however, another bill, accomplishing by indirection the same ends, had been quietly slipped into the Assembly. The first bill was speedily discovered and exposed by the legislative agents of the Prairie du Chien Company. Upon their threat to flood the market with new issues of common stock, Stimson was compelled to order it dropped. He further agreed not to introduce any new measure of such a character at that session, though he said nothing concerning the secret bill which was at that very moment quietly working its way through the Assembly. The vigilance of the railroad officials was relaxed, and the operations of Stimson's attorney were not detected. The latter represented to the committee before which his bill appeared that it was intended to apply solely to a corrupt Madison pelroleum mining company, and since some forty-five or fifty other measures relating to petroleum companies were before the legislature, this explanation was readily accepted. The close of the session was near at hand and in the usual rush of legislative business bills were passed without careful scrutiny. On the last day of the session the fateful "petroleum bill" was signed by Governor Fairchild, together with scores of other measures, and as a result Stimson and his associates had come into control of the Milwaukee & Prairie du Chien Railway.[1]

[1] For details concerning the passage of this measure see Wis. *Assem. Jour.*, 1866, 692, 864, 933, 937, 1124, 1154, 1157; *id.*, 1867, 1282–1291; Wis. *Sen. Jour.*, 1866, 652, 929; *id.*, 1867, 277–80, 336–38; Wis. *Gen. Laws*, 1866, chap. 88.

Stimson at once entered into negotiations with the officers of the Milwaukee & St. Paul Company to sell out to them the holdings which he possessed. His offer was eagerly accepted. At the end of April, 1866, just when the pooling arrangement between the two railroads, to which reference has been made, was to have gone into effect, control of the Prairie du Chien Railway passed into the hands of its rival. For Stimson and his associates the operation had been an extremely profitable one. For their common stock, amounting to some 29,200 shares, they received an equal number of first preferred shares of the Milwaukee & St. Paul Company and 25 per cent more of common.[1] The unhappy officers of the Prairie du Chien Company fought for a time to retain possession of their road, but near the close of 1867 became discouraged and sold out their interests to their victorious rivals.

In acquiring possession of the Prairie du Chien properties the Milwaukee & St. Paul Company also secured control of the McGregor & Western Railroad. Thereafter for many years its chief interest lay in expanding westward as swiftly as possible over Iowa, Minnesota, Nebraska, and Dakota. However, the construction of these feeders did not so entirely engross its energies as to preclude new consolidations in Wisconsin. In 1868 a lease of the West Wisconsin Railway, then under construction from Tomah to Hudson, was obtained. In the winter of 1868–69 Alexander Mitchell, while on a visit to his native

[1] Cary, *The History of the Chicago, Milwaukee & St. Paul Railway Company*, 81; see also statement of Judge Jason Downer in Milwaukee *Sentinel*, Mar. 4, 1867.

home in Scotland, purchased from the City Bank of Glasgow a controlling interest in the Racine & Mississippi. By the end of 1869 the Milwaukee & St. Paul Company controlled every Wisconsin through route leading from the lake shore to the Mississippi River.

Surprising as was this swift integration of the Milwaukee & St. Paul system, it was but a counterpart to a similar development of the Chicago & Northwestern. The latter corporation, like the Milwaukee & St. Paul, arose out of the panic of 1857.[1] It, too, represented an association of bondholders and creditors, in this instance of the bankrupt Chicago, St. Paul & Fond du Lac Railroad Company. Being at that time quite as much a Wisconsin as an Illinois organization, it was incorporated under the laws of both Wisconsin and Illinois in 1859.[2] During the early sixties it rapidly extended its line by way of the valleys of the Rock and Fox rivers to Green Bay. Its road differed in two notable respects from most Wisconsin railroads: First, it ran north and south; second, it served a variety of interests instead of a single one. From the well-settled Rock River Valley it drew wheat and agricultural products; as it proceeded northward it drained the pineries of the Wolf River and Green Bay, serving at the same time the aspiring young manufacturing communities of the lower Fox; and when in 1864 the "Extension" across the Michigan peninsula was built it tapped the rich iron mines of the Lake Superior region.

[1] For the early history of the Chicago & Northwestern Railway see W. H. Stennett, *History of the Chicago and North Western Railway System* (Chicago, 1910); Milwaukee *Semi-Weekly Wisconsin*, Sept. 8, 1869; letter of Pres. W. B. Ogden in Chicago *Tribune*, June 5, 1868.

[2] Chicago & Northwestern Railway Company, *Report*, 1865, 3–45.

The Chicago & Northwestern Company began its remarkable career of consolidation in January, 1864, when it acquired a controlling interest in the bankrupt Kenosha, Rockford & Rock Island Railroad, a line recently completed from Kenosha to Rockford.[1] In the spring of the same year it undertook to eliminate the severe and injurious competition which had for years been carried on with the Galena & Chicago Union Railroad, and its efforts were entirely successful. On June 3, 1864 to the surprise of the whole railroad world it absorbed its rival, though it was apparently the weaker and less prosperous road of the two. A suit to dissolve the combination was instituted by stockholders of the Galena & Chicago Union, who alleged that both this and the Kenosha consolidation had been accomplished by the machinations of a corrupt inner ring of the Chicago & Northwestern. However, the action had no other effect than to depress the value of Northwestern stock.[2]

In acquiring the Galena & Chicago Union, the Chicago & Northwestern also secured control of the Beloit & Madison Railroad. In the spring of 1865 it quietly purchased a majority of the stock of the Chicago & Milwaukee Railroad, thereby heading off a similar move on the part of the Milwaukee & St. Paul Company.[3] By 1868 the Chicago & Northwest-

[1] *Ibid.*, 24–26.

[2] For information concerning this consolidation and the legal proceedings growing out of it see *ibid.*, 3–45; *id.*, 1866, 19–26; Elliott Anthony, Brief before the United States Circuit Court for northern Illinois in the case of *Wadsworth et al. vs., C. & N. W. R. R. Co., Wm. B. Ogden et al.* (Chicago, 1865); James Parton, *Manual for the Instruction of "Rings" Railroad and Political* (New York, 1866).

[3] Chicago & North Western Railway Company, *Report*, 1865, 36–37; Milwaukee *Sentinel*, Feb. 14, 1865; Milwaukee *Daily News*, Feb. 12, 1865;

ern and the Milwaukee & St. Paul owned or controlled every important railroad line in Wisconsin.

It was not long before these two companies moved to secure harmonious relations with each other. At the annual stockholders' meeting of the Chicago & Northwestern in the spring of 1868 four of the directors and influential owners of the Milwaukee & St. Paul, one among them being President Mitchell, were chosen to its board.[1] A few days later the stockholders of the Milwaukee & St. Paul Company, not to be outdone, elected President Keep of the Northwestern road to membership on their board. The keen rivalry that had hitherto marked the relations of these two corporations was now for a period of two years at an end, and the Northwestern gave up a long contemplated plan of constructing a competitive line from Madison northwest to the Mississippi River.

In the summer of 1869 the amity between the two corporations became still closer when the president of the Northwestern died and the president of the Milwaukee & St. Paul was chosen to fill his place.[2] Alexander Mitchell was in 1869 and 1870 the railroad king of the world, representing, with one possible exception, the greatest concentration of railroad mileage in existence. Some 2,300 miles of railroad

J. D. Butler, "Alexander Mitchell, The Financier," in *Wis. Hist. Colls.*, XI, 447.

[1] Chicago *Tribune*, June 2 and 5, 1868; Milwaukee *News*, June 5 and 6, 1868; Milwaukee *Sentinel*, June 6 and 11, 1868; Milwaukee *Semi-Weekly Wis.*, June 10, 1868.

[2] For comments upon this election see Milwaukee *Sentinel*, Sept. 2, 13, and 22, 1869; Milwaukee *News*, Sept. 3, 1869; Green Bay *Gazette*, Sept. 9, 1869; New York *Times*, Sept. 2, 1869; New York *Herald*, Sept. 3, 1869.

lines reaching northward to Lake Superior and westward to Omaha were under his supervision. He and his associates controlled by ownership, lease, or otherwise every desirable railroad property in Wisconsin, amounting in all to some 1,045 miles. Only two insignificant companies, owning together but eighty-six miles of track, were at that time operating independently within the Badger State. The Chicago *Post* commenting facetiously upon this situation observed:

> History repeats itself. The tears of Alexander the Great, because he had no more worlds to conquer, are familiar to every school-boy, and here we have another Alexander, surnamed Mitchell, who starting out with the Milwaukee and St. Paul railroad, first gobbled the old Milwaukee and La Crosse, then the Prairie du Chien, then half a dozen small railroads in Wisconsin, Iowa, and Minnesota, then the Western Union, and now, eheu iam satis! the Northwestern, with all its branches, spurs, divisions, and ramifications! As there are still other lines to gobble, however, we suppose the weeping will not commence until such little side-tracks as the Union Pacific, New York Central, etc., are added to the inventory.[1]

In many ways this wave of consolidation served a useful and beneficial purpose. It gathered together the numerous local, fragmentary, and isolated lines left bankrupt by the panic of 1857 and welded them into several comprehensive and powerful through-route systems, affording conveniences of transportation and economies of management that had hitherto been unknown. The railroads of Wisconsin, formerly bound by local jealousies and limited by State borders, were now able to leap even the natural barrier of the Mississippi River[2] and fling their lines hundreds of miles over the rich and flourishing prairies of the

[1] Reprinted in Milwaukee *News*, Sept. 4, 1869.

[2] The first through line from Milwaukee to St. Paul was completed in 1867.

far West. They were developing speedily into continental systems, and their plans for securing connection with the distant Pacific Ocean were no longer merely idle dreams.

Much of the consolidation, on the other hand, particularly such as involved parallel lines, was calculated solely to eliminate desirable competition. Where this was the case, the companies kept their operations secret, and the public learned of them only when resistance was too late. Unfortunately the people of Wisconsin were only partially aroused to the danger of such concentrations. As a matter of abstract theory they were opposed to all consolidations, but when brought face to face with concrete instances they were either indifferent, actually favorable, or vacillating in their policy.

A notable exception to this uncertainty occurred in the summer of 1863. It was a time when more consolidation movements were on foot in Wisconsin than at any subsequent time in the entire period. The Milwaukee & St. Paul Company was just emerging out of a court receivership and was about to take over three other lines elsewhere mentioned. The Milwaukee & Chicago Railroad and the Chicago & Milwaukee Railroad were undergoing consolidation with Mitchell as president. The Chicago & Northwestern was in the process of taking over the Kenosha, Rockford & Rock Island and was well known to have designs on the Racine & Mississippi. Particularly disquieting was the report published in New York and Wisconsin newspapers that the newly born Milwaukee & St. Paul Company was negotiating with the Milwaukee & Prairie du Chien Company either to consolidate outright or pool earnings.[1] Even more menacing in the eyes of Wisconsin people was the intelligence that the Chicago & Northwestern was negotiating for a consolidation with both of these Milwaukee railroads.[2]

The people of the State were dismayed, and with good reason, at the prospect of having fastened upon them so immense a transportation monopoly. The press of Wisconsin, notwithstanding the distraction of exciting events at the front, gravely turned to the new domestic problem. A broadside printed by the Milwaukee *Daily Life* on June 27, 1863,[3] in which the alleged project of the "consolidationists" was described and its disastrous consequences upon the future of Wisconsin vividly pictured, gained State-wide circulation. In Milwaukee, where the agitation centered, a brisk campaign of open letters and editorials was conducted in the daily newspapers, which culminated during the autumn of 1863 in two largely attended and highly interesting public meetings.[4]

The friends of the projected consolidation, who were for the most part railroad representatives,

[1] See New York *Herald*, June 17, 1863; Milwaukee *Daily Wis.*, June 20, 1863; Milwaukee & Prairie du Chien Railway Company, *Directors' Proceedings*, June 24, 1863.

[2] New York *Herald*, July 31, 1863; Milwaukee & Prairie du Chien Railway Company, *Directors' Proceedings*, Nov. 19, 1863 and July 15, 1864.

[3] Bound with Milwaukee & Prairie du Chien Railway Company, *Reports*, 1861–66. See also Milwaukee *Daily Wis.*, June 13 to Sept. 1, 1863; Milwaukee *Sentinel*, June 27, 1863; Prairie du Chien *Courier*, July 9, 1863; La Crosse *Democratic Journal*, Nov. 25, 1863; La Crosse *Democrat*, Dec. 8, 1863; B. H. Meyer, "Early Railroad Legislation in Wisconsin," in Wisconsin Academy of Sciences, *Transactions*, XII, 364–79.

[4] For reports of the proceedings of these meetings see Milwaukee *Daily Wis.*, Aug. 24, 1863; Milwaukee *Sentinel*, Aug. 25 and Sept. 10, 1863; Wis. Acad. of Sciences, *Trans.*, XII, 365–71.

usually ignored the charge that the Chicago & Northwestern was to be included in the combination and directed their defense chiefly to the necessity for combining the Milwaukee lines. Shrewdly making capital of the rivalry existing between Milwaukee and Chicago, they pictured the Chicago & Northwestern as a greedy, all-devouring octopus, that was encircling Milwaukee with its tentacles and carrying off to Illinois the riches of the Badger State. They represented it as being interested not so much in earning dividends for its stockholders as in building up the city of Chicago at the expense of the Wisconsin metropolis. They maintained that, by intersecting both of Milwaukee's east and west railroad lines and by holding out to each of them the bribe of the through business to Chicago which it controlled, it was able to pit these roads against each other in competition ruinous alike to themselves and to Milwaukee. Against such a policy the only safety for the Badger city lay in the consolidation of her lines.[1] A consolidated railroad would add to the prosperity of the Cream City by erecting tap lines into the wheat fields of Iowa and Minnesota and extending much-desired branch lines into Wisconsin. Since it could be operated more economically than a number of small units, it would be able to grant the public cheaper and better service, while the State would be guarded against any abuse of monopolistic power by the regulatory power of the legislature, the competition of other routes in Illinois, and considerations of enlightened self-interest.[2]

[1] Milwaukee *Daily Wis.*, June 13 and 29, and Aug. 24, 1863; Milwaukee *Sentinel*, Mar. 4, 1867; Cary, *The History of the Chicago, Milwaukee and St. Paul Railway Company*, 87–88; *Wis. Hist. Colls.*, XI, 447.

[2] Wis. *Sen. Jour.*, 1867, 799–809.

To such reasoning the "anti-monopolists" replied that the consolidation, far from benefiting Milwaukee, would actually destroy her future. The combination was to include not merely the Milwaukee roads, but also the hated Northwestern, and in a union of such elements it was easy to foresee which would predominate. The Milwaukee roads, nursed by the city in their infancy, and in behalf of which it had plunged itself deeply into debt, would end by becoming feeders of the Northwestern; the proud Cream City would become but the tail to the kite of Chicago. Wall Street and Chicago speculators, who were engineering the consolidation and who in the event of its consummation would line their pockets with $20,000,000 of watered stock, would be the only ones to profit by the transaction. Upon the farmers and merchants of Wisconsin would fall the crushing burden of paying dividends upon a more than doubled railroad valuation, while freight tariffs, already so excessive that honest toil went unrequited, would be still further increased. The farmers of Wisconsin, like their unhappy brethren of Illinois, would find it cheaper to burn their grain for fuel than to ship it by rail to the East. The monopoly would "control the legislation, overawe the courts, override the constitution when and as it pleased, and hold every public man at its mercy, from Governor down to county officers."[1] Owned and controlled outside of the State, it would be another Camden & Amboy and Wisconsin would be the ignominious New Jersey of the Northwest.[2]

[1] Report of a committee of the Milwaukee anti-consolidation mass meeting printed in Milwaukee *Sentinel*, Sept. 10, 1863.

[2] For an account of the Camden & Amboy Railroad see Fite, *Social and Industrial Conditions*, 169–74.

While the people of Wisconsin were thus anxiously debating the dangers of consolidation, negotiations between the railroads concerned quietly continued in New York. Apparently an arrangement of some kind was very nearly concluded between the Milwaukee & St. Paul Company and the Milwaukee & Prairie du Chien Company in June, 1863 when, as the result of an announcement that a consolidation had actually taken place, the stock of the Prairie du Chien road took a sudden rise in value.[1] For the time being, however, it proved impossible for any of the roads to agree upon the terms of union, and the anti-consolidation movement quietly disintegrated.[2]

After 1863 the people of Wisconsin were not again actively aroused against railroad consolidations. Indeed, even the forcible absorption of the Prairie du Chien road by the Milwaukee & St. Paul in 1866 failed to excite any hostile comment. On the contrary it was formally approved in 1867 by the Milwaukee Chamber of Commerce and a mass meeting of Milwaukee citizens.[3] When in 1869 Alexander Mitchell was elected president of the Northwestern road the entire press of Milwaukee and the press of the State in general expressed only gratification.

The course of the State legislature was marked by the same vacillation.[4] In 1857, during the last week and a half of the session, the railroad interests of Milwaukee and Chicago quietly slipped into en-

[1] New York *Times*, June 18, 1863.

[2] New York *Herald*, July 10, 1863; New York *Times*, July 11, 1863.

[3] Milwaukee *News*, Feb. 6 and 12, and Mar. 3, 1867.

[4] For early legislation relating to consolidations see Wis. Acad. of Sciences, *Trans.*, XII, 365–71.

actment a bill which gave to railroads within Wisconsin practically unlimited powers of consolidation.[1] During the panic years following 1857 no notice was taken of this extraordinary act, but in 1860 it was discovered and exposed by L. P. Harvey, newly elected secretary of state, and later governor of the State. A bill was at once introduced in the session of 1860 to repeal the law. It passed the Senate but was defeated in the Assembly.[2] During the consolidation excitement of 1863 a baseless tale gained wide acceptance in the State, and was repeated with variations by such prominent public men as Matt H. Carpenter and Josiah A. Noonan, to the effect that the repeal measure had been unanimously passed by the legislature, had been signed by the governor, and duly filed in the secretary of state's office, but had been stolen by unscrupulous agents of the consolidationists[3] before it could be published. The story was denied by the senator who had introduced the measure, by the secretary of state, and by the evidence of the legislative journals, but it persisted for many years as a popular charge against the railroads.[4]

The agitation of 1863 bore somewhat empty fruit in 1864 when the consolidation law of 1857 was actually repealed.[5] It is to be observed, however,

[1] Wis. *Gen. Laws*, 1857, chap. 55; see also "Bill No. 396 A" in Wis. *Sen. Jour.* and Wis. *Assem. Jour.* for 1857, indexed under "Railroads."

[2] See "Bill No. 168 S" in Wis. *Sen Jour.* and Wis. *Assem. Jour.* for 1860, indexed under "Amendments to Revised Statutes."

[3] Milwaukee *Daily Life*, June 27, 1863; Milwaukee *Sentinel*, Aug. 25, 1863; Milwaukee *Daily Wis.*, July 2, 1863; La Crosse *Republican*, Dec. 2, 1863.

[4] *Wis. State Jour.*, Sept. 12, 1863; Milwaukee *Sentinel*, Sept. 21, 1863; Wis. Acad. of Sciences, *Trans.*, XII, 365–68.

[5] Wis. *Gen. Laws*, 1864, chap. 49.

that no statute expressly forbidding combinations was enacted in its place. Nor did the railroads of Wisconsin find any great difficulty in persuading subsequent legislatures to authorize by special enactments such consolidations as they desired, or to legalize consolidations effected without the sanction of law.

In 1867, it is true, an act was passed, much to the satisfaction of the State press, prohibiting forever the consolidation of the Milwaukee & St. Paul or Milwaukee & Prairie du Chien companies with the hated Chicago & Northwestern.[1] It was a somewhat suspicious circumstance, however, that one of the foremost advocates of the measure was Alexander Mitchell. The position which he and his associates assumed was that such a law protected the State against the encroachments of the powerful Chicago railroad.[2] Unfriendly critics asserted, however, that this bill had been introduced solely to ward off opposition to two other of Mitchell's bills legalizing and completing the consolidation of the Milwaukee & St. Paul and the Milwaukee & Prairie du Chien.[3] That the much-touted anti-consolidation law was never taken seriously by those whom it was intended to affect was sufficiently shown within the following year when Mitchell and his friends were elected directors of the Chicago & Northwestern Railroad.

The wave of consolidation that thus swept over Wisconsin during the decade of the sixties left many

[1] Wis. *Priv. Laws*, 1867, chap. 433. See Wis. *Sen. Jour.*, 1867, 799–809 for a committee report frankly urging railroad consolidations.

[2] Speech of Alexander Mitchell in Milwaukee *Daily Wis.*, Mar. 4, 1867.

[3] Wis. *Priv. Laws*, 1867, chaps. 431 ana 435.

difficult problems in its wake. So long as railroads operated independently their competition had protected the public, at least in a measure, against overcharges. In 1870, however, practically the entire transportation service of the State was controlled by two allied railroad corporations, and it was necessary to find a new safeguard against oppression. Wisconsin eventually obtained this in public regulation. In the Granger laws of 1874 she answered the challenge of a previous decade of railroad combination.

CHAPTER XII

THE ANTIMONOPOLY REVOLT

While the people of Wisconsin were apparently indifferent to railroad consolidations, they were thoroughly aroused over an allied transportation problem, the rapid increase of freight charges. No other question in the State, excepting always national issues, called forth during the years 1863 to 1866 such widespread popular feeling. The agitation extended not only over Wisconsin but Illinois, Minnesota, and Iowa; in fact over all that region west of Lake Michigan which ten years later was the seat of the Granger uprising. Gathering force during the temporary depression that attended the close of the Civil War, it culminated in the so-called "antimonopoly" revolt of 1865–66, an outbreak which, although little known, is extremely significant in the transportation history of the Northwest.

The railroad companies of this region were not wholly to be blamed for this popular disturbance. They were themselves the victims of war conditions. The advances which they made in freight rates were to a considerable extent but compensatory for the depreciation of currency due to greenback inflation. The prices of railroad supplies, materials, and labor were increasing by leaps and bounds, and they justly maintained that rates of transportation must rise in corresponding measure. In addition, they were subject to burdensome Federal and State war taxes, both direct and indirect, which they felt obliged to shift upon their patrons.[1] According to an estimate of Alexander Mitchell the Milwaukee & St. Paul Company paid into the United States treasury in 1865 not less than 20 per cent of its gross earnings, "so that a farmer who pays us 15 cents per bushel for bringing wheat to market, pays to us really but 12 cents, and to the Federal Government 3 cents."[2]

The blockade of the lower Mississippi was likewise responsible for forcing up freight rates, indirectly, by removing the wholesome competition of the water route, directly, by thrusting upon the railroads running to the East the additional burden of the northern commerce that formerly was transported by the river route. How great was the strain of this double burden may be seen by comparing the tonnage statistics of Wisconsin's chief east and west railroads before and after the opening of hostilities.

The La Crosse & Milwaukee Railroad (Milwaukee & St. Paul) in 1860 carried westward from La Crosse only 28,627 tons of freight. In 1861 it carried from that city 84,939 tons and in 1865, 118,778 tons. Its

[1] In 1862 the State tax upon railroads was increased from 1 per cent on gross earnings to 3 per cent. For a complete discussion of railroad taxation in Wisconsin during the years 1860–70 involving several important legal decisions of the State supreme court see G. E. Snider, *History of the Taxation of Railway Corporations in Wisconsin* (Ms. thesis, 1901, in the University of Wisconsin Library); Wis. Acad. of Sciences, *Trans.*, XII, 378–88; Gov. E. Salomon, "Annual Message," in Wis. *Mess. and Docs.*, 1863, p. xii.

[2] Milwaukee & St. Paul Railway Company, *Report*, 1865, 5–6.

total east and west freight in 1860 was but 157,680 tons; in 1861 it was 274,174 tons and in 1865, 319,656 tons.[1] Statistics for the Milwaukee & Mississippi (Prairie du Chien) Railroad for 1860 are not available, but, judging from such data as are at hand, its eastward traffic from Prairie du Chien in that year was not over 35,000 tons. In 1861 it was 100,599 tons, and in 1865, 131,202 tons. Its total east and west traffic in 1859 amounted to only 163,970 tons; in 1861 it was 305,794 tons.[2]

These Wisconsin railroads, as we have seen, had been completed but a short time when the war broke out. They had been built, moreover, with an eye to developing a pioneer country rather than to carrying an existing commerce. For the most part they were poorly and uneconomically constructed, and their equipment was inadequate to the needs of even their normal business. They were ill prepared for the sudden deluge of traffic that poured upon them in 1861 and they responded, naturally enough, by forcing up their rates.[3]

Freight tariffs at competitive points, and notably those between the Mississippi River and the lake shore, were at this time customarily established by

[1] La Crosse & Milwaukee Railroad Company, *Reports*, 1852–63; Milwaukee & St. Paul Railway Company, *Reports*, 1865–69.

[2] Milwaukee & Mississippi Railroad Company, *Reports*, 1849–61; Milwaukee & Prairie du Chien Railway Company, *Reports*, 1861–66.

[3] Agricultural products ordinarily moved only during the spring and autumn months when Lake Michigan and the Mississippi River were free from ice. As a result the railroads of Wisconsin were annually swamped with traffic during the shipping seasons and comparatively idle during the remainder of the year. This difficulty, peculiar to agricultural regions, was accentuated by the war and no doubt accounts in part for the increase in rates.

agreement among the several competing railroads. There was then nothing unlawful or improper about such a course, and no effort was made to hold it secret. Each spring or oftener, as occasion required, the representatives of the five railroad lines running to the lake shore from La Crosse, Prairie du Chien, and Dunleith met in convention at Chicago or Milwaukee and agreed upon rates between River and Lake.

The most important question which came up for decision at such conventions was the charge upon wheat. Wheat was the staple of agriculture, not only in Wisconsin but in all the states west of Lake Michigan. Increased rates for transportation of this grain came home directly to practically every inhabitant of the region, a circumstance pregnant with danger for the railroad companies as they were later to discover in the Granger uprising. It is necessary to examine in some detail, therefore, the movement of wheat tariffs during the years of the Civil War. Roughly such a study will indicate the trend of other transportation charges during the same period.

In the spring of 1860 the wheat charge from La Crosse or Prairie du Chien to Milwaukee or Chicago was 10 cents per bushel. In the spring of 1861, a month after the assault on Fort Sumter, it rose to 13 cents per bushel.[1] Thereafter for a year and a half it fluctuated considerably, though with a slightly downward tendency. In the spring of 1863 it again bounded upward and now continued swiftly to increase until the end of the war. By April, 1865

[1] This was an unfortunately timed advance since prices of all kinds were at that time swiftly declining and wheat in particular was suffering in the depression.

it reached the extraordinary height of 20 cents per bushel, the highest rate the region has ever known.[1]

Intimately associated with the railroads in the carrying trade were the Mississippi River steamboats. The latter performed the service of collecting the grain carted to the river towns by the farmers of northwestern Wisconsin, eastern Minnesota, and eastern Iowa, and transporting it to the railroad terminals, La Crosse, Prairie du Chien, and Dunleith. Three prominent corporations were engaged in this labor during the Civil War: the La Crosse & St. Paul Packet Company, which ran in connection with the Milwaukee & St. Paul Railway at La Crosse; the Galena, Dubuque, Dunleith & Minnesota Packet Company, which made running connections with the Milwaukee & Prairie du Chien at Prairie du Chien and the Illinois Central at Dunleith; and the Northern Line Packet Company which ran to St. Louis.[2]

The transportation charges imposed by these lines upon freights local to the river depended under normal conditions upon two factors: the pressure of traffic and the depth of water in the river channel. Usually in the spring of the year when traffic was light and the water was of sufficient height to be navigable by the largest steamboats, the charges

[1] Data relating to transportation charges on Wisconsin railroads are extremely scattering and difficult of access. That which is here presented is the result of a laborious search through newspaper files in the Wisconsin Historical Library for the years from 1860 to 1867. See particularly Milwaukee *Sentinel;* Milwaukee *Daily Wisconsin;* Prescott *Democrat;* Prescott *Transcript;* La Crosse *Republican; Polk County Press;* St. Paul *Pioneer;* Hudson *Star and Times;* Chicago *Tribune;* and Chicago *Times.*

[2] A number of unimportant "wild" boats were also in operation, following no definite schedule, but proceeding wherever traffic chanced to take them. See *post,* chap. xiv.

were low. In July or August, however, when scant water set in and the new crop pressed to market, they rose. Invariably they were higher in the fall than at any other time of the year.

The local river rates of the packet lines were of far less importance, however, than the so-called through charges. The latter were the tariffs imposed upon traffic the origin or destination of which was the lake shore. Freight of such a nature was handled by both railroads and steamboats, and consequently the charges imposed upon it were established jointly. In practice through rates were fixed at the railroad rate conventions held in Chicago or Milwaukee during each shipping season.[1]

The forces that led to the increase of railroad charges during the years of the war have already been touched upon. The extraordinary advance of river charges is to be accounted for by three factors. One was the scarcity of steamboats on the upper Mississippi, resulting from the repeated government requisitions for vessels to be used in the military service. Another was the unusually low stage of water that prevailed in the river during the seasons 1863 and 1864, rendering navigation difficult and expensive. The chief and deciding factor, however, was the complete suppression of steamboat competition on the river as the result of the organization in the spring of 1863 of an extraordinary combination of river-and-rail transportation interests.

Railroads ever since their construction had dominated the steamboat trade. They were in a position

[1] When freight was shipped to Milwaukee or Chicago via La Crosse or Prairie du Chien from river points above Trempealeau, the steamboat company customarily received one-third of the through rate and the railroad company two-thirds.

to make and unmake river carriers. The through traffic which they controlled was the life of the river commerce. No steamboat owner had any chance of subsistence if railroads discriminated against him. Railroads, it is true, had always favored the regular packet lines. They had uniformly turned over to the latter all west-bound passengers and freight not specifically consigned to independent vessels. Such favoritism, however, was not necessarily fatal to the independent vessels. So long as the latter obtained equal treatment in the transportation of east-bound through freight, they could manage to maintain themselves.

Events occurring in 1862 and 1863, however, removed every vestige of equality. The first of these, which will be discussed later, was the absorption by a single great steamboat corporation, of practically the entire vessel interest north of Dubuque. The second, still more important, was the entrance as directors and heavy stockholders into this corporation of prominent officials of the several railroads terminating at the river.[1] A practical monopoly of all the railroad and steamboat interests of this region came thus into being. Needless to say competition on the river came at once to an end.

Independent steamboats now received short shrift. By an amazing system of discriminations the railroads drove them from the upper river.[2] In the autumn of 1865, for example, the railroads charged independent vessels 6 cents per bushel more for transporting

[1] See *post*, chap. xiv; also *Minn. Hist. Colls.*, VIII, 408–9.

[2] Milwaukee *Sentinel*, Mar. 26 and 28, and April 1, 1864, Sept. 6 and 12, 1865; Chicago *Tribune*, April 5, 8, and 16, 1864; Milwaukee Chamber of Commerce, *Record Book B*, Feb. 11, 1865; *Ibid.*, 21.

through wheat to the lake shore than they charged their own monopoly packets. A similar discrimination upon flour amounted to the surprising figure of 28 cents per barrel.[1] Outside vessels found it exceedingly difficult, moreover, to obtain facilities for unloading at the railroad elevators. The merchants of St. Croix and Polk counties in Wisconsin, and Chisago and Washington counties in Minnesota, in the winter of 1864–65 built a steamboat and several barges with which they essayed to do their own carrying. The railroads, however, utterly refused to receive their shipments upon equitable terms unless they first agreed to pay over to the monopoly packet line $9,000 in "damages," and further agreed never to compete with any of the steamboats of the packet line. The merchants after several months of negotiation abandoned their project in despair and withdrew their vessel.[2]

Freight rates reflected this destruction of competition. In the spring of 1860 farmers residing at Prescott or Hudson, the northernmost river points in Wisconsin, paid a through rate of 10 cents a bushel to ship their wheat by steamboat and railroad to Milwaukee or Chicago.[3] During the autumn of 1860 the tariff varied, falling for a time as a result of a fierce steamboat and railroad war to 4 cents per bushel, and later rising, when the immense crop of 1860 was thrown upon the market, to the maximum height of 15 cents

[1] Milwaukee *Sentinel*, Sept. 6, 1865.

[2] See report of the St. Paul anti-monopoly convention printed in St. Paul *Weekly Pioneer*, Feb. 16, 1866; also Milwaukee *Sentinel*, Feb. 14, Sept. 6 and 12, 1865; Wis. *Private Laws*, 1864, chap. 229.

[3] The steamboat rates quoted in the river newspapers are usually through rates.

per bushel. In the spring of 1861 it was 12 cents; immediately upon the outbreak of the war it again rose to 15 cents. During the fall of 1861 and the spring of 1862 it was once more 12 cents and 15 cents respectively. Beginning with 1863, however, it ceased to fluctuate. In the spring of that year it was fixed for all points above La Crosse at 18 cents. In the autumn of 1863, it was increased to 25 cents. In the spring of 1865 it rose to 35 cents from Hudson and 34 cents from Prescott.[1]

In order to grasp the full import of these advances it is desirable to analyze them, apportioning to the steamboat and railroad companies their respective shares. In the spring of 1860 the farmers of Prescott and Hudson paid only 3 or 4 cents to packet companies to carry a bushel of wheat to La Crosse or Prairie du Chien. In the spring of 1865 they paid 15 cents.[2] In the spring of 1860 they paid to railroad companies only 6 or 7 cents to complete the shipment of this grain to the lake shore. In the spring of 1865 they paid 20 cents.

The price of wheat, it is true, had also risen rapidly, but the advance did not compare with the increased cost of transportation.[3] During the shipping season of 1864 the value of this grain reached a higher average than at any other period in the Civil War. It

[1] During the early sixties the through rate on wheat was ordinarily the same for all points on the Mississippi River above La Crosse, so that Trempealeau paid as high a rate as St. Paul which was over one hundred miles farther up the river. During the closing years of the war through rates began to be graduated somewhat like local rates, according to distance of shipment.

[2] Milwaukee *Sentinel*, April 7, 1865; Prescott *Journal*, April 8, 1865.

[3] See *ante*, chap. i.

was then but one and seven-tenths as great as during the shipping season of 1860.[1] In the same interval the cost of transporting it from River to Lake had increased two and a half times. In April, 1865 the price of wheat had fallen in Milwaukee to nearly the level of April, 1860. Carrying costs, however, were three and a half times greater.[2] The farmers of northwestern Wisconsin in the spring of 1865 paid transportation companies nearly one-third of their crop for the short river-and-rail carriage of the remaining two-thirds across the State. This they were compelled to do despite the fact that economies of a vital character had been effected in grain transportation during the early years of the Civil War.[3]

It is instructive to compare the rates charged by this river-and-rail combination with the rates in vogue on the Great Lakes. To ship a bushel of wheat from Milwaukee to New York by way of the Great Lakes and the Erie Canal, a distance of some 1,350 miles, including transfer charges at Buffalo and tolls

[1] Statistics relating to wheat prices are from Milwaukee Chamber of Commerce, *Reports*, 1860–70.

[2] According to Fite, *Social and Industrial Conditions*, 15–16, 44–45, grain rates on railroads in the North as a whole actually declined after 1861. This appears to be contradicted, however, by data printed in an article by William P. Grosvenor in the *Atlantic Monthly* for November, 1873, 599–60. According to Grosvenor the average per ton per mile receipts of the five great through roads carrying western produce to the Atlantic in competition with the lake and canal route during the decade 1860–70 were:

1860	2.01 cents	1866	2.74 cents
1861	(slightly less than 1860)	1867	2.36 "
1862	2.05 cents	1868	2.11 "
1863	2.16 "	1869	1.89 "
1864	2.58 "	1870	1.53 "
1865	2.83 "	1871	1.48 "

[3] See *post*, chaps. xiv and xv.

through the Erie Canal,[1] cost 5 cents less in April, 1865 than to carry it from Hudson to Milwaukee, a river-and-rail carriage of but 330 miles. To ship a bushel of wheat from Milwaukee or Chicago to Buffalo, a lake carriage of approximately 1,000 miles, cost 5 cents less than a river carriage of but 130 miles from Hudson to La Crosse.[2]

[1] Freight rates from Milwaukee or Chicago to New York for the years 1860 to 1870 are printed in U. S. *Statistical Abstract*, 1902, 416. For transfer charges at Buffalo during this period, see U. S. Inland Waterways Commission, *Preliminary Report*, 1908, 232, note a. See also Milwaukee Chamber of Commerce, *Reports*, and Chicago Board of Trade, *Reports*, for the years 1860 to 1870.

From St. Paul to St. Louis, a distance of 800 miles, the charges by steamboat, averaged for each season, from 1857 to 1873 were:

	Wheat per bu.	Flour per bbl.
1857	15	50
1858	14	50
1859	15	50
1860	16	52
1861	15	50
1862	18	60
1863	19	62
1864	25	75
1865	24	73
1866	23	72
1867	21	70
1868	20	68
1869	20	68
1870	18	60
1871	15	50
1872	15	50

See 43 Cong., 1 sess., *Senate Report*, No. 307, *Transportation Routes to the Seaboard* (Washington, 1874), pt. II, 594; also pt. I, 204.

[2] Milwaukee Chamber of Commerce, *Report*, 1865, 49–51; also Chicago

No doubt it was cheaper to carry freight on the Great Lakes than on the Mississippi, for the carrying capacity of lake vessels was greater than that of river craft and the difficulties of lake navigation were less than those on the river. Yet ignoring absolute rates and comparing only relative increases for the five-year period under review, we find the same striking discrepancies. We have seen that river rates increased from April, 1860 to April, 1865 more than threefold. Lake rates, on the other hand, were practically the same in April, 1865 as in April, 1860.[1]

During the early years of the Civil War shippers occasionally found relief from such exactions in the dissensions of the railroad and the steamboat companies. The quarrels of the steamboat companies dated back to the very beginnings of the river traffic. Those of the railroads were more recent, as their lines had come into competition with each other only upon the completion of their tracks to the Mississippi.[2] The through trade of the river was the bone of all such contentions. Secret tariff cuttings or the granting of special favors or free passes to influence traffic constituted the usual cause. The packet companies,

Tribune, Feb. 2 and 14, 1866; *Proceedings* of the Mississippi River Improvement Convention, held at Dubuque, Iowa, Feb. 14 and 15, 1866 (Dubuque, 1866). For passenger rate increases during this period see Wisconsin Railroad Commissioner, *Report*, 1874, Official Papers, 113–29.

[1] Milwaukee Chamber of Commerce, *Reports*, 1860–65; Chicago Board of Trade, *Reports*, 1860–65.

[2] Rate wars were particularly frequent and severe on railroads running between river and lake during the hard times which marked the later fifties. They contributed not a little to the financial embarrassment of these roads following the panic of 1857. See Thompson, *Wheat Growing in Wisconsin*, 146–48.

in addition to their own disputes, invariably became involved in those of the railroads, in which they ranged themselves each on the side of its respective railroad patron. Shippers joyfully welcomed these wars because of the cheap transportation that accompanied them.

A notable conflict, out of which arose the great steamboat corporation that shortly monopolized the traffic of the upper river, raged during the summer of 1860. It had its roots in the personal grievances of several officials of the La Crosse & Milwaukee Railroad Company, who in 1859 had attempted to secure from the steamboat company, with which their road was then affiliated, an interest in the latter's immensely profitable business.[1] They had been refused, and, disgruntled, had induced a new packet line to organize. To it they had granted all the patronage that they controlled.

The new steamboat organization, the La Crosse & St. Paul Packet Company, familiarly known as Davidson's Line, entered upon its career in the summer of 1860. The old organization, the Galena, Dubuque, Dunleith & Minnesota Packet Company, was determined to crush it at the outset. For years the latter had enjoyed undisturbed the patronage of the railroads terminating at the river. It did not propose to surrender any part of it without a struggle.

Between these two companies and their respective railroad allies there developed during the summer and autumn of 1860 one of the fiercest conflicts ever known upon the upper river. The through rate on wheat from St. Paul and other river points to the

[1] *Minn. Hist. Colls.*, VIII, 408–14.

lake shore fell to 4 cents a bushel. Both steamboat companies for a time carried through freight from La Crosse to any river point above absolutely free of charge. One company transported approximately 3,000 tons of freight without a cent of compensation. Passenger rates from Prescott to the lake shore fell from $11.25 to $3.50, and later to $1. A dollar ticket included, besides transportation, meals and berth aboard the packets. It was far cheaper in the autumn of 1860 to live, eat, and sleep on the palatial river steamboats than in the humblest country tavern. Before the fight was over the Galena Company was nearly ruined.[1]

Again in June, 1861, and once more in the autumn of that year, short-rate wars were in progress in which the same belligerents were arrayed against each other.[2] In 1862, however, the Davidson Line absorbed its older rival, and thereafter until near the close of the decade these controversies came to an end.

Inland shippers in Wisconsin paid even higher proportionate transportation charges than those on the Mississippi River. Entirely at the mercy of railroad companies, they were losers even during rate wars. The railroad companies invariably reimbursed themselves for their losses during rate conflicts by increasing their charges upon local freights. Not infrequently cities halfway across the State

[1] Prescott *Transcript* and Prescott *Democrat* for August to November, 1860; La Crosse *Weekly Republican*, Sept. 18, 1867; *Minn. Hist. Colls.*, VIII, 408–14. See also *post*, chap. xiv.

[2] Milwaukee *Daily Wis.*, July 11, 1861; Milwaukee *Sentinel*, July 12 and 19, 1861; Milwaukee Chamber of Commerce, *Proceedings*, July 10, 1861; La Crosse *Democrat*, Oct. 4, 1861.

like Madison, Portage, Beaver Dam, and Ripon actually paid more per bushel to transport their wheat to Milwaukee than the cities of La Crosse, Prairie du Chien, and Winona.[1]

The farmers and merchants of Wisconsin had many other grievances against the railroads. Rate favoritism and particularly the "drawback" or rebate system were sources of constant complaint. Published rates applied only to the small and occasional shippers; the larger ones usually secretly received more favorable terms. Employees of the railroads were often permitted to engage in wheat speculations, being allowed special railroad rates by reason of which they were able to crowd out of business bona fide commission merchants. Milwaukee millers and warehousemen faced a local problem of excessive and discriminatory storage charges in the railroad elevators of that city. The southern portion of the State was incensed at the refusal of the railroad companies to carry cordwood during the busy shipping seasons. The problems of the railroad farm mortgagors and the municipal railroad bonds added their portion to the general discontent. Truly, the railroads of Wisconsin were not without critics during the years of the Civil War.

As early as the fall of 1861 public resentment was stirring, though the issue was then overshadowed in the popular mind by the more pressing problems of the war. In the consolidation excitement of 1863, however, the rate question occupied a conspicuous

[1] *Wis. State Jour.*, April 28, 1863; Hartford *Home League*, Jan. 30, 1864; Portage *Register*, Aug. 12, 1865; Milwaukee *Sentinel*, Sept. 3, 1865; Wis. *Sen. Jour.*, 1867, 649; B. H. Hibbard, "History of Agriculture in Dane County," University of Wisconsin, *Bulletin*, No. 101, 140–42.

part and thereafter came more and more to the foreground. When the schedules of the spring of 1864 were announced the settlers of western Wisconsin and Minnesota were stirred to action. In every important river shipping center they held mass meetings of indignation and protest. On Mar. 3, 1864 they assembled to take counsel in a spirited convention at Red Wing, Minnesota.

However, conventions and indignation meetings served only to reveal their helplessness. The resolutions of condemnation that they adopted fell upon deaf ears. The only constructive proposal that the Red Wing convention could pursue was to dispatch a delegation of its members with an account of its grievances to the politically powerful lake-shore region. The committee succeeded in stirring up considerable interest and sympathy in Milwaukee and Chicago but accomplished little else. The Chicago Mercantile Association and the Chicago Board of Trade adopted resolutions condemning the tariff and denouncing the policy of discrimination that closed the Mississippi River to steamboat competition. The Milwaukee Chamber of Commerce and the Milwaukee Merchants' Association in still more vigorous terms called upon the Wisconsin legislature to correct these abuses.[1]

At a meeting called in Chicago on April 12, 1864 the railroad companies, however, curtly justified their rates as reasonable, and upheld the policy of discrimination as necessary in order to secure regularity of service.[2] How little they were impressed by all the

[1] La Crosse *Republican*, April 20, 1864; Milwaukee *Sentinel*, Mar. 28, 1864 and Jan. 1, 1866.

[2] Chicago *Tribune*, April 16, 1864.

agitation was seen a year later when, in the face of industrial depression, they increased the through rates on wheat to 35 cents per bushel.

In despair the farmers of the upper Mississippi now turned to the almost abandoned river route via St. Louis to New Orleans and New York. Much to the alarm of the merchants of the lake ports, wheat once more moved in considerable quantities to the lower river during the shipping season of 1865.[1] Railroad apologists asserted that this was the natural result of the reopening of the river, and no doubt their explanations contained some truth. Others believed, however, with the Chicago *Tribune*, that the exactions of the river-and-rail monopoly were responsible. "Let them reflect," observed that journal, "that the war is now over, that the Mississippi is unobstructed, that under the most favorable circumstances a considerable portion of the trade which has enriched us during the past four years must now be attracted to that channel. Can we afford to add to the natural attraction of the Mississippi the powerful repulsion of exorbitant railroad freights on all lines crossing that river or adjacent to it? Can we afford to allow it to be done?"[2]

At length in May, 1865 the railroad and steamboat companies consented to modify their charges. By a single stroke they cut 7 cents per bushel from their wheat rates between the upper Mississippi and the lake shore.[3] However, even this reduction failed

[1] La Crosse *Democrat*, May 29, 1865; Chicago *Tribune*, Dec. 13 and 15, 1865; Milwaukee *Sentinel*, Dec. 11, 1865. The wheat rate from Prescott to St. Louis in the spring of 1865 was 27 cents per bushel.

[2] Chicago *Tribune*, Dec. 11, 1865.

[3] *Polk County Press*, May 27, 1865; Prescott *Journal*, May 20 and 27, 1865.

to appease the now thoroughly aroused farmers. The exactions which they had borne with such patience as they could during the prosperous years of the war were now, in a time of low prices, no longer to be endured. Wisconsin, Minnesota, northern Illinois, and northern Iowa were ablaze with anti-railroad and anti-steamboat excitement. The entire region west of Lake Michigan was in the grip of its first reaction against transportation companies, an uprising known in history as the "anti-monopoly revolt."

Too brief to attain political importance, this popular dissatisfaction found expression chiefly in vehement indignation meetings. One of the latter, the St. Paul Anti-Monopoly Convention of Feb. 7, 1866, was typical, and of considerable importance to Wisconsin.[1] Several hundred delegates from the river counties of Minnesota and the Badger State attended its deliberations, which were presided over by the lieutenant-governor of Minnesota. The convention spent much of its time in denouncing railroad and steamboat offenders, particularly Davidson's Line. To the legislature of Wisconsin it sent a memorial demanding State regulation of her railroads and a suggestion that the through rate on wheat between river and lake be fixed at 12 cents per bushel. Likewise it appointed a special delegation of its members to attend the sessions of the Wisconsin legislature and secured a law forbidding any further discrimination by Wisconsin railroads against independent steamboats on the upper Mississippi.

[1] For a complete report of the proceedings of this convention see St. Paul *Weekly Pioneer*, Feb. 16, 1866; see also Milwaukee daily papers from Feb. 8 to Feb. 16, 1866.

It advocated four proposals for restoring competition in the packet and railroad trade. Like all antimonopoly gatherings it emphasized the improvement of the Mississippi River channel, which it made the subject of an urgent memorial to Congress. It encouraged the revival of the former river-and-ocean trade via New Orleans to New York, by offering its support to the various steamboat lines below St. Louis that made connection with ocean liners. In order to secure more active railroad competition it advocated the construction of a railroad line from the head of navigation on the Mississippi River to the head of Lake Superior.

Most important and unique of all its plans was that of establishing a coöperative steamboat line on the upper Mississippi, owned and controlled entirely by shippers in the several river towns. This had been suggested by a proposal to organize a shippers' league, advocated at a preceding St. Paul meeting, which should give all the patronage it controlled to a selected antimonopoly packet company.[1] Four steamboat owners, among them Captain Davidson himself, offered to sell or lease their vessels to the convention members. None of their tenders was accepted, however, and the organization of the coöperative line continued apace. Its capital stock was set at $500,000, and a large committee of delegates was appointed to solicit subscriptions among the merchants of the river towns. Eventually an association known as the Minnesota Transportation Company was incorporated under the laws of Minnesota, to whose stock the St. Paul Board of Trade

[1] St. Paul *Weekly Pioneer*, Jan. 12, 1866.

conditionally subscribed $50,000.[1] In the end, however, the project came to naught because of the inability of the committee to secure sufficient subscriptions.

However, the railroad and the steamboat companies of the upper valley had taken alarm at these manifestations of public resentment. A few days before the assembling of the St. Paul convention the Milwaukee & St. Paul Railway and the Milwaukee & Prairie du Chien promised, in public letters, to abandon the policy of a "closed river" and thereafter accord equal terms to all steamboats irrespective of ownership.[2] Freight rates likewise came tumbling down. Notwithstanding wheat had risen in value 26 cents per bushel between April, 1865 and April, 1866, the steamboat rate for transporting it from Hudson to La Crosse fell from 15 to 4 cents per bushel, and the railroad rate between La Crosse and Milwaukee dropped from 20 to 15 cents.[3]

As a result of these concessions and the return of prosperity in 1866 the antimonopoly movement quietly disintegrated. Freight rates remained comparatively stationary until 1868 when, owing to the vigorous competition of the St. Louis market and a fall in the value of gold, they steadily declined. In the spring of 1870 the through wheat rate from upper river towns to Milwaukee was 18 cents; in the summer of 1871, 15 cents; in the spring of 1872, 12 cents.[4] Rate wars again made their appearance, the

[1] *Ibid.*, Mar. 2 and 9, 1866.

[2] *Wis. State Jour.*, Feb. 6, 1866.

[3] Milwaukee *Daily News*, Mar. 29, 1866. During the summer of 1866 as a result of steamboat consolidations the steamboat rate again advanced to 7 cents.

[4] Eau Claire *Free Press*, April 7, 1870; Milwaukee *Daily News*, Aug. 4, 1871; Milwaukee *Sentinel*, April 19, 1872.

Milwaukee & St. Paul Company fighting the Illinois Central, much to the delight of the river shippers. Inland towns continued to complain of high charges and discriminations, particularly during the depression of 1869, yet even their dissatisfaction was scattering. On the surface it seemed that the antimonopoly revolt had passed into history leaving behind no record of permanent achievement.

To careful observers, however, it was apparent that this popular movement had profoundly impressed the region west of Lake Michigan. Farmers and merchants had been confronted with the startling realization that they were well nigh helpless before the power of transportation companies. Jurists had learned that existing laws offered no protection against the oppressions of public carriers. Legislators had discovered that a mighty revolution in transportation had been suffered to take place during the past fifteen years without having received recognition on the statute books. Public opinion in short had been prepared to receive the new conception of state regulation of railroads.

CHAPTER XIII

THE GENESIS OF RAILROAD REGULATION IN THE UNITED STATES

For a number of years after the upper Mississippi River had lost its importance as an independent thoroughfare of commerce it still served the region west of Lake Michigan as a regulator of railroad rates. Never as useful in this respect as was the lake and canal route to the region east of Lake Michigan,[1] it was yet a power not to be disregarded. Whenever railroad charges became unreasonable shippers sent their products by steamboat to southern markets, and the usual result of such competition was to restore a proper balance.

Even before the outbreak of the Civil War, however, the regulative influence of the river was on the decline. The surplus of the upper valley had grown to be too enormous for consumption in the South, and as an independent route to the sea the old highway was out of the question. Suddenly the war shut off even the remnants of this river competition. The farmers living west of Lake Michigan were forced to seek their markets wholly in the East. During the four years of the conflict they were taught to depend upon the speed, directness, and certainty of overland transportation, and when the river was reopened to commerce they no longer cared to use it.

[1] The direction of the Mississippi River was contrary to the general trend of northern commerce. See *post*, chap. xiv.

It was not long, however, before shippers learned the full import of the decadence of the river route. Freed from the fear of water competition, railroad companies no longer hesitated to be arbitrary and exacting. Their new power became only too apparent during the closing years of the Civil War. Regretfully the antimonopoly reformers attempted to reëstablish the old equilibrium by improving the channel of the Mississippi, by removing obstructions from its bed, and by cutting away the sand bars formed at its mouth. To every section of the river valley they carried the campaign for river improvement, and during the later sixties and early seventies Congress never heard an end of their demands.

The more farsighted understood, however, that the departed power of the Mississippi could never return. They realized that if the railroads were to be curbed at all the restraining power must be found elsewhere. The program which they suggested was State regulation, and in the antimonopoly agitation they first prominently urged it upon the public.

Naturally public regulation was obnoxious to the railroad companies. They protested against it with all their powers of argument and persuasion. Upon five general grounds they rested their case.[1] They maintained that no reasonable cause for such interference existed, that it would be dishonest and unconstitutional, that it would render them unable to compete with the unhampered companies of Illinois, that it would drive railroad capital from the State,

[1] This account is compiled from a wide variety of sources, but chiefly from speeches delivered in the legislature and elsewhere, reports of legislative committees, and newspaper editorials.

and finally, that it could not properly be undertaken by any governmental authorities because of lack of knowledge and training.

In substantiation of their first argument they earnestly contended that their freight rates were just, even though apparently high. The cost of building their roads, they maintained, had been unusually large, due to the fact that the early promoters had been inexperienced in the art of railroad construction and that investments for this far-western region had been procured only at heavy discounts and high rates of interest. Their costs of operation were likewise higher than in the East, for this was a new country, undeveloped in its resources and unable to produce a profitable supply of traffic. Under such circumstances the freight rates which they demanded were if anything still inadequate. Indeed, the net earnings of their lines were scarely ever sufficient to pay stock dividends equal to the interest rates ordinarily accorded productive capital.[1]

To such a stand the reformers replied that the high cost of railroad construction in Wisconsin had not been due so much to inexperience or natural difficulties as to fraudulent financiering. As victims of railroad mortgages and local bonds they could testify only too intimately to this fact. Wholly beside the point, however, was any argument concerning the original cost of the roads. The present owners had purchased them under the hammer and for a

[1] Wis. *Assem. Jour.*, 1864, 717–36; *id.*, 1867, 641–49; Wis. *Sen. Jour.*, 1868, 280. For earnings of a conservatively managed road see Milwaukee & Prairie du Chien Railway Company, *Reports*, 1860–66; S. B. How v. Milwaukee & Prairie du Chien Railway, *Bill of Complaint*, in U. S. District Court, Milwaukee; New York *Times*, Nov. 6, 1865.

mere song after the panic of 1857. The only real losers by the forced sales had been the small stockholders, notably the railroad mortgagors. They had received short shrift in the devious process of reorganization. If, indeed, the roads paid meager dividends, this was to be attributed not to actual high costs or to insufficient earnings but to the watering of capital stock, fraudulent management, and the necessity for regenerating impaired and deteriorated lines.

The historian seeking to weigh these conflicting contentions is embarrassed by the meagerness of the evidence that accompanies them. Railroad managers whether honest or dishonest were not eager to admit the public into their confidence. Only on rare occasions did information of a trustworthy character find its way into print. No doubt the gross forms of high finance prevalent from 1850 to 1860 were less common during the following decade. However, it is apparent from the stray scraps of data that have been preserved that managers and directors of Wisconsin railroads still enriched themselves at the expense of the stockholders and the public. The investigations instituted by the Granger reformers in 1873 show, for example, that of the several railroads constructed within the State under approximately the same conditions, some had cost two or even three times as much per mile as others.[1] There seems little room for disagreement with the conclusions arrived at by the investigators that this

[1] Wis. Railroad Commissioner, *Report*, 1874, pt. 1, 51–56; U. S. Internal Commerce, *Report*, 1876, pt. 2, 161–63; Milwaukee *Daily Wis.*, Aug. 20 to Aug. 29, 1863; Milwaukee *Sentinel*, Mar. 2, 1867; Hartford *Home League*, Sept. 8, 1860 and June 27, 1863; Wis. *Assem. Jour.*, 1864, 730.

was the result chiefly of corrupt financiering, in which the railroad officials themselves shared the profits.

Exceptional opportunities for stock watering and irregular financing were presented by the numerous railroad consolidations that marked the decade of the sixties. Stock watering was carried on in Wisconsin and other states of the Union so freely and openly as to approach respectability. Of more direct dishonesty there were also a number of instances. Roads of little intrinsic value were purchased at excessive prices and incorporated into consolidated systems at inflated values, those privy to the proceedings dividing the spoils.[1] Even when consolidations were undertaken in good faith they invariably resulted in an undue increase of the nominal capital upon which dividends had to be paid.

The extent and the character of such maneuvering may be judged from a few well-substantiated illustrations. The figures which they involve may not be impressive to the present generation, but for their day they were large. In 1863 Russell Sage, Washington Hunt, and others purchased the Milwaukee & Horicon Railroad under foreclosure proceedings for $670,000. A few weeks later it was placed in the Milwaukee & St. Paul consolidation on a stock-and-bond basis of $1,050,000.[2] When the Chicago & Northwestern Railway Company consolidated with the Galena & Chicago Union in 1864 the latter com-

[1] See *ante*, 290, note 1; Milwaukee *Sentinel*, Mar. 4, 1867; Portage *Register*, Sept. 5, 1863; Milwaukee *Daily Wis.*, Aug. 30, 1863. See also notes on consolidation.

[2] Portage *Register*, July 4 and Sept. 5, 1863; Milwaukee *Daily Wis.*, Aug. 20, 1863; Hartford *Home League*, Nov. 15 and Dec. 6, 1862. See also notes on Milwaukee & St. Paul consolidation.

pany, whose total stock issues amounted to but $6,000,000, was credited in the new corporation with $12,000,000. The president of the Chicago & Northwestern frankly defended the increase on the ground that Northwestern stock had been so diluted prior to 1864 as to render it necessary to issue the additional $6,000,000 bonus to the owners of the Chicago & Galena Union in order to equalize in the consolidation the interests of the two sets of stockholders.[1] In the forced absorption of the Milwaukee & Prairie du Chien Company, there was involved approximately $3,000,000 of common stock. A few days prior to the Prairie Dog Corner this had been worth but 70 cents on the dollar. It was exchanged by the Milwaukee & St. Paul Company for $3,000,000 of its preferred stock plus a $750,000 bonus of its common stock. Almost without exception the consolidations of this period resulted in forcing upon the public enormous issues of securities of wholly fictitious value.[2]

Faced by such facts the conservative Milwaukee *Sentinel* laid down the following principle of railroad regulation in a series of editorials published in 1866, containing perhaps the ablest discussion of this subject written in the State at that time: "The proposition will hardly be disputed that a railroad company should have the right to maintain such charges upon its business as will pay a net profit upon capital prudently and economically invested, corresponding to the average net profit on capital other-

[1] New York *Times*, June 4, 1864; New York *Tribune*, Mar. 20, 1865; Chicago & Northwestern Railway Company, *Report*, 1865, 23–25. See also notes on Chicago & Northwestern consolidation.

[2] Poor, *Manual of Railroads*, 1868–69, 24, 30–31; Wis. *Assem. Jour.*, 1864, 728–31.

wise employed. The public is not bound to pay this net profit on the whole nominal cost of the road, if one half, or any other proportion of the capital has been squandered or stolen by the managers. The company cannot justly demand the usual net profit on capital for stock diluted in this or any other way, but only on the cash cost of the road, economically and faithfully constructed."[1] This was the answer of the reformers to the complaint of the railroad managers that their earnings were insufficient to pay proper dividends upon capital stock.

The second ground upon which railroad representatives objected to State regulation was its unconstitutionality. They maintained that the State had no more right to fix transportation charges than to fix the price at which the farmer sold his grain or the merchant his wares. Some granted the legal right of the State but asserted that regulation would constitute a moral violation of the promises made to railroad capital in the original liberal railroad charters.

The reformers in reply emphasized the quasi-public nature of the railroad industry, as recognized by the companies themselves when they accepted land grants and exercised the rights of eminent domain. They insisted that the enormous power of the railroads required some legislative check, some means of protection to the public. They denied that regulation constituted any legal or moral violation of the original charters. They pointed out the clause in the State constitution which expressly reserved to the legislature the privilege of altering or repealing

[1] Milwaukee *Sentinel*, Feb. 22, 1866.

the franchise of any company incorporated under the laws of Wisconsin.[1]

The third contention of the railroad companies was that regulation would so restrict and handicap their powers that they would be unable to compete successfully with the unhampered lines of Illinois. In particular they would be forced to surrender the important through freights moving between the Mississippi River and the lake shore. They would inevitably be ruined and in their downfall would drag with them the flourishing towns and cities that had grown up about this trade.

Even more persuasive was the argument that regulation would frighten railroad capital from the State. No capitalist, the railroad representatives declared, would think of investing his money in Wisconsin when once it was shown that the State legislature had violated the solemn contracts entered into with the companies in the original charters. Even under the best of conditions the Badger State found it difficult to attract railroad investors in competition with its western neighbors. Obviously a policy of restricting and harassing transportation companies could result only in increasing the handicap and perhaps halting entirely the railroad development of Wisconsin.[2]

Such an argument appealed powerfully to every locality eager to secure railroad connections, and in particular to the northern half of the State. Here

[1] Wisconsin *Constitution*, art. XI, sec. 1. See address of M. H. Carpenter in Wis. Agric. Soc., *Trans.*, 1869, 138–50; Milwaukee *Sentinel*, Mar. 21, 1866.

[2] Wis. *Assem. Jour.*, 1864, 717–36; Wis. *Sen. Jour.*, 1867, 643–45; *id.*, 1868, 280; *Wis. State Jour.*, Mar. 14 and 24, 1864; Milwaukee *Sentinel*, Mar. 20, 1866 and Mar. 4, 1867; Milwaukee *Daily Wis.*, April 10 and 26, 1867.

the agitation for rate regulation was looked upon as "a dishonest political hobby-horse ridden by popularity-seeking demagogues." "These tariff agitators know full well the disastrous consequences that would follow the success of such a bill, in the way of discouragement to railroad enterprise, thus subjecting the [north]western portion of the State for years to the inconvenience of stage coach travel and transportation of freight by wagon."[1]

Spurning the policy of regulation the northern portion of Wisconsin demanded only further encouragement to railroad investors. Not by restriction but by stimulation of construction was the danger of railroad extortion to be met. New railroads would increase competition, which by natural laws would reduce rates to a reasonable level.[2]

In these opposing methods of dealing with the same problem we have an interesting study in public psychology. One region, possessing no railroads, associated with them only the blessings of quick and easy transportation. The other, to whom these blessings had become a matter of course, thought only of high charges and inadequate service. So long as a large portion of the State remained without railroad facilities these conflicting points of view neutralized each other and the transportation companies were comparatively safe from interference. When, however, railroads had penetrated with some degree of uniformity all the settled portions of Wisconsin grievances came to a majority, and in the legislation of the Granger period they gained expression.

[1] Eau Claire *Free Press*, June 13, 1867.

[2] *Ibid.*; Wis. *Sen. Jour.*, 1869, 276–85.

Undoubtedly the most cogent argument advanced against rate regulation was that State authorities possessed no adequate basis of information upon which to undertake so difficult a task.[1] This was an objection not easy to answer. In Wisconsin as well as elsewhere in the country the only persons who knew anything of the technique of railroad administration were those in the employ of the carrying companies. Overland rail transportation was too recent a development in America to be fully understood in its manifold implications. The railroad managers themselves knew but little of the fundamental principles of rate making. They frankly fixed all their noncompetitive charges upon a rough basis of what the traffic would bear.

In the simply organized agricultural state of Wisconsin rate making, it is true, was not the intricate problem that it is today. It required, however, a special knowledge and training which public officials did not possess. In view of this obstacle it is fortunate that the efforts to enact regulatory legislation from 1864 to 1870 failed. It was upon this rock that the Granger laws were wrecked a few years later.

The railroad reformers averred that other than legitimate arguments were used to defeat regulation. It was impossible for them to substantiate their allegations, and it is probable little direct corruption existed. However, it was painfully apparent that the atmosphere which surrounded railroad legislation was far from ideal.[2] It prompted one disgusted assembly-

[1] Poor, *Manual of Railroads*, 1868–69, 31; *id.*, 1870–71, p. xxxiii; *id.*, 1871–72, p. xxxi; *Wis. State Jour.*, Jan. 4, 1866; Milwaukee *Sentinel*, Mar. 20 and 21, 1866.

[2] *Wis. State Jour.*, Mar. 29 and April 1, 1864; Madison *Patriot*, June

man in 1864 to propose the following resolution: "That the Sergeant at Arms of this House be directed to furnish the Railroad Lobby Agents that now infest this chamber, with a room, and the necessary liquid comforts, in the basement of the Capitol, where they can carry on their log rolling without annoyance to the proceedings of this body."[1] In discussing the regulation bills of 1866 the Janesville *Gazette*, an administration paper, gave somewhat homely expression to a belief commonly entertained in Wisconsin: "A wet rag about a washerwoman's thumb is not

21, 1862; *Waukesha County Democrat*, Mar. 1, 1864; Milwaukee *Daily News*, Feb. 9, 1866; Wis. *Assem. Jour.*, 1864, 563; *id.*, 1866, 123; Wis. *Sen. Jour.*, 1866, 782, 867; *id.*, 1867, 765; and Stephenson, *Recollections*, 193. The following account, published in *Wis. State Jour.*, April 1, 1864, may be cited as an illustration. It occurred in the Assembly in 1864 while the important railroad regulation bill of that session was under consideration. It was permitted to go by without creating even a demand for an investigation.

"After some further discussion Mr. McGarry asked leave to read a letter showing how the railroad operators and speculators influence the legislature.

"Cries of 'read' 'object' etc.

"Mr. Geo. B. Smith [speaker] said he had no objection to the reading of the letter. He knew what it was. It was a year old and did not relate to this House at all.

"Mr. McGarry began reading the letter, saying that he would omit names.

"Cries of 'names' 'read the names,' and great confusion and excitement on the floor.

"Mr. McGarry continued reading the letter and omitting the names. It seemed to have been written from New York by some railroad man, either to a member of the legislature or 'lobby member,' urging the importance of securing the passage of some measure on the subject of mortgages to railroads. The writer said the passage of the bill would be worth $5,000 'to us,' and that that amount would be paid to the order of the recipient of the letter if he got the bill through. It mentioned certain other gentlemen who would aid in getting it passed, but who knew nothing of the $5,000, that being 'between us.' The letter closed with the vigorous injunction: 'Yoke up the forty bullocks and put it (the bill) through.' "

[1] Wis. *Assem. Jour.*, 1864, 563.

more pliable than some of our Wisconsin solons are in the hands of these shrewd and skillful lobbymen."[1]

The custom of issuing free railroad passes to members of the legislature was the subject of numerous though unsustained complaints. Public opinion on the whole condoned the practice as it condoned others that would not be tolerated now. The legislative and business methods of Wisconsin were, it must be remembered, the methods of a period whose ethical standards were far different from our own. The Milwaukee *Sentinel* probably honestly reflected public sentiment at this time when in a caustic editorial upon the action of an assemblyman who had attracted notice by rejecting a railroad pass it declared that free passes were merely "an act of good fellowship on the part of the companies." "We are not among those who believe that Wisconsin legislators are so cheap that a pass will buy them. If that were so, would it not be questionable whether such cheap trash was worth purchasing at all?"[2]

By one means or another the railroad companies succeeded in defeating every effort that was made to regulate their conduct. As early as 1860 a bill to establish their charges was introduced in the legislature,[3] which they brushed aside with contemptuous ease. They granted the same scant consideration to other sporadic efforts of this kind during the early years of the Civil War.

[1] Janesville *Gazette*, Jan. 5, 1866.

[2] Milwaukee *Sentinel*, Jan. 28, 1871.

[3] Similar measures were at this time before the legislatures of New York, Pennsylvania, and Ohio. See *ibid.*, Feb. 21, 1860; Milwaukee *Daily News*, Mar. 28, 1866; *Wis. Farmer*, April 1, 1860; Fite, *Social and Industrial Conditions*, 161.

In the legislative session of 1864, however, a rate regulation measure, known as Assembly Bill No. 298, was the most urgent domestic question under consideration. The State was thoroughly aroused against the railroads, and memorials from all quarters demanding the passage of the bill poured in upon the lawmakers. More petitions on this subject found their way to the capitol in 1864 than had been presented on any other subject for years. "No measure," declared the *Wisconsin State Journal* on Mar. 15, 1864, "has ever been so universally demanded by the people."

The bill thus popular in Wisconsin was very sweeping in character. It proposed to divide freight into sixteen classes, enumerating the several articles to be included in each and the rate which each should bear. It forbade preferences of any kind in transporting the several classes, and in particular required the railroads to carry wood by the carload with reasonable dispatch. Passengers traveling first-class were to be charged not exceeding 3 cents per mile, those journeying second-class, not exceeding 2 cents per mile. State officers, judges, and members of the legislature were to be carried without charge. Any corporation that deliberately violated the law was at once to forfeit its charter.[1]

The railroad interests of Wisconsin arrayed against this measure the most formidable lobby that the legislature had seen since the land-grant days of 1856. Before many weeks they had succeeded in amending the bill to death. In the form in which it

[1] La Crosse *Democrat*, Mar. 15, 1864. For two instructive committee reports on this bill see Wis. *Assem. Jour.*, 1864, 717–36.

eventually passed it contained but two provisions, one of which prohibited railroad agents from transporting produce or lumber over roads with which they were officially connected, and the other authorized transportation companies to refuse to carry wood during their busy shipping seasons.[1]

At every subsequent legislative session until 1874 one or more measures to regulate railroad charges and service were up for consideration. Thirteen such bills were before the lawmakers in 1865, eight in 1866, seven in 1867.[2] Some of these were crude maximum rate bills, which like the measure of 1864 attempted to fix rigid schedules of charges and service. Others were carefully thought out and elaborately framed plans for regulatory commissions, which would be regarded as creditable even by the present generation. A number contemplated commissions with power merely to enforce the rates and regulations imposed by the legislature; others had in view boards with wide discretionary powers; still others, intended authorities with but advisory and supervisory powers. None had any chance for passage. Wisconsin legislatures were too completely dominated by railroad influences to admit of the acceptance of any substantial reform of this kind.

The antimonopoly uprising thus failed entirely to impress itself upon the statute books of Wisconsin. It made contributions of extreme importance, however, to popular and legislative knowledge. It familiarized the people of the State on the one hand

[1] Wis. *Gen. Laws*, 1864, chap. 482.

[2] See Wis. *Assem. Jour.* and Wis. *Sen. Jour.* for the years 1865, 1866, and 1867. The legislature of Minnesota requested such legislation of Wisconsin in 1866.

with the idea of public regulation. On the other it afforded an opportunity for the gradual development of the methods by which regulation could best be accomplished. It foreshadowed, while it prepared the way for, the Granger legislation of 1873.

Today one of the marked tendencies of American industrial life is the extension of government control over the service and charges of public carriers. To the antimonopoly revolt belongs the distinction of having for the first time turned public opinion in this direction.

CHAPTER XIV

COMMERCE OF THE UPPER MISSISSIPPI

Wisconsin possessed unusual natural advantages for the conduct of a profitable inland commerce. On three sides her shores were washed by the greatest inland watercourses on the North American continent. On her western border flowed the Mississippi River, pouring into her lap the products of Minnesota and northern Iowa and affording the products of her own western counties an exit to market; on her eastern boundary the broad waters of Lake Michigan offered her easy access to the sea; on her northern shore rolled Lake Superior, the largest of all the northern chain of fresh-water lakes. These magnificent highways supported an internal commerce, unparalleled in all the rest of the world, and to it Wisconsin contributed an important part.

The conditions of navigation on the Mississippi River differed widely from those on the Great Lakes.[1] The upper Mississippi in frequent stretches is but

[1] No adequate study has yet been made of the steamboat commerce of the Mississippi River. The best works thus far published are biographical in nature, those of George B. Merrick, a former river pilot, being especially useful. See G. B. Merrick, *Old Times on the Upper Mississippi* (Cleveland, 1909), "Western River Steamboating," in Wis. Hist. Soc., *Proc.*, 1911, 97–148; and "Joseph Reynolds and the Diamond Jo Line Steamers, 1862–1911," in Mississippi Valley Historical Association, *Proceedings*, 1915, 217–61; George Gale, *Upper Mississippi* (Chicago, 1867), 388–414; E. W. Gould, *Fifty Years on the Mississippi* (St. Louis, 1889); S. L. Clemens, *Life on the Mississippi* (New York, n. d.). For the best contemporary source see the annual reviews of steamboat trade on the upper river printed at or near the close of each shipping season in the St. Paul papers.

a few feet deep; it fluctuates greatly from season to season; and above Keokuk in our period it was impeded by a chain of rapids thirty miles in length. The Great Lakes, on the other hand, offered to commerce almost the same facilities as were to be found on the ocean. The vessels employed on the two water systems naturally reflected these differences. The lake vessels were of the familiar type employed on the sea; the river steamboats on the contrary were of a genus known only to river navigation.

Mississippi River steamboats represented a comparatively recent development in boat building, the first having been constructed but fifty years before the outbreak of the Civil War. They were of two kinds, sidewheelers and sternwheelers, the former being the newer and more popular type on the upper river. Both types were light of draught, of great speed and good carrying capacity, and were excellently adapted to the requirements of the commerce in which they were engaged.[1] Steamboat men on the upper river proudly boasted that their vessels "could float on a heavy dew."

Usually they were arranged for both passenger and freight service. The transportation of passengers, particularly immigrants bound for Iowa, Minnesota, and western Wisconsin, constituted during the fifties and sixties one of their largest and surest sources of profit. Immigrants as a rule contented themselves with the cheap deck passage, but for those who could afford better accommodations there were cabins comfortably and often elegantly fitted out. The better-class packets were referred to in the newspaper notices of the day as "floating palaces" and such in

[1] Wis. Hist. Soc., *Proc.*, 1911, 96–148.

fact some of them were. To the simple westerner, accustomed to the rude life of the frontier, they represented the height of magnificence and in particular their sumptuous bills of fare filled him with delighted amazement.

There was a picturesqueness about steamboating on the Mississippi that was less pronounced in the more important commerce of the Great Lakes. One feature of it which particularly caught the public eye was the occasional racing between rival vessels. Speed was a prime requisite for any successful passenger packet, and river captains were under constant temptation to establish new records or "show their heels" to a competitor when the river was at a good stage and freight was meager. On the lower river such contests were scheduled and carefully prepared for, but on the upper river they were as a rule impromptu "scrub races," as the steamboat men called them. Often in the excitement of a close match safety valves were tied down and boilers recklessly crowded with dried pine, rosin, and other highly inflammable materials. Many boats constantly carried with them barrels of rosin for no other purpose than that of producing high steam pressure in an emergency. Now and then as the result of such encounters boilers exploded or red-hot smokestacks set boats afire, and the most painful catastrophes followed. This was the case with the steamboat "John Rumsey," destroyed near St. Paul in the fall of 1864, her engineers having in the course of a race forced her boilers until they burst.[1]

[1] G. B. Merrick, "Steamboats and Steamboatmen of the Upper Mississippi," in Burlington *Sat. Evening Post*, Oct. 11, 1913.

The difficulties of river navigation produced along the Mississippi an interesting social class known as steamboat pilots. These men possessed a minute knowledge of the river—its twists and bends, the vagaries of its current, and the location of its unseen snags and rocks. Their skill at the wheel was proverbial, as was their courage and presence of mind in a crisis. Their long period of apprenticeship and the heavy responsibility resting upon them gave them standing and power among the rivermen. This they increased during the fifties by an effective organization known as the Pilots' Benevolent Association.[1] Their wages were often higher than those of the captains under whom they served, reaching their maximum just prior to the Civil War, when first-class men received from $500 to $600 per month, and a number of the best "lightning pilots" running between St. Paul and St. Louis were paid as high as $800 or $900 per month.[2]

The Civil War destroyed their strong organization and loosened their hold upon the river traffic. The derangement of the commerce of the lower river threw hundreds of them out of employment with the result that the wages of all came tumbling down.[3] Even more damaging to them than the war were the economic changes of the later fifties, sixties, and seventies, which not only ruined their profession but altered and eventually destroyed the river commerce itself.

[1] Clemens, *Life on the Mississippi*, 127–40.

[2] *Ibid.*; Merrick, *Old Times*, 163.

[3] During the season of 1867 pilots employed by the Northwestern Union Packet Company received $250 per month. La Crosse *Republican*, Dec. 18, 1867.

The lucrativeness of upper Mississippi steamboating during the fifties and sixties was astonishing. This was the golden era of the river trade, when settlement was rushing into Minnesota, Iowa, and western Wisconsin. Passenger and freight rates were high, and the steamboats were busy with cargoes, coming and going, from the opening of navigation to its close. On the up-trip they carried eager crowds of immigrants and loads of supplies from the great wholesale entrepôts of the lower river. On the down-trip they were laden to their capacity with wheat and other agricultural products. Their gains from a single round trip were sometimes sufficient to pay half the cost of a new boat.

The net profits of the La Crosse & St. Paul Packet Company, one of the most prominent companies on the upper river, were, according to its secretary, a trifle over $249,000 for the season of 1865. "This above all expenses," observes the La Crosse *Democrat*, "makes quite a fine showing, being in excess of the entire capital stock of the company."[1] In individual cases the gains were even higher. Thus the "Burlington," the smallest sidewheeler of the Northern Line Packet Company, representing an investment of $30,000 at the utmost, earned in the season of 1866 a net income of $70,000.[2] Boats in regular lines, particularly if they enjoyed railroad connections, ordinarily won greater profits than the "outside" or "wild" boats, yet even the latter flourished during the years between 1850 and 1870.

During the early years of the Civil War there

[1] La Crosse *Democrat*, Jan. 29, 1866.
[2] Burlington *Sat. Evening Post*, Feb. 7, 1914.

appeared on the upper river a more important improvement than it had seen in several decades. This was the introduction of grain barges, designed chiefly for the carrying of wheat but capable, also, of transporting other bulky commodities. No more economical freight carriers than these have ever been devised on the upper river. They required but a small investment of capital, for they were merely great wooden hulks. They were economical of operation for, being towed by the regular steamboats, they required no crew. They were light of draught for they were unencumbered with machinery or cabin accommodations. They possessed carrying capacities often as great as those of the steamboats that towed them.[1] Though they slackened the speed of the packets, they compensated for this to some extent by decreasing the delays of loading and unloading. A vessel merely left its empty grain barges at the desired shipping point on the up-trip and picked them up loaded on the return.

This improvement was the result to a large extent of changing conditions along the upper river. By 1860 Minnesota and northwestern Wisconsin had completely outgrown the carrying capacity of their steamboat service. They needed not only greater but cheaper transportation, particularly for their surplus grain and this, barges alone could provide them. "What would some of the Erie Canal 'skiff' owners say," boasted the La Crosse *Democrat* in the spring of 1864, "to see one of our steamers ploughing her way to market with fifteen thousand bushels of

[1] Steamboats of the first class plying the river above Dubuque were usually not much over 250 or 350 tons burden.

wheat on her decks, and from one to three barges in tow, each loaded with from ten to fourteen thousand bushels of wheat."[1] The steamboat "Ocean Wave" in the spring of 1866 took to market on a single trip with the aid of her barges a load of 61,395 bushels of grain, the largest cargo it was said that up to that time had ever been taken down the river.[2]

The number of grain barges thus employed multiplied with astonishing rapidity during the decade of the sixties. The increase was particularly noticeable during the years 1863 and 1864 when, owing to the unprecedentedly low stage of water in the Mississippi, it was difficult for the larger steamboats to navigate the upper reaches of the river. By the close of 1866 a single great packet company operating between Dubuque and St. Paul possessed more than a hundred of the new carriers, the total grain capacity of which was 325,000 bushels.[3] In the trade of St. Paul in 1866 were over 180, the total tonnage of which was three times as great as the volume of all the steamboats entering that port.[4]

The economies of the new system were extended by other improvements during the early sixties. Originally it was the custom for the barges to carry wheat in two-bushel bags, an expensive practice that held over from the days when grain was carried only upon the decks and in the holds of the packet boats. During the early sixties the construction of improved

[1] La Crosse *Democrat*, May 5, 1864.

[2] Prescott *Journal*, May 19, 1866.

[3] St. Paul *Weekly Pioneer*, Dec. 21, 1866. The same article contains an excellent summary of the commerce of the upper river for the year 1866.

[4] *Ibid.*

elevators at the river-shipping centers[1] rendered possible the far cheaper method of shipping grain in bulk.[2] At the same time another change crept in. Towing by the regular steamboats was found to be too expensive, and small but powerful craft, especially built for this purpose, came into use. The latter were light of draught, so that they could penetrate with their barges to the uppermost reaches of the Mississippi or its tributaries. They were comparatively cheap of construction as well as inexpensive of operation, for they were small and able to dispense with costly crews. They could, despite their diminutive size, haul down the river surprising quantities of grain.[3]

Originally these towboats contented themselves with taking to market three or four barges at a time. Soon, however, competition forced them to accept seven or eight, or even more. In the early seventies it was not unusual for one of the powerful craft of the "Diamond Jo" line to take to market at one trip a fleet of barges carrying 100,000 bushels of grain.[4] We have already seen in a previous chapter how towboats at this time assumed the function of hauling rafts of pine to market. Puffing their vigorous way through placid waters, with huge lumber hulks or grain barges at their front or sides, they represented the new order of events on the Mississippi River.

[1] See *post*, chap. xv.

[2] Owing to the necessity of lightering at the Keokuk rapids grain descending the river to St. Louis was carried in bags as late as the seventies.

[3] St. Paul *Weekly Pioneer*, Dec. 21, 1866; Milwaukee *Sentinel*, May 25, 1864; New York Produce Exchange, *Report*, 1872–73, 250–52.

[4] Miss. Valley Hist. Assn., *Proc.*, 1915, 227–28.

In the meantime the number of steamboats in service slowly but steadily declined. In 1857 approximately one hundred such vessels ran into St. Paul; in 1866, not more than sixty-three; in 1876, scarcely a dozen.[1] In 1857 the number of arrivals at St. Paul was 1,025; in 1866 it had fallen to 777; in 1874 it was only 218.[2] As sure and as striking as had been the rise of the barge trade of the upper Mississippi was this decline in the packet trade. The stately steamboats, once the pride of the entire valley, had been supplanted by the noisy towboats with consorts of clumsy barges.

Concentration of ownership was a marked characteristic of the packet industry of the upper Mississippi during the sixties and seventies. As in the case of railroads, this was an outgrowth of unregulated competition. It was not so much, however, competition between river carriers themselves, as that offered by overland transportation. Indeed, it was only after the railroads had well started the decline of the commerce of the upper river that the greatest combinations of steamboat capital made their appearance.

In 1860 concentration was already well under way. At that time there were in the service in Wisconsin, Minnesota, and Iowa two prominent packet companies maintaining regular lines, and a few unimportant "outside" steamboats. The former possessed a decided advantage over the latter in that they were able, by virtue of their regular service, to monopolize the jobbing and railroad trade of the great wholesale entrepôts on the river.

[1] Merrick, *Old Times*, 83; St. Paul *Weekly Pioneer*, Dec. 21, 1866.
[2] U. S. Internal Commerce, *Report*, 1876, pt. 2, app., 188.

One of these steamboat organizations, the Northern Line, plying between St. Paul and St. Louis, until 1860 was nothing more than a pooling agreement among individual steamboat owners. As such it had originated in 1857, the aftermath of a period of ruinous competition. In 1860 its loose organization was exchanged for the more compact unity of a stock company, a consummation of such arrangements not infrequent on the river.

The other organization was the Galena, Dubuque, Dunleith & Minnesota Packet Company, organized in 1847 while Wisconsin, Minnesota, and Iowa were still territories. Until 1860 it had contrived to suppress its most active competitors by the simple device of absorbing them as soon as they became formidable, and it was at this time the richest and most powerful steamboat company in the trade of the upper reaches of the Mississippi River. At Galena it received the railroad traffic of the Illinois Central and its connecting railroad lines; at Prairie du Chien it had an exclusive contract with the Milwaukee & Prairie du Chien Railroad; at La Crosse it made running connections with the La Crosse & Milwaukee Railroad. Its only important rival within its own territory was the Northern Line Packet Company, with which it contrived in 1860 to form a satisfactory traffic agreement.[1] In many of the river towns of Wisconsin it was condemned as an oppressive monopoly that should be destroyed.

A third organization, the La Crosse & St. Paul

[1] Milwaukee *Daily Wis.*, Jan. 31, 1860; Prescott *Transcript*, April 27, 1860; G. B. Merrick, *History of Upper River Packet Companies*, Ms., 26; Russell Blakeley, "Advent of Commerce in Minnesota," in *Minn. Hist. Colls.*, VIII, 408.

Packet Company, began operations at La Crosse in 1860.[1] Its leading spirit was Capt. W. F. Davidson, a typical western steamboat man of great energy and ability, who soon became the dominating figure in the steamboat industry of the upper river. Peculiarly advantageous were his connections with the La Crosse & Milwaukee Railroad. That corporation, by reason of possessing the most direct overland route from Minnesota and northwestern Wisconsin to the lake shore, was in a position to control and share with him the richest portion of the through commerce of the upper river.

His line flourished from the very outset. Into the developing tributaries of the upper Mississippi, particularly the Minnesota, St. Croix, and Chippewa, he ran prosperous branch lines, all of which gathered for the railroad at La Crosse millions of bushels of grain and carried back in return thousands of tons of merchandise and tens of thousands of immigrants.

In the meantime the old Galena line, nearly ruined by the rate war of 1860, and possessing only roundabout railroad connections with the lake shore, steadily declined in power. In 1861 it was obliged to transfer a number of its vessels to the vigorous service of its rival,[2] and in 1862 its owners quietly permitted Davidson to secure a controlling interest in its stock.[3] In 1863 its property was formally sold to an association consisting of Davidson and officials of the several railroads centering at Dunleith, Prairie du Chien, and

[1] See *ante*, chap. xii.

[2] Prescott *Transcript*, Aug. 17, 1861; La Crosse *Weekly Republican*, Sept. 18, 1867; Milwaukee *Sentinel*, Aug. 14 and 16, 1861.

[3] See *ante*, chap. xii; La Crosse *Weekly Republican*, Sept. 18, 1867; *Minn. Hist. Colls.*, VIII, 408–11.

La Crosse,[1] and in the following year it was reorganized as the Northwestern Packet Company.[2]

A single group of interests now controlled practically the entire river commerce between Galena and St. Paul. The Northern Line, to be sure, still maintained a regular, if infrequent, service between St. Paul and St. Louis, but its potential competition was stifled by an agreement whereby upon freight carried north of Galena it charged the rates demanded by the Davidson lines, in return for which it was permitted to fix its own rates upon freight carried south of that city.[3] How complete was the control exercised by this combination and how oppressive was its alliance with the railroads of Wisconsin and Illinois became startlingly apparent during the closing years of the Civil War.

For a number of years the public was not permitted to know that Captain Davidson controlled the affairs of both his own line and the Northwestern Packet Company. In the spring of 1866, however, shortly after the antimonopoly reformers had forced the separation of the railroad and steamboat interests on the upper river, it was formally announced that the two interests had combined.[4] The consolidated corporation, known as the Northwestern Union Packet Company, was the most powerful steamboat organization on the entire Mississippi River. It owned at the end of 1866 thirty steamboats, of which

[1] Prairie du Chien *Courier*, Nov. 5, 1863; La Crosse *Democrat*, Nov. 10, 1863; La Crosse *Weekly Republican*, Jan. 27, 1864 and Sept. 18, 1867; Prescott *Journal*, Dec. 5, 1863; Milwaukee *Sentinel*, Dec. 5, 1863.

[2] L. Kessinger, *History of Buffalo County*, 330.

[3] Chicago *Tribune*, Dec. 11, 1865; Milwaukee *Sentinel*, Dec. 13, 1865.

[4] Prescott *Journal*, May 5, 1866.

eleven were palatial sidewheelers and nineteen, sternwheelers. In addition it possessed 115 barges. According to the river press this was the finest fleet ever afloat on western waters. The property of the corporation was capitalized at $1,500,000, including its boats, two large dockyards, and 15,000 acres of woodland from which it secured its fuel.[1]

The entire river trade of Wisconsin and Minnesota was thus monopolized in 1866 by a single great corporation. The Northern Line was still independent, but the length of its run from St. Louis to St. Paul rendered it unable to furnish a sufficiently frequent service for effective competition. The rivals were, moreover, ordinarily able to maintain harmony by rate agreements and a judicious division of territory. A rate conflict did, indeed, break out in the season of 1868, when the Northwestern Union Packet Company invaded the southern precincts of its rival, but this quarrel was shortly composed and a joint agreement entered into which endured until the early seventies when the two companies were merged into one.[2]

We may best judge of the extent to which concentration had worked itself out during the Civil War by a glance at the steamboat records of St. Paul. In the season of 1866, of the sixty-three steamboats running into this port, forty-four were owned by the Northwestern Union and the Northern Line companies; of the 180 barges employed in its trade

[1] St. Paul *Weekly Pioneer*, Dec. 21, 1866; La Crosse *Weekly Republican*, Sept. 18, 1867.

[2] Oshkosh *Times*, April 27, 1868; Green Bay *Advocate*, June 25, 1868; Milwaukee *News*, Mar. 6, 1869; Prescott *Journal*, Feb. 10, 1870; *Minn. Hist. Colls.*, VIII, 414–15.

they owned 175.[1] The steamboat industry like many others had outgrown its old-time individualism. It had entered upon a new era of concentrated corporate control, which became more and more marked during the seventies as the river commerce declined under the effects of railroad competition.[2]

Thus far we have considered only incidentally the influence of railroads upon the commerce of the upper river. We must now trace this out in some detail, sketching hastily in introduction the conditions existing prior to the advent of the overland carriers.

In 1823 for the first time a steamboat succeeded in ascending the Mississippi River to the present site of St. Paul. Others followed as the northern country developed, bringing merchandise and goods for the Indian trade, carrying away lead from the Galena, Dubuque, and Potosi mines, and furs brought by native trappers to St. Paul and Prairie du Chien. Such of this traffic as was bound for Atlantic seaports followed the exceedingly indirect and expensive river route via St. Louis and New Orleans. Frequently it occurred that lead, mined in the Mineral Point region and carried thousands of miles by water to New York, was destined for Milwaukee, where it arrived after months of travel but 175 miles from the place where it had been mined.

During the fifties all these conditions were transformed. The Illinois & Michigan Canal was completed in 1851, providing a continuous watercourse from the Mississippi River to Lake Michigan. In

[1] St. Paul *Weekly Pioneer*, Dec. 21, 1866.

[2] Near the close of the sixties the Diamond Jo Line of steamboats, which later became the greatest on the upper river, was organized. See Miss. Valley Hist. Assn., *Proc.*, 1915, 217–61.

1854 the first railroad line from the lake reached the Mississippi at Rock Island. Thereafter in rapid succession other railroad lines in Illinois and Wisconsin arrived at the river, tapping it ever nearer and nearer its source.

The new commercial paths thus established by way of the Great Lakes and the Erie Canal to the Atlantic were so much more direct and economical than the old route that by the time western Wisconsin and Minnesota were sufficiently developed to have a large grain trade the trend of commerce was already away from the river. We have seen how little the closing of the lower Mississippi at the outbreak of the Civil War disturbed the people of the upper valley. Within a few months they had adjusted themselves to the new conditions, and the only effect of the blockade was to hasten the inevitable diversion of the river traffic to these new northern highways.

For a number of years the competition of the railroads did not decrease the steamboat commerce of the upper river. On the contrary the packets were never more busily and profitably employed than during the years between 1855 and 1865. Railroads were few and far between; they penetrated only the comparatively well-settled country. The newer regions about the headwaters of the Mississippi were still obliged to rely chiefly upon steamboats for the transportation of their surplus.

A notable change had taken place, however, in the character of the packet commerce. It no longer descended the river to St. Louis and New Orleans as formerly, but a large part was deflected at the railroad terminals. Steamboats gathered their cargoes at

St. Paul, Hudson, Red Wing, Winona, and a dozen other river landings, only to deliver their accumulated burdens to the waiting cars at La Crosse, Prairie du Chien, and Dunleith. The river was employed merely to gather up, as the agent of the railroads, the surplus of the upper country and to distribute, as the agent of the railroads, the supplies which the latter brought from the East. It had become but a feeder, subsidiary to rival trade courses.

The lower river towns were loth to admit that this change was the result of immutable economic laws. They clung to the belief that the bulky products of the upper valley must return to what they were pleased to term the natural route. The increasing diversion of traffic to the northern highways they attributed chiefly to obstructions in the channel of the river. They ascribed their failure to retain the trade of the Northwest particularly to the rapids above Keokuk and at Rock Island and the silt bars formed at the mouth of the Mississippi. Their remedy consisted in the removal of these obstructions.[1] Between 1866 and 1873 they held convention after convention memorializing Congress upon the subject. In the upper valley their demands were sanctioned and reënforced upon other grounds by the discontented antimonopolists. Congress responded readily and many improvements were made. Commerce, however, stubbornly refused to be coaxed back to its old haunts.

[1] See *Proceedings* of the Mississippi River Improvement Convention of Dubuque, Feb. 14 and 15, 1866; *Proceedings* of the River Improvement Convention of St. Louis, Feb. 12 and 13, 1867; *Memorial* adopted at New Orleans, Keokuk, and Louisville conventions in 1869; *Transportation Routes to the Seaboard*, I, 187–215, II, 591–715.

A prospect for the revival of the river traffic seemed to be held out during the later sixties by the rapid development of barge and towboat transportation. St. Louis, in particular, was sanguine of regaining thereby her lost trade with the upper river. She set out in this hope to improve her facilities for handling bulk grain, erecting elevators for the first time and establishing a regular barge line to New Orleans.[1] Her efforts attracted considerable attention in the upper valley, especially in 1869, when hard times and the low price of wheat forced that region to look about for cheaper avenues to market.[2] However, the advantages of the northern highways were not easy to overcome, and the railroads running between Lake Michigan and the Mississippi promptly met the potential competition of the river in 1869 by cutting their rates in half.[3] The commercial centers on the Great Lakes likewise jealously guarded their new accessions. They diligently spread the impression, erroneous though effective, that wheat sent to market via the southern route would heat and spoil owing to the humidity and high temperatures prevailing in the zone of the Gulf.[4] Thus promptly were

[1] St. Louis Union Merchants' Exchange, *Reports*, 1865–70; New York Produce Exchange, *Report*, 1872–73, 250–52; 57 Cong., 1 sess., *House Executive Documents*, 17, No. 2, serial No. 4284, *Mississippi River Commission Report*, 1901, 33–40; *Transportation Routes to the Seaboard*, II, 598–99.

[2] One of the expressions of this movement in Wisconsin was the organization in the winter of 1869 by the merchants of St. Croix and Pierce counties of the St. Croix Valley Exporting Association. This was a coöperative shipping company, organized under the auspices of a local branch of the Patrons of Husbandry for the purpose of shipping wheat to St. Louis in barges.

[3] See *post*, chap. xv.

[4] So wide a credence did this impression gain that in 1869 the St. Louis Grain Association felt called upon to demonstrate its falsity by shipping to

the advantages of barge transportation met and neutralized.

The northern railroads, having captured the southern traffic of the upper river, were soon reaching out to absorb even the remaining local commerce. The close of the war found them rapidly pushing into the very heart of the country from which the steamboats had hitherto drawn their sustenance. In 1867 they struck the first blow when the Milwaukee & St. Paul Railway extended its Minnesota line to St. Paul, the head of steamboat navigation on the Mississippi.[1] In 1870 the Lake Superior & Mississippi Railroad gave St. Paul new railroad connection with the flourishing young port of Duluth at the head of Lake Superior. On the Wisconsin side of the river the Milwaukee & St. Paul Railway completed a second route to the Minnesota metropolis via Winona in 1871. Shortly afterwards the West Wisconsin Railroad provided a third. From every direction railroads penetrated the region that for a score of years had nourished and sustained the river steamboats.[2]

The first railroad whistle heard within the precincts of St. Paul sounded the doom of the waning river commerce. At the very outset the rich passenger traffic, later the general merchandise trade, and eventually the bulky grain, passed to the new high-

Liverpool, via New Orleans, at regular intervals during the season, test cargoes of wheat, all of which arrived in good condition. *Mississippi River Commission Report*, 1901, 33–40; *Transportation Routes to the Seaboard*, I, 201–3, II, 596–97, 858–60.

[1] After the opening of this road freight rates from Wisconsin and Minnesota river towns to Milwaukee were usually the same as to St. Louis by river.

[2] St. Paul Chamber of Commerce, *Reports*, 1869–73.

ways. After 1867 even barges declined in number, and their activities outlived those of the steamboats only a few years. For some decades the river was busy with lumber rafts from northern Wisconsin and Minnesota, but the gradual extinction of the forests brought this occupation also to a close. The proud sway of the river over the destinies of the upper valley was at an end, its picturesque steamboats and barges supplanted by the prosaic but efficient box car. Today it may be said with almost literal truth, the Father of Waters goes unvexed to the sea.

CHAPTER XV

COMMERCE OF THE GREAT LAKES

We turn now to Wisconsin's commerce on the Great Lakes, taking up as with the river trade, first its development, second its transportation agents, and third its competition with the railroads. The most obvious characteristic of this commerce was its dependence upon the crude products of the extractive industries. Wheat, corn, flour, in general, heavy foodstuffs, constituted its entire eastward movement. Lumber, coal, salt, and stone made up the bulk of its westward and southward movement. The water route was the carrier only of such commodities as did not require swift transportation and were too bulky to be carried by rail.

Like the commerce of the upper Mississippi River this was almost wholly "through" in character. Freights originating at Milwaukee, Racine, or Green Bay were destined for the lower lake ports, there to be transferred to canal boats and railroads running to New York, Philadelphia, and Boston; or sent directly without transshipment to Montreal by way of the Welland Canal. Of a local commerce from port to port or lake to lake, such as flourishes today, there was then almost none.

The richest grain-producing areas in the world at this time lay west and northwest of Lake Michigan. Draining them of their immense surplus were the two rising young lake ports, Chicago and Milwaukee.

Milwaukee contested with her neighbor the trade of the northern wheat-raising portions. Wheat and flour constituted the chief reliance of her commerce. In striking contrast to her singleness of interest was the variety of pursuits of the Illinois metropolis. Situated between a notable corn belt and a notable wheat belt Chicago was unrivalled as a corn, wheat, and oats market. She boasted the greatest primary hog and beef trade in the country, ranked as the greatest lumber distributor in the world, and in addition maintained manufacturing interests of no small importance. She but reflected in all this the nature of the region which she served.

So, too, did Milwaukee in her commerce mirror the development of her hinterland. Wisconsin, northern Iowa, and Minnesota lay just north of the great corn line, leaving the Cream City without an important corn traffic. Its hog and beef trade, therefore, was small compared with that of Chicago. Large portions of the territory tributary to it were either covered with forest or situated so near the pine supply as to preclude the possibility of any lumber trade with a central distributor. It was only as a wheat market that Milwaukee could hope at this time to compete with her aspiring rival to the south.

At the beginning of the Civil War the career of Milwaukee as an exporter of wheat extended back only a score of years. Her first shipment seems to have been made in 1841, consisting of a small cargo of about 4,000 bushels. In order to gather so large a consignment at that time the shippers had been obliged to circulate handbills "far and near through the country, announcing to the inhabitants thereof the somewhat startling and quite unexpected intelligence that cash was being paid in Milwaukee for wheat."[1] From such humble beginnings grew a trade that by 1860 amounted to 7,500,000 bushels.[2]

Milwaukee was elated over her wheat exports in 1860. Nor was this elation without good reason. Her exportation in 1860 had nearly doubled that of any previous year. Yet in 1861 the amount exported again nearly doubled,[3] and during the remaining years of the war continued to average nearly 12,000,000 bushels. In 1862 Milwaukee could proudly proclaim herself the greatest primary wheat market in the world, a distinction which Chicago had previously held, and which now passed back and forth between these two cities during the remaining years of the decade.

Several other Wisconsin lake centers, particularly Racine, Green Bay, and Sheboygan, at this time exported small quantities of the great northern staple. Together with Milwaukee they sent eastward during the five years of the war approximately 67,000,000 bushels, of which the Cream City exported 60,000,000.[4]

The rapidity of this development was in part the cause, in part the result, of a revolution west of Lake Michigan in the methods of shipping and transferring grain. Prior to 1857 wheat elevators for the handling of bulk grain were known only in the East. Conditions in the new West were such that merchants felt

[1] *Address* of Thomas Whitney before Milwaukee Chamber of Commerce, Feb. 3, 1863; Milwaukee Chamber of Commerce, *Report*, 1858, 6–7.

[2] *Id.*, 1860, 23.

[3] *Id.*, 1861, 16.

[4] *Id.*, 1860–65.

compelled to adhere to the antiquated and cumbersome methods of dealing with grain in bags. Old-fashioned private warehouses for transferring bagged wheat were the only facilities that even such export centers as Milwaukee and Chicago afforded.

So soon, however, as Milwaukee had carried to completion her railroad lines to the Mississippi and had felt the resulting pressure of the grain trade of the upper valley she set about to secure adequate elevator facilities. The rapidity with which she moved during the decade of the sixties was equalled only by the swiftness with which her commerce expanded. In 1857 she erected her first modern elevator.[1] By 1860 she had three, by 1866, seven or eight.[2] The daily capacity of these establishments for transferring bulk grain in 1858 was 80,000 bushels; in 1860, 120,000 bushels; in 1866, 1,100,000 bushels.[3] A single enormous structure, said to have been the greatest in the world, which the Milwaukee & St. Paul Railway built in Milwaukee in 1865 had a storage capacity of 1,500,000 bushels and a daily shipping capacity of 450,000 bushels.[4] In all the grain-gathering centers on the upper Mississippi River, in the receiving centers of interior Wisconsin, and in the exporting centers on Lake Michigan, a similar rapid development was taking place.[5] St. Louis on the

[1] *Id.*, 1858, 24–25.

[2] Milwaukee *Sentinel*, Jan. 1, 1861; Milwaukee Chamber of Commerce, *Report*, 1866, 32.

[3] *Id.*, 1858, 24–25; *id.*, 1866, 32; Milwaukee *Sentinel*, Jan. 1, 1861.

[4] Milwaukee Chamber of Commerce, *Report*, 1866, 32; Milwaukee *Daily Wis.*, Feb. 25, 1865; *Wis. State Jour.*, Mar. 7, 1865.

[5] Milwaukee & La Crosse Railway Company, *Report*, 1860, 520; *id.*, 1861, 4; Milwaukee & Prairie du Chien Railway Company, *Report*, 1861, 11; Chicago & Northwestern Railway Company, *Report*, 1863, 4;

other hand did not build her first elevator until 1865. Until then she had facilities only for bagged grain, a striking confession on her part of the decadence of her trade with the upper river.[1]

The successful transportation of grain in bulk, which became feasible with the introduction of the elevator system, was the most signal achievement of its kind since the advent of railroads in the region west of Lake Michigan. Coming into full operation just in time to be of service during the war, it affected economies to which were due in no small part the abounding prosperity of the farmers of this region and the swiftness of their agricultural expansion during the critical years of the slavery conflict.

The grain-exporting centers of the new West found it impossible to pattern their grain-elevator system after the accepted eastern model. Perhaps this was one of the reasons why they clung as long as they did to the outworn warehouse methods. Geographical differences permitted Milwaukee and Chicago to adopt the eastern plan of operation only after radical alterations.

Buffalo, Oswego, and New York received their grain by water. They had shipments come to them by the boatload, a single consignment containing thousands, often tens of thousands, of bushels. It was feasible in their elevator bins to handle each shipment as a distinct and separate unit. From the very beginning, therefore, they bought and sold grain by sample.

Prescott *Transcript*, June 1, 1861; *Wis. State Jour.*, Dec. 16, 1862 and Feb. 25, 1864; Green Bay *Advocate*, Aug. 10, 1865.

[1] St. Louis Union Merchants' Exchange, *Report*, 1865, 11–12.

In the region west of Lake Michigan this was impossible. Lake centers like Milwaukee and Chicago received their wheat not in large, but in small parcels. Not more than 350 bushels was the capacity of the railroad car of that day. Had the elevators been forced to maintain separate each small consignment as it arrived, the chief economy of the new system would have been lost. The handling of grain in large masses was the great objective of elevator operation and this could be achieved only by combining in the bins the hundreds of little shipments that the railroads brought in.

If all wheat were of the same quality this would have occasioned no difficulty. No two shipments, however, are ever exactly alike, and between the best and the worst there is a wide difference. It was obviously out of the question to mingle or combine indiscriminately good and bad consignments. The farmer or merchant whose grain passed into a Milwaukee elevator would never permit its identity to be lost in the great bins unless first its quality had been exactly and impartially recognized.

In response to this situation the boards of trade of Milwaukee and Chicago during the later fifties evolved a system for rigidly inspecting, grading, and weighing grain.[1] They maintained at the elevators for that purpose disinterested inspectors, whose function it was to determine the quantity and quality of every carload of incoming produce before it was hoisted into the bins. These officials were required to provide shippers with receipts specifying exactly

[1] Milwaukee established its grading system in October, 1858. See Milwaukee Chamber of Commerce, *Report*, 1858, 13.

the quality and weight of the wheat or corn which they had received. An elevator receipt of this kind entitled the holder at any time to receive a like amount and grade of grain. If the shipment was made in winter it remained in the elevator at small cost until the opening of navigation in the spring. If it arrived during the season of navigation, it was upon proper order spouted into a lake vessel and sent onward to Buffalo or some other lower lake port.

The merchants of Milwaukee and Chicago thus established the now universal practice of handling grain by grades. Eastern centers continued for a time to buy and sell by sample. In the early seventies, however, the trunk railroads running from Milwaukee and Chicago to the Atlantic coast became able to compete successfully with the Great Lakes for the carriage of grain to the seaboard. The East was then compelled to adopt the western plan of elevator operation.[1]

Excellent though the grading system was, it had some obvious limitations. It could make only a rough classification of grain. Considerations of economy in storage and transfer demanded as few grades as possible. Considerations of accuracy in fixing the quality of shipments demanded as many as possible. A working basis lay between the two extremes.

In actual operation a shipper whose grain fell ever so little below the quality known as No. 1 was obliged to accept a receipt specifying common No. 2. If his wheat were of better quality than No. 1, though not quite equal to Extra, his receipt entitled him only to average No. 1.

[1] Buffalo Board of Trade, *Report*, 1869, 10; *Transportation Routes to the Seaboard*, I and II.

This natural difficulty was accentuated by the conduct of the grain-carrying railroads running to the lake shore. Usually the latter owned or controlled large elevators to which they insisted delivering whatever grain they were called upon to transport. Merchants, millers, and independent warehousemen protested that this created a monopoly with power to fix unlimited charges for storing and transferring grain. They asserted that railroad elevators defrauded them by corrupt mixing of grades. "We purchase from the farmers," they complained, "a superior grade of No. 1 wheat, weighing nearly sixty pounds to the bushel. It passes through the railroad elevators and that is the last we see of it. In its place we are given the average No. 1 mixture that flows from the elevator bins, weighing only fifty-eight pounds to the bushel. Who gains by this strange exchange? None but the owners of the railroad elevators. They seize upon our fancy grain, mix it with their own inferior qualities, and behold, they have brought their cheap lots up to a grade passing inspection."[1]

These grievances came to a head in Milwaukee in 1863. The railroads of that city under no circumstances permitted bulk grain to pass to other than their own elevators. They allowed bagged wheat to be taken elsewhere, but discouraged its shipment by imposing an extra charge of 4 cents a sack for transporting it.[2]

The merchants, millers, and warehousemen were united in their protest. They insisted that the rail-

[1] Paraphrased from accounts in Milwaukee *Sentinel*, July 2, 1862, Jan. 9, 1863, Mar. 7, 15, 26, 27, 29, and 30, 1864; Milwaukee *Daily Wis.*, Jan. 14, 1863; *Wis. State Jour.*, Mar. 30, 1864.

[2] See references in preceding note.

road companies remove their discriminatory rate against bagged wheat, and that they permit bulk wheat to be taken to other elevators than those belonging to the railroads. After some discussion the railroad companies agreed to the first demand but turned a deaf ear to the second.[1] In the spring of 1864, however, the merchants of Milwaukee carried the matter to the State legislature and there eventually won their point. The statute which they secured compelled the railroad companies to deliver bulk grain to any elevators designated by the shippers, provided only such elevators were equipped with adequate sidetracks.[2] Apparently the new law operated satisfactorily, for it was not until the Granger excitement of 1873 that there was again united agitation against the elevator companies. In Illinois the solution of these difficulties was less prompt, and there the elevator question occupied a prominent place in the antimonopoly revolt.[3]

Closely identified with the wheat trade was the flour trade. In this, also, Milwaukee led the Wisconsin lake ports. During the five years of the Civil War she exported nearly 3,000,000 barrels, an amount equivalent to 13,500,000 bushels of wheat.[4] Her trade, however, was then only in its infancy. It remained for the years after 1865 to establish her real strength in this traffic.

Between 1865 and 1873 Milwaukee first effectually shook off her provincialism, extending her railroads into the developing states of Minnesota and Iowa

[1] See references cited *ante*, 370, note 1.

[2] Wis. *Gen. Laws*, 1864, chap. 390.

[3] Chicago *Tribune*, Feb. 14, 1866.

[4] Milwaukee Chamber of Commerce, *Reports*, 1860–65.

and drawing to herself their vast flour and wheat trade. Her commerce became more and more closely identified with their farming development and less dependent upon the unstable agricultural fortunes of the home State. By 1873 her flour exports had climbed to 1,805,200 barrels and her wheat exports to 24,994,266 bushels.[1] She ranked at that time as the greatest flour market as well as the greatest wheat market on all the upper lakes.[2]

Green Bay, Racine, and Sheboygan, together with a number of other Wisconsin ports on Lake Michigan, were likewise flour markets of some importance. Their combined exports during the five years of the Civil War amounted to some 600,000 barrels.[3] Their geographical position, however, barred them from anything more than a local trade and their importance consequently continued to be merely local.

For the transportation of this produce to the seaboard in 1860 Wisconsin depended almost wholly upon the great chain of northern lakes. We turn now to an account of this inland highway and particularly to the merchant marine that found employment upon its waters. When the season of 1860 opened the marine faced depression everywhere from Lake Michigan to distant Lake Ontario. No interest had been struck a more crushing blow by the panic of 1857. Vessels went begging for freights over the entire chain of lakes; dozens were laid up or dismantled; many went into the ocean trade; a number of tugs departed by way of the Mississippi for the

[1] *Id.*, 1873, 52.

[2] The number of clearances from the port of Milwaukee in 1858 was 2,113; in 1866, 3,572; in 1873, 5,535.

[3] *Id.*, 1860–65.

more prosperous waters of New Orleans.[1] The total number of ships plying the northern lakes fell from 1,548 in 1858 to 1,457 in 1860; their total tonnage decreased from 404,301 tons to 377,825.[2]

The year 1860, however, witnessed a swift recovery. In that year the Northwest reaped a greater grain crop than it had ever before known. As if by magic the fortunes of the lake fleet were reversed. No sooner did the extent of the crop become established than carrying rates doubled and trebled, and many a vessel owner earned during this one season more than the total value of his boat.[3] Even more prosperous was the season of 1861. Although almost every other interest in the Northwest was prostrate owing to the outbreak of the war, the shipping interest flourished.[4] Never in the history of the lakes had carriers received such rates. A succession of excellent crops and the closing of the Mississippi River route had

[1] For a graphic description of conditions in 1860 see extract from New York *World*, printed in Oshkosh *Northwestern*, Jan. 4, 1861. See also Milwaukee Chamber of Commerce, *Report*, 1858, 25; *id.*, 1859, 39–40.

[2] There are no thoroughly reliable statistics showing the total tonnage of the lake marine for the early sixties. Those contained in the annual reports of the U. S. Register of the Treasury in "Commerce and Navigation of the U. S." are worthless. The best are to be found in the board of trade reports of the various lake-shipping centers. For the period 1858 to 1863 see Chicago Board of Trade, *Reports*, for those years, and U. S. *Sen. Docs.*, 38 Cong., 1 sess., Ser. No. 1176, no. 54, 143–47; for the period 1860 to 1869 see Buffalo Board of Trade, *Reports*, for those years, especially that of 1869, and *Report on the Vessels, Commerce and Trade of the Lakes and Erie Canal* (Buffalo, 1861), 4. The statistics contained in the Buffalo *Reports* appear to have been compiled from the Marine Register of the Board of Lake Underwriters, and are probably fairly accurate; for the period after 1868 see G. G. Tunnel, *Statistics of Lake Commerce*, U. S. *House Ex. Docs.*, 55 Cong., 2 sess., Ser. No. 3679, no. 277, 1–28.

[3] Milwaukee *Sentinel*, Jan. 1, 1861; Oshkosh *Northwestern*, Jan. 4, 1861; Milwaukee Chamber of Commerce, *Report*, 1860, 44–45.

[4] Milwaukee Chamber of Commerce, *Report*, 1861, 26, 29–30.

conspired to thrust prosperity upon them. New vessels from all quarters entered the thriving service. By 1863 the number on the lakes was 1,870; 470,034 tons measured their total capacity.[1]

In 1863, however, a reaction set in. The equilibrium between supply and demand had been restored, and severe competition kept rates low and rather unprofitable. There was a sudden return of great prosperity in 1866, when rates shot up to heights almost equal to those of 1861, and a similar revival in 1872,[2] but with these exceptions the decade between 1863 and 1873 proved a disappointing one. The tonnage of the lake fleet during those years little more than held its own. In 1872 it stood almost exactly where it had been in 1863,[3] and the only advance that the decade saw was an increase in the efficiency of some of the vessels employed.

The service which this lake marine rendered Wisconsin and in general the Northwest during the years of the Civil War is beyond calculation. Railroads were still new and wholly unprepared to transport at small cost for long distances the bulky wheat and lumber that constituted the exports of the Badger State. Cheap transportation to the seaboard, the key to the prosperity of the agricultural Northwest, only the shipping of the Great Lakes was then prepared to give.

By far the largest part of this shipping in 1860 was composed of sailing vessels. Popular among the

[1] See references cited *ante*, 373, note 2.

[2] For lake rates see the *Reports* of the Milwaukee, Chicago, and Detroit boards of trade for the years 1857–73. See also Tunnel, *Statistics of Lake Commerce*, 1–52; *Transportation Routes to the Seaboard*, I, app., 35–36.

[3] See references cited *ante*, 373, note 2.

latter were the so-called schooners, constituting 80 per cent or more of the total.[1] Other common types, classified according to their rigging, were barks, brigs, brigantines, and sloops. To their lot fell the transportation of the exceptionally bulky freights—lumber, coal, salt, wheat, corn, ore, and stone.

In 1858 sailing vessels numbered 1,208 and their capacity was 263,512 tons. By 1868 they totalled 1,855, the highest record ever attained, of 293,978 tons burden. By 1875 their count had fallen to 1,710, but their tonnage, owing to the increased average size of new boats, had risen to 339,787.[2] After 1875 their construction fell to minor proportions, and by the end of the century these white-winged carriers of the lakes had almost disappeared. On Lake Michigan they remained longest of all, for they were especially fitted to the lumber commerce that flourished on its waters.

Steam-driven vessels, in the meantime, maintained a steady growth. They possessed every advantage over wind-propelled craft. In a storm a steamer could hold its course in the teeth of the heaviest gale, whereas a sailing vessel was in constant danger of being dashed to pieces upon the rugged shores that hem in these landlocked waters. As for efficiency, a steamer could accomplish from two to two and a half times the work of a sailing vessel of like capacity, a most important consideration on a body of water that is closed to navigation at least a third of the year. Reflecting these advantages, the number of steam-driven vessels in the lake marine increased

[1] *Ibid.*

[2] *Ibid.*

from 242 in 1857 to 802 in 1873,[1] a rate of growth that before very long placed them in control of the carrying service of the northern lakes.

Three distinct types of steam-driven vessels plied the lakes—tugs, side-wheel steamers, and propellers. Tugs were employed, as they are today, chiefly for the duty about canals and harbors. The side-wheel steamers were the passenger carriers of the Great Lakes, though like the Mississippi River steamboats they also carried freight, particularly merchandise, wheat, and flour. They had come into prominence when the transportation of passengers, and particularly immigrants, from the Atlantic coast to the West was the business exclusively of the northern waterway. Like the steamboats of the Mississippi River their first-class cabins were usually elegant and often luxurious, though their steerage facilities left much to be desired. As soon as railroads were completed to Chicago and Milwaukee from the East their better passenger traffic deserted them, and they were left with the transportation of only the poorer. Their costly construction and expense of operation forbade their entrance into the freight service, and during the sixties and seventies, as a result, they slowly disappeared from the lakes.

Screw-driven propellers, first employed in the early forties, gradually took the place of the steamers as favorites of the merchant marine. Though slower they possessed the great advantage of economy of operation. They, too, were fitted up for both passenger and freight service, though usually they placed

[1] J. C. Mills, *Our Inland Seas* (Chicago, 1910), 158; Tunnel, *Statistics of Lake Commerce*, 26.

their emphasis upon the transportation of freight. On Lake Michigan they were engaged chiefly in the carrying of grain and flour destined for Buffalo and other lower lake ports. On the return trips they brought back immigrants and transported such commodities as merchandise, salt, and coal. During the sixties they grew rapidly in numbers, and in 1873 occupied among steam craft on the lakes nearly the same relative position that schooners occupied among sailing vessels.

A specialized form of propeller which first came into use during the early sixties was the steam barge. This was a vessel containing no accommodations for passengers but devoted wholly to the carrying of freight. For cheap transportation of grain and lumber it had no peer on the Great Lakes, and its entrance into the inland marine marked an important advance.

A specialized form of the steam barge which came into use during the same period was the "rabbit," so called because of its peculiar shape. It was a vessel built especially for the freighting of commodities like salt, stone, and coal, and was less used on Lake Michigan than on other lakes in the chain.

An improvement of quite another character was the extension of the towing or "hooker" system from the lumber to the grain commerce. This occurred near the close of the sixties.[1] Productive of great economies, it was soon universally adopted. It was an innovation of much significance in the history of the lake marine, for it marked the beginning of the end of the old sailing fleet.[2]

[1] See *ante*, chap. iii. See also Buffalo Board of Trade, *Report*, 1869, 5; Mills, *Our Inland Seas*, 187–88.

[2] Unfortunately "hookers" are classed as sailing vessels in government statistics because they retained a small spread of canvas. This renders

Along with these changes went a slow but steady increase in the size of lake vessels. As on the Mississippi River, the tonnage of boats was here conditioned by the depth of water at necessary passageways. The lakes in general were deep enough to support craft of any size. This was of little avail, however, so long as harbors were unimproved and the channels connecting the several members of the chain were shallow. Especially troublesome restrictions of this kind were the meager capacities of the Erie and the Welland canals, and the obstruction in the channel uniting Lakes Huron and Erie known as the St. Clair flats.

The St. Clair flats were deepened somewhat just prior to the Civil War, and in 1862 the state of New York completed its enlargement of the Erie Canal. At once lake vessels were built of larger dimensions. In 1856 the largest vessel afloat on the Great Lakes had a grain capacity of not more than 33,000 bushels.[1] In 1873 it was not at all unusual for a steam barge to clear from Milwaukee or Chicago with from 55,000 to 60,000 bushels of wheat in her hold and like amounts in the holds of one or two tows.[2] In 1858 the largest propeller entering Chicago was of 1,223 tons burden; in 1873 there were eight propellers of between 1,400 and 1,600 tons burden plying the Great Lakes.[3] Unfortunately the ability of the

it difficult to determine the rapidity with which towing developed and sailing declined.

[1] R. G. Plumb, *History of Navigation on the Great Lakes* (Hearings before U. S. House Committee on Railways and Canals, Washington, 1911), 25; Manitowoc *Pilot*, Feb. 17, 1910.

[2] Buffalo Board of Trade, *Report*, 1873, 41–42; Milwaukee Chamber of Commerce, *Report*, 1873, 13–14.

[3] Chicago Board of Trade, *Report*, 1858, 40–43; Buffalo Board of Trade, *Report*, 1873, 40-43.

Federal government after the Civil War to undertake extensive harbor and channel improvements was limited by its heavy financial obligations. Correspondingly the increase in the tonnage of lake vessels was checked.

Nearly all the vessels plying the Great Lakes during this period were wooden. A few were constructed of iron, the first merchant vessel of the latter type having been launched in Canadian waters as early as 1845. During the sixties and early seventies a limited number of excellent ships of iron construction were built. In all, however, probably not more than two score ever sailed the lakes. They are interesting chiefly as representing the transition from the old-time wooden craft to the modern steel leviathans of our inland seas.

Almost without exception in 1860 steamers and propellers on the Great Lakes burned wood for fuel. The same was true, also, of the Mississippi River steamboats and of the railroads of the Northwest. Manitowoc on the Wisconsin shore of Lake Michigan was a favorite "wooding up" point for vessels running between Milwaukee, Chicago, and Buffalo. Wood, however, though cheap and abundant, was cumbersome to handle, and in the early sixties propellers began to install boilers designed for the consumption of coal. It was an important advance, which during the following decades found gradual acceptance among the steam-driven vessels of the northern waterways.

No such concentration of ownership marked the vessel interests of the Great Lakes as developed during the sixties in the steamboat industry of the

Mississippi River. Centralization on the lakes was favored neither by natural nor artificial conditions. Sailing vessels were usually owned individually, frequently by the captains that commanded them. Steam-driven vessels were more likely to be owned by companies, for they represented larger investments of capital. The panic of 1857 forced the consolidation of some of the weaker propeller organizations, and the stronger ones increased largely the number of boats that they operated. During the sixties, however, new companies were again established, as steam craft came more and more into favor.[1]

The regularity with which propellers were able to make their runs encouraged organizing them into lines. During the later fifties and sixties these fell almost without exception into the hands of the eastern railroads that were competing with the Erie and the Welland canals. It became the practice for propeller lines to deliver exclusively to their affiliated railroads whatever cargoes they carried, destined for the seaboard.[2] In return they were given all the westward-bound traffic which their associated railroads controlled.

These arrangements possessed all of the advantages and few of the objectionable features that attended steamboat agreements on the Mississippi River. On the one hand they produced regularity of service, on the other they were powerless to increase rates

[1] Milwaukee Chamber of Commerce, *Reports*, 1860–70.

[2] In dividing the through rate from the lake shore to the seaboard the propeller lines were allowed one-third and the railroads appropriated two-thirds. The propeller carriage from Chicago or Milwaukee to Buffalo was about 1,000 miles, that of the railroads from Buffalo to New York was 423 miles. *Transportation Routes to the Seaboard*, II, 366.

owing to the competition of sailing vessels. By 1873 hardly a propeller plying out of Milwaukee or Chicago ran "wild" as in the earlier days.[1]

Propeller companies usually sought out the larger lake ports that possessed deep harbors for their regular service, leaving the uncertain trade of the smaller and less accessible ports to the sailing vessels. The Wisconsin cities which enjoyed regular and frequent propeller service were Milwaukee, Racine, Kenosha, and Green Bay. In 1860 Milwaukee was served by five lines, in 1867, by eleven, giving her daily, and in some instances more frequent, connection with the lower lake ports, the eastern shore of Lake Michigan, and also its western shore.[2]

In important marine centers like Chicago, Buffalo, Cleveland, and Detroit local associations of vessel owners and some associations purporting to cover the entire chain of lakes attempted during the sixties to regulate carrying conditions, the wages of seamen, and, to a limited extent, rates. Like the sailors' unions, however, they were loosely organized and, on the whole, ineffective. It remained for a later generation to bring about concentration in the vessel interest of the Great Lakes.

During the sixties the shipping of these northern waterways came face to face with the problem of railroad competition. For a time the same fate appeared to await it that had already overtaken the steamboats on the Mississippi River. The lake route, however, had this decided advantage over the river,

[1] *Ibid.*, I, 58–59, 66, II, 220–28.

[2] Milwaukee *Daily Wis.*, April 25, 1867; Milwaukee Chamber of Commerce, *Report*, 1860, 39–40.

that its general direction was east and west, coinciding with the trend of northern commerce. The slump in its traffic which began in the later sixties proved to be only temporary. Since the eighties the traffic of the Great Lakes has kept full step with the development of the territory tributary to them.

The cheapness of water transportation afforded the lake shipping an enormous advantage in resisting the aggressions of the overland carriers. Fortunately this was not neutralized, as on the Mississippi, by the operation of a transportation monopoly. On the contrary, competition on the Great Lakes was so vigorous that rates were constantly changing. Sometimes they fluctuated with utmost violence from day to day, always a good deal from year to year. Ordinarily they were high during the spring movement of grain, fell materially during the slack summer months, and reached their climax during the fall, when the new crop was pressing to market.

How great the changes sometimes were in a single season may be judged from the experiences of 1861. During the first two weeks of navigation the rate upon wheat was 16 cents per bushel; during the summer months it ranged at from 5 to 7 cents; in August it rose to 13 or 14 cents; in October it soared to 24 cents; in November it fell back to between 14 and 20 cents; closing the season on November 25 at 16 cents.[1] The graph shown on the opposite page represents the average wheat rate from Milwaukee or Chicago to Buffalo by years from 1857 to 1873.[2]

[1] *Id.*, 1861, 29–30.

[2] Lake rates from Milwaukee to the lower lakes were the same as from Chicago. All rail rates to the seaboard were likewise the same from Milwaukee and Chicago.

Freight Rate on a Bushel of Wheat by Lake from Chicago or Milwaukee to Buffalo

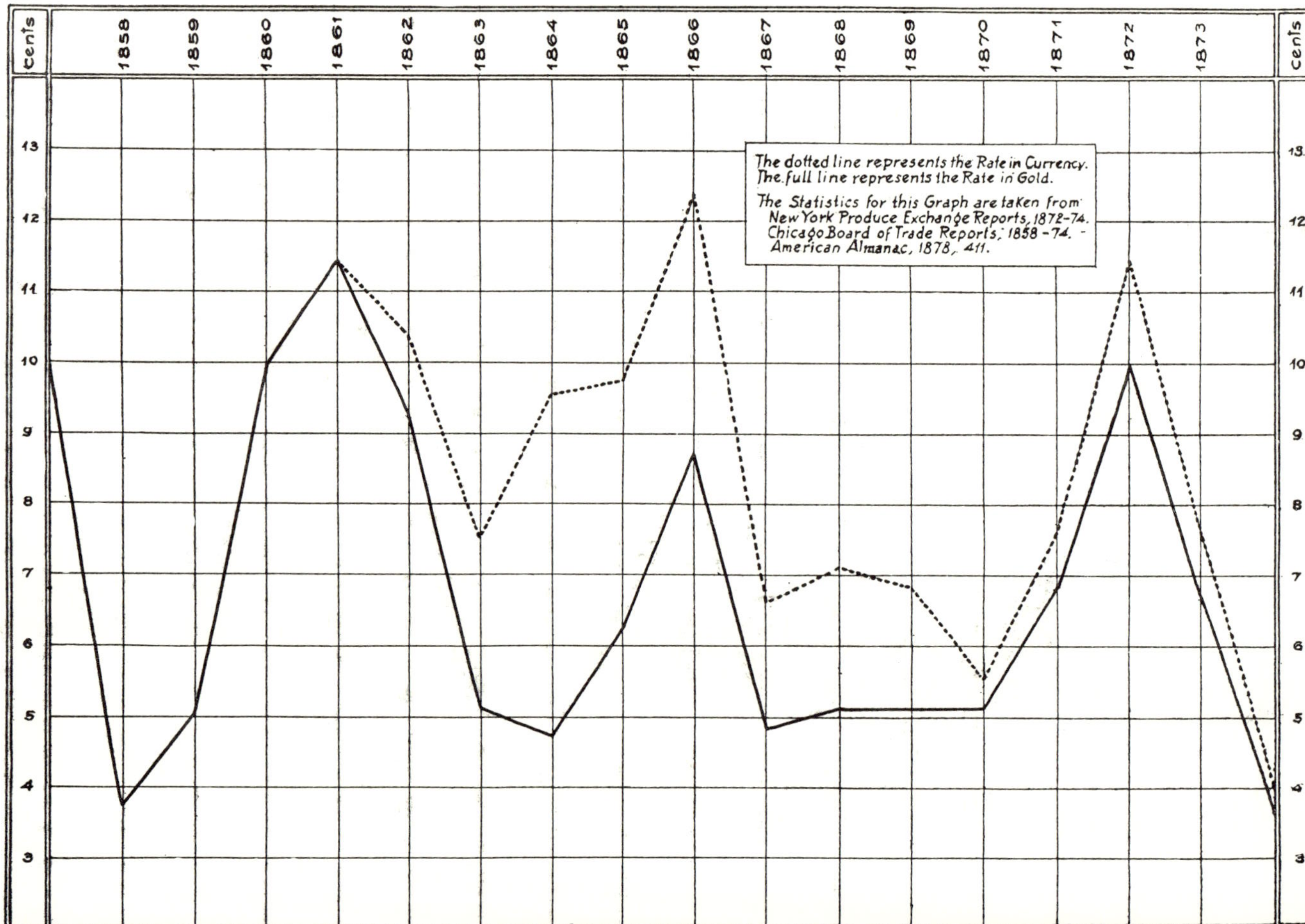

It indicates that the general movement of charges during this period was downward, a tendency that became more marked after the panic of 1873.

The cheapness of water transportation was to some extent offset on the Great Lakes by difficulties from which there was no escape. The lakes were closed by ice for more than a third of the year, during all of which time the capital invested in vessels was forced to lie idle. Owing to the necessity for rounding the lower peninsula of Michigan, the water route was exceedingly indirect and wasteful. From Milwaukee to New York by lake and canal was a distance of approximately 1,400 miles; by rail it was not more than 1,000 miles. Transfer charges were a heavy burden. Wheat from interior Wisconsin had to be transferred twice on its way to the seaboard, first at Milwaukee and again at the lower lake ports. Owing to the danger of shipwreck on these storm-tossed seas cargoes had to be insured, an expense obviated in overland shipments. Finally, lake vessels obtained full cargoes only one way. Westward they were obliged to travel either very light or with freights that little more than paid the cost of transportation. The competing trunk lines, to be sure, were confronted with the same difficulty, for the imports of the West never equalled in bulk the exports. They were favored, however, with a considerable local westward traffic that the boats entirely lacked.

The overland carriers on their part labored under numerous disadvantages. The chief of these, prior to the war, was lack of organization. The roads had originally been built as short, local lines, isolated and unconnected, with tracks, even, of different gauges. The traveler from New York to Chicago was subjected to the vexation and delay of constantly changing trains. Freight suffered, in addition, the expense, loss of time, and often breakage that attended frequent transshipment. Upon the carrying of bulky commodities this obstacle placed a complete ban.

However, a rapid improvement in this respect was secured during the fifties and early sixties as the result of a wave of consolidation similar to that which later passed over Wisconsin.[1] Lines were united, others were purchased or leased, and new links and extensions built, until out of the maze of isolated trackage in this region there emerged great trunk railroads stretching half way across the continent.

Even more important was the development during the middle sixties of "through freight" or "fast freight" companies. The latter were of several varieties.[2] One feature, however, was common to all. They all owned large numbers of freight cars, distinguished from common cars by color and general appearance, which they contracted with railroad companies in every part of the country to send "through" from shipper to consignee. A single fast freight line, the Star-Union, whose advertisements appeared in Wisconsin papers early in 1865, owned or controlled "nearly a thousand new cars so constructed as to *Run Through* between Eastern and Western Cities *Without Transfer*." It guaranteed to

[1] Fite, *Social and Industrial Conditions*, 159–62.

[2] *Transportation Routes to the Seaboard*, I and II.

have its cars carried from Chicago to Philadelphia in six days, to New York in seven, to Boston in eight, and for every day's delay after contract time it allowed a forfeit of 5 cents per hundred weight of freight.[1]

Early in 1867 there appeared in the Milwaukee press advertisements of four such lines, the Red, Star-Union, Empire, and Diamond, all operating in connection with the Chicago & Northwestern Railway. "Milwaukee shippers," ran the advertisement, "can load their property into the cars of any of the above named lines at the freight depot of the Chicago & Northwestern Railway in this city, lock the car, and have the property promptly forwarded to their correspondents without change of car."[2]

Along with these improvements in organization went swift improvement in the physical equipment of the railroads, particularly the substitution of steel for iron in rails, double tracking, standardization of gauges, increase in the size and power of locomotives, betterments of bridges and roadbed, and improvements in terminal facilities.[3]

Speed, safety, and directness of shipment, the rewards of such improvements, soon won from the lake carriers not only their profitable passenger traffic, but a considerable part of that class of freight known as general merchandise. Not content with these considerable conquests, however, during the middle sixties the trunk lines set out to capture the remaining heavy freight.[4] They found their oppor-

[1] *Wis. State Jour.*, Feb. 13, 1865.

[2] Milwaukee *Daily Wis.*, April 18, 1867; Milwaukee *Sentinel*, Aug. 23, 1866.

[3] *Transportation Routes to the Seaboard*, I, 27–28.

[4] Milwaukee Chamber of Commerce, *Reports*, 1860–73; *Transportation Routes to the Seaboard*, I, app., 28.

tunity to do this in the unusually high water-charges prevailing in 1866.

Their first important prize was flour. Of the total shipments from Milwaukee in 1866 more than a third went eastward by rail. By 1873 the proportion had grown to more than five-ninths,[1] a gain that the lake carriers were never able permanently to win back.

Corn followed a few years after flour. In 1869 the New York legislature was informed that "nearly two million bushels of grain [chiefly corn] per month for the past six months had been carried by railroad from the lake cities to all the minor markets in the country, that although railroads had begun carrying grain long distances less than two years before, and then only in winter, they now continued to carry it to their utmost capacity even after the lakes and canals were open to navigation, and that as a consequence, our lake marine, although they offered charters at rates barely covering expenses, were lying idle at our docks."[2]

Wheat, too, at length succumbed to the enticements of the railroads. As the result of a season of high lake charges in 1872, similar to that of 1866, nearly a million bushels of the 11,570,000 shipped from Milwaukee were carried to the seaboard by rail.[3] Since 1872 overland carriers have never ceased to be formidable competitors for the grain trade of the Northwest.

Shipping centers both on the upper and lower lakes were gravely menaced by this diversion. The pros-

[1] Milwaukee Chamber of Commerce, *Report*, 1866, 11; *id.*, 1873, 39.

[2] Milwaukee *Sentinel*, May 17, 1869.

[3] Milwaukee Chamber of Commerce, *Report*, 1872, 36.

perity of Milwaukee, in particular, was at stake. So long as the Great Lakes remained the carriers for her agricultural hinterland large quantities of wheat were forced to pass into her elevators for storage and transfer. Once in the city, the grain could be handled by her merchants, ground by her millers, and forwarded by her shipping interests. As soon, however, as the railroads took upon themselves the carrying of this staple to the interior of New England and New York, as soon as direct communication was established between western harvest fields and eastern consumers, the Badger metropolis, like other lake-shore shipping centers, was eliminated from its profitable middleman position.

Chicago on account of her commanding railroad position was less likely to be adversely affected by such a change than Milwaukee. Buffalo, which during the sixties was accustomed to receive from one-half to three-fourths of all the wheat shipped from Milwaukee, as well as large portions of the grain and flour trade of Chicago,[1] was seriously endangered. Detroit, Oswego, Kingston, and the lower lake ports of Canada, which shared to a less extent in the trade of Milwaukee and Chicago, were likewise imperiled.

These ports took early and vigorous steps to guard the water route against the aggressions of the railroads. They united in the spring of 1869 in calling together at Chicago a convention of the boards of trade of all the important shipping centers on the Great Lakes.[2] The program which they there out-

[1] *Reports* of the Milwaukee Chamber of Commerce and of the Chicago Board of Trade for the years 1860–70.

[2] Milwaukee *Sentinel*, May 17, 1869.

lined was to cut the cost of water transportation "so low as not only to defy [railroad] competition in summer, but low enough to induce the storing of grain at receiving points in the winter, with a view to cheap transportation on the opening of navigation in the spring."

They did not expect to do this by reductions in lake charges which were already low, but rather by savings in the terminal expenses of the shipping and receiving ports. They hoped materially to reduce the transfer charges of Milwaukee and Chicago, which on wheat were still the same as before the war, 2 cents a bushel.[1] They hoped also to cut the cost of marine insurance which on the value of grain cargoes averaged four-tenths of 1 per cent.[2] In these expectations they were disappointed.

They succeeded, however, in securing reductions in transfer charges at Buffalo, Oswego, and Toledo, amounting to from 50 to 75 per cent.[3] They were unexpectedly successful in securing from the railroad companies running between the lake shore and the Mississippi River a cut of one-half in rates on wheat and flour.[4] Their greatest victory came to them in

[1] *Ibid.;* Milwaukee Chamber of Commerce, *Record Book B,* June 23, 1869; Chicago *Tribune,* April 28, 1869. The Milwaukee Chamber of Commerce *Reports* after 1862 print besides transfer charges the customary commission rates for buying and selling grain and costs of inspection.

[2] Buffalo Board of Trade, *Report,* 1869, 23.

[3] Milwaukee Chamber of Commerce, *Record Book B,* June 23, 1869. See also Buffalo Board of Trade, *Report,* 1869, 41; *Supplementary Report,* 1869, 43.

[4] This triumph, which temporarily brought transportation charges between river and lake to the level of 1860, was ostensibly a concession to the lake ports. In reality it was a recognition of hard times in the Northwest, and an answer to the competitive menace of barge transportation on the Mississippi. See *ante,* chap. xiv; see also Milwaukee Chamber of

1870 when the state of New York reduced the wheat tolls on the Erie Canal from 6 to 3 cents a bushel.[1]

Despite these efforts the eastern trunk railroads continued their inroads upon the lake commerce. Each reduction in lake-carrying rates they met in kind. Their charges were never quite as low as those of their competitors, but the difference was sufficiently compensated for by the superior attraction of overland transportation. Eventually, in the middle seventies, a state of equilibrium between the rival routes was established, after which they continued their struggle upon substantially even terms.

For the Northwest it was fortunate that the water route was thus able to reassert itself. Unlike the Mississippi River, it afforded a constant regulative influence upon overland carriers. How effective its competition was, the railroads themselves made clear. Uniformly, year after year, they raised their rates a third or two-thirds as soon as ice closed the lake channels. With the same regularity they returned to the competitive basis as soon as navigation was resumed in the spring. So consistently was this process repeated that shippers came to take as a matter of course the wide differences between winter and summer rail rates.

Another tribute to the Great Lakes route was the fact that almost without exception the eastern railroads competing with it charged lower rates than the roads west of Lake Michigan. To be sure, the nature

Commerce, *Record Book B*, June 23, 1869; Milwaukee *Sentinel*, May 20, 1869; Prescott *Journal*, May 28, 1869; *Mississippi River Com. Report*, 1901, 36–37.

[1] Buffalo Board of Trade, *Report*, 1869, 7–9, 68; *Supplement*, 1869, 21; *id.*, 1873, 16.

of the service and the conditions of operation of the two groups of overland carriers differed. However, there is no reason to doubt that the presence of water competition in the one case and its absence in the other was an important, if not the major, cause for the unusual differences in their rates. That the Granger revolt against railroads secured a slighter foothold east of Lake Michigan than west of it was one of the results of this situation.

The commercial changes brought to pass in the period 1857–73 were fairly revolutionary in character. During these years the mighty Mississippi was virtually eliminated as an economic influence in the affairs of the region west of Lake Michigan. The proud marine of the Great Lakes likewise met the shock of railroad competition, and was compelled by the overland carriers to relinquish to them the most desirable portion of the carrying trade of the Northwest.

The North succeeded in 1865 in restoring the Union and destroying slavery not because its people were more patriotic, its soldiers braver, or its generals more skillful than those of the South. Victory in that great contest rested with the side that could bring to bear the weight of superior resources. To the loyal workers of the North, who manned the ships of commerce, cultivated the fields, and turned the wheels of industry was due the happy outcome of the conflict quite as much as to the fighting armies. Wisconsin, as we have seen in this volume, did her share in providing the government with the sinews of war. Her industries vied with her soldiery in upholding the arm of President Lincoln. Not only were these industries more productive than ever before, but they were more diverse and complex. With the return of peace the young Badger commonwealth was prepared to set out upon a new era of progress, whose fruits and whose problems confront us today in our modern industrialism.

Index

Index